The Literature
of Post-Communist
Slovenia, Slovakia,
Hungary and Romania

The Literature of Post-Communist Slovenia, Slovakia, Hungary and Romania

A Study

ROBERT MURRAY DAVIS

McFarland & Company, Inc., Publishers
Jefferson, North Carolina, and London

LIBRARY OF CONGRESS CATALOGUING-IN-PUBLICATION DATA

Davis, Robert Murray.
　　The literature of post-communist Slovenia, Slovakia, Hungary and Romania : a study / Robert Murray Davis.
　　　p.　　cm.
　　Includes bibliographical references and index.

　　ISBN-13: 978-0-7864-3207-3
　　softcover : 50# alkaline paper ∞

　　1. East European literature — 20th century — History and criticism. 2. East European literature — 21st century — History and criticism. 3. Post-communism — Europe, Eastern.　　4. Literature and state — Europe, Eastern.　　5. Literature and politics — Europe, Eastern.
I. Title.
PN849.E9D38　　2008
809'.8949 — dc22　　　　　　　　　　　　　　　　2007031781

British Library cataloguing data are available

©2008 Robert Murray Davis. All rights reserved

No part of this book may be reproduced or transmitted in any form or by any means, electronic or mechanical, including photocopying or recording, or by any information storage and retrieval system, without permission in writing from the publisher.

Cover image ©2007 Shutterstock.

Manufactured in the United States of America

McFarland & Company, Inc., Publishers
　Box 611, Jefferson, North Carolina 28640
　　www.mcfarlandpub.com

In Memoriam: Ottó Orbán, 1936–2002

Tremors

"'we remember' is in itself resurrection. —Ottó Orbán,
"Keats"

Shaken by tremors all your life.
Midway through what should have been
the middle of our journeys,
I could not read the lines
squiggled by the instrument that sensed them:
the war, "My father murdered by my mother's relatives."
Pest basement, German shells, Russian occupation.
The orphanage. Upheavals from incautious tastes in poems.
Midlife palsy. Heart finally shaken and then stilled.
Almost last words to me about our "sunny and young days...
much better than this Waste Land of coming old age
with desolate days of illness, death.
But leave all these to the poems; that is what they are for."
All but the final tremor marked on paper,
recording, with irony and courage,
symptoms of the strains beneath
that you left to move us.

Acknowledgments

Much of the material that follows has been revised and expanded from articles and reviews published in *Commonweal* and in *World Literature Today*. Thanks are due to the editors and staff for their encouragement of my work. Support for travel has come from the University of Oklahoma Research Council, the Fulbright Commission of Romania, the PEN Clubs of Slovakia, Hungary, and Slovenia, the Center for Slovenian Literature, and the Vilenica conference. Adam Sorkin, Ioana Ieronim, Ferenc Takács, Éva Tóth, Gustáv Murín, Iztok Osojnik, Aleš Debeljak, Brane Mozetič, and Lela Bajda Njatin have been especially but not uniquely helpful.

Finally, thanks are owed to the writers, editors, and translators who provided books and granted interviews. I hope that I have not misrepresented them too grossly. I also hope that the admiration and affection for them and their work is clear.

Parts of Chapters 2, 3, and 5 originally appeared in *Commonweal* as "Old Enemies Endure: Church and State in Slovenia," ©2000; "In Hungary, Coping with Freedom," ©1997; and "Report from Romania," ©2001, respectively. All are reprinted with permission.

Material in chapters 1 through 6 has been adapted from material originally published in *World Literature Today* and is reprinted by permission, including: Chapter 1: "The High White Wall and the Hospital Bed: Central European and Western American Poets," *World Literature Today*, 74:4 (Autumn 2000), 779–782; Chapter 2: "Out of the Shadows: Slovene Writing After Independence." *World Literature Today*, 75:1 (Winter 2001), 59–65; Chapter 3: "Desperate but Not Serious: The Situation of Hungarian Literature in the Nineties," *World Literature Today*, 74:1 (Winter 2000), 81–89, and "Disapora's Children," *World Literature Today*, 80:6 (November-December 2006), 55–58; Chapter 4: "Slovak Writers After 1993," *World Literature Today*,

73:1 (Winter 1999), 93–96; Chapter 5: "Romanian Writing Redivivus," *World Literature Today*, 76:2 (Spring 2002), 76–83; and Chapter 6: "East Goes West: New Ventures in Eastern European Publishing," *World Literature Today*, 78:2 (May-August 2004), 53–55.

Permission to reprint material is gratefully acknowledged: Northwestern University Press for Pavel Vilikovsky, *Ever Green Is...: Selected Prose*, Translated by Charles Sabatos (Evanston, IL: Northwestern University Press, 2002); Alvin Greenberg, Walter McDonald, George Economou, Éva Tóth (and her translator Peter Zollman) for permission to reprint their poems; Jascha Kessler for material from his translation of Ottó Orbán's *Our Bearings at Sea: A Novel in Poems* (Xlibris Books, 2001), a non-linear narrative of prose poems which provided many quotations for my characterization of his work, and I am grateful to Jascha Kessler, not only for permission to use them, but for his years of effort devoted to setting such sophisticated Hungarian into his equally complex and racy English; Bruce Berlind for material from his translation of Ottó Orbán's *The Journey of Barbarus* (Pueblo, CO: Passeggiata Press, 1997).

Acknowledgment of other quoted copyright material is given in the works cited list at the end of each chapter.

Contents

Acknowledgments vii
Preface 1
Introduction 3

1. Very Different: Central European and American Poets — 9
2. Out of the Shadows: Slovene Writing After Independence — 22
3. Desperate but Not Serious: Hungarian Writing After 1989 — 66
4. Slovak Writing in Transition — 111
5. Romanian Writing Redivivus — 144
6. Transition — And After? And Beyond? Geopolitics, Marketing and Literary Anxieties in the New Central Europe — 165

Epilogue — 180

Appendix: Memorial Poem *by Éva Toth* — 189
Index — 193

Preface

The only excuse for a monoglot writing about central European literature is that most Anglophones know less about the region and its writers than I do. Over the past quarter century, I have traveled to Hungary, Slovakia, Slovenia, and Romania to lecture, to participate in writers' conferences, and to interview many of the writers and editors mentioned in the following pages.

My approach has obvious limitations. For one thing, each of the chapters depends on the kind and amount of information I was able to obtain. The chapter on Slovakia relies more heavily on published materials than on interviews; that on Hungary more on interviews; that on Slovenia on a balance. Inevitably, my first and in most cases subsequent contacts have been with what used to be called the nomenklatura, the writers who hold official positions in the cultural network of these countries. (The cultural organization and politics of the United States are much less definite, but as with our class system, the fact that it is somewhat amorphous does not mean that it does not exist.) In any case, I have been able to interview only those who speak English and to read only work that is available in translation. Some of that work, published by cultural organizations, is available only in the country of publication. Happily, more and more work previously inaccessible has begun to appear on the Internet, although this requires a sometimes tedious search by the names of individual writers.

Of course, working with translations poses problems. If only one version of a work in English is available, the reader can rest in happy ignorance. But when two translators give different versions, one's confidence is shaken. While poetry may not be entirely what is lost in translation, different translations make for very different poems. For example, Michael Biggins and Sonja Kravanja have rival translations of some poems by Edvard Kocbek

(*Edvard Kocbek* [Ljubljana, Slovenia, 1995], by Biggins, *Embers in the House of Night* [Santa Fe, NM, Lumen, 1999], by Kravanja).

On the whole Kravanja's versions seem more direct and colloquial. In "Black Sea," for example, she chooses "murmur" rather than Biggins' "purl," and "our bodies / sink into you" and "we have become a part of your depth" rather than "our bodies reach / their last stop in you" and "we are one with your very depths." Her translations make Kocbeck seem more modern.

A different kind of problem arises in variant translations of Aleš Debeljak's "Bosnian Elegy." For example, Andrew Wachtel begins "Bosnian Elegy" with "Sing, young poet, touch my inflamed skin, tanned by lengthy treks" (*The Imagination of Terra Incognita: Slovenian Writing 1945–1995* [Fredonia, NY: White Pine, 1997]). Debeljak and Christopher Merrrill's version begins "Sing, young poet, touch my burning skin, darkened by long treks" (*Mosaic of Seven Pebbles: Insight into Contemporary Slovenian Literature* [Ljubljana: Center for Slovenian Literature, 1999]). Wachtel's speaker hasn't crossed a threshold, Debeljak's and Merrill's a line, which seems more appropriate in the context of gunpowder. Those literate in Slovenian might be able to tell whether the Wachtel translation of "Migrations" is literal. If so, Debeljak and his collaborator have not only rendered but revised the poem in their translation, for "How quiet the house is now" (*Terra Incognita* 285) becomes "The magic of words is dying out" (*Mosaic* 42). No translator can be that far off.

Despite these problems, I take some consolation in Andrej Blatnik's justification for this kind of book. In "The Future of Literature Can Be Discerned in the Last Sentence" (*The Slovenian Essay of the Nineties* [Ljubljana: Slovene Writers' Association, 2000]) he argues that "the future of (not only Slovenian) reading will in general consist of knowing the majority of world authors through their translations into major world languages" because there is not enough market for direct translation from one small language to another. But if a translation falls on the bookstore shelf and no one picks it up, does it exist?

Also, of course, I approach the work from a background in English and American literature. But so does the audience I seek to address. In any case, I hope that making known the names and works of the writers I have encountered, in person or in print or both, can give American readers a sense of the nature and quality of their work. This in turn may lead to wider circulation of books already published, to a greater demand for additional translations, and to wider discussion of the role of writers in cultures reclaiming their heritage after more than four decades of confusion at best and suppression at worst.

Introduction

Central Europeanism is not a state citizenship but a view of the world. — György Konrád

What do they mean by Central Europe, when with all the curtains around it, you can't see past your own barn! — Pavel Vilikovský

On a visit to Central Europe less than ten years after the end of Communist domination of the region, a friend asked, "Why can't these people just get along with each other?"

I replied that since we were only going to be there two weeks, I couldn't possibly unravel the complexities of language, culture, and religion, let alone account for the fact that eight hundred years ago someone did something to someone else and they were still angry about it. And this doesn't even attempt to account for what was done in the last century or the last year.

Many of the problems can be traced to what Slovakia, Hungary, Slovenia, and large parts of Romania — the countries I am dealing with — have in common: all were part of the Austrian and, after 1867, the Austro-Hungarian Empire. That domination was cultural and linguistic as well as political and architectural. One sign of "Central Europe" is that the major towns have at least two names, one German, one in the local language. More, or less, fortunate cities like Cluj-Klausenberg-Kolozsvár and Bratislava-Pressburg-Pozsony have three.

The physical legacy — sober, turn of the previous century stuccoed buildings, peeling from neglect under the Communists — is everywhere evident. Other imposed influences require a little more ingenuity for the outsider to discover because this region has, to American and even Western European eyes, a peculiar character.

While everyone agrees that there is, or was, a Central Europe, the boundaries are fluid. One survey I saw several years ago excluded Spain but was vague about everything else. Milan Kundera, who is more experienced, described it as an "indefinite area of small nations between Russia and Germany" (quoted in Mikuláš Huba, "Instead of the Prologue: Values for a Sustainable Future," www.czp.cuni.cz/values/citanka/Heartofeurope/huba1.htm). Lajos Grendel, an ethnic Hungarian living in Slovakia, puts it roughly in the same area and adds that some defining characteristics are "multiculturalism, nationalism (somewhere hidden under the surface, elsewhere expressed in bloody conflicts), non-existing modern national and societal self-definition, chronic crisis of identity and related to that value of chaos, or bluntly, a value of nihilism, severance of natural historical development which comes out and adapts to given conditions of the area. The consequences are: liquidation of citizens (as a stratum and also as an attitude) and elimination of civic values from tradition" (Huba's paraphrase).

Elsewhere, Grendel doubts the future value of the whole idea of "Central Europe," which before 1989 was a way of wishful orienting these countries away from Eastern (i.e., Communist) Europe and towards the West. Certainly my Hungarian friends in the early 1980s corrected, sharply, anyone who placed their country in "Eastern Europe." But now, Grendel argues, the concept of Central Europe can prevent integration into the West. And Huba notes in the collection he introduces that "most writers find Central Europe to be an illusion or ghetto, unnecessarily restricting exchange of ideas across the whole Europe."

Still, as he says, a train ride between any of these countries indicates that they have a good deal in common — not least, I repeat, buildings covered with mustard-colored stucco built under or under the influence of the Hapsburgs and allowed to flake and peel under the communists.

Furthermore, the histories, literary and otherwise, of the countries I deal with are not identical, but they have enough in common for the writers to understand each other's situation because all four nations — now independent states — achieved political and linguistic autonomy relatively late in comparison with the rest of Europe.

In Western Europe, vernacular literatures began to appear in the early Renaissance, partly as the result of emerging nationalism. But in the countries I am dealing with, tourist information points with pride to the first recorded use in print — not literature; any record at all — of the national language. Even in Hungary, which had a flourishing culture in the Renaissance, the development of literature was deflected or halted by more than a century of Turkish occupation, followed by Austrian domination. Slovaks and Slovenians had not been politically independent since the first millennium, and large parts of Romania were dominated by Austrians and other invaders.

As a result, the role of writers in the nineteenth century was not, as Mallarmé put it, to give a purer sense to the words of the tribe but to use the language to assure the tribe and to convince the outside world that the tribe existed as a cultural force. Literature was inextricably linked with politics. Sometimes, as in the movement led by Slovakia's Ľudovít Štur and in less formal terms in the work of Slovenia's France Prešern, it took the form of what is now called "identity politics." Sometimes, as in the political and literary work of Hungary's Sándor Petőfi, it was revolutionary action.

In either case, literature had a clearly political function, and writers became the unofficial, though not the unacknowledged, spokesmen (gender-specific in those days) for the ethos of peoples who had no political voice. This was a glorious, if sometimes dangerous, time for writers who could become not just the authors of national anthems, when the people became a nation, but architects of national consciousness.

By the beginning of the twentieth century, although the Hapsburgs still ruled, some writers enjoyed the luxury of turning outward to join the larger world, which for them meant Western Europe—as in the Hungarian magazine *Nyugat*, the word for "west."

After 1918, Hapsburg domination ended, but Slovakia was merged with and felt culturally overshadowed by the Czechs, and Slovenia got third billing in the newly constituted Kingdom of Serbs, Croats, and Slovenes, which became Yugoslavia, with Serbs replacing Austrians as the dominant culture. Romania regained control of Transylvania but had numerous internal problems.

After World War II, the Soviet empire took control of the area, except, after 1948, Yugoslavia, and Russian language and culture were supposed to dominate as German had in the previous century. Once again, writers were forced into a political role, either to support the programs of new puppet regimes or, simply by enunciating democratic political and humane cultural values, to become dissenters. And once again, writers achieved a cultural importance difficult for Americans or even western Europeans to appreciate, though dissent was praised and sometimes rewarded in the West regardless of literary quality. As Andrej Blatnik puts it, "The prevalent attitude to Eastern European literature seemed to be: sorry, dear author, but if you were never thrown in jail back home, your writing can't amount to anything much" (*The Slovenian Essay of the Nineties* [Llubljana: Slovenia Writers Association, 2000]).

After the fall of communist regimes in 1989, some of the dissidents moved into formal politics, some by replacing apparatchiks in government positions, some by establishing new institutions. As writers, all had to deal with changing conditions in publishing, in support for cultural programs, and in broader changes in transitional economy — and even more so in a transitional literary climate, where the terms of dissent are no longer easily and automatically honorable.

Writers who came to maturity before and during the communist era have had a more difficult time than those who began their careers after 1989. For the latter, the socialist regime is becoming as remote as Vietnam already seems to America's younger generation of writers. In Ljubljana, the Slovenian capital, a fashionable bar is named "Tito" in a nostalgia that will seem complicated only to those who lived through the regime.

But even the younger writers are reluctant to face the fact that — Blatnik again — "A book will never again hold the status it had merely a few decades ago," not just because of television and genre trash but "because the rhythm and way of life are changing in general, and everything has to adjust to that" (*Slovenian Essay*). There is also globalization, in literature as well as everything else, and Americanization, so that more than half of the songs played on the 1000-watt station in the Slovene town of Kočevje are in English, and a very good jazz band in Congress Square in Ljubljana, the capital, accompanies a vocalist who, if you closed your eyes, you would identify as American as she sings "Route 66." Someone responded to the Romantic poet's line "I accept the universe" with "By gad, he'd better." Not quite the same thing, but close enough.

Certainly the countries once under Communist rule seem eager to reach out to the larger world. Referendums on joining the European Union passed easily in Slovakia, Hungary, and Slovenia, and, given the chance, Romania will join the EU in 2007, willing to give up some economic and political sovereignty for greater financial security. Writers from these and other countries in the region have long been members of an even broader if less formal cultural union without at all weakening ties to local cultures and languages. It seems pointless to predict what they will do but valuable to see and celebrate what they have already done.

There are humanistic as well as literary reasons for doing so. As Vilikovský's character says, "A man can spend his whole life in Central Europe without necessarily being a Central European." On the other hand, he adds later, "a man can be a Central European his whole life without ever coming here at all" (*Ever Green Is*...see Chapter 4). Any reader can benefit from a sharper sense of irony and of the way that history creates social and psychic as well as physical conditions. These qualities are Central European, but they are also human. And, of course, love, loss, ennui — all the private emotions —

are peculiar neither to Central Europe nor America. Thus, the writers and works I have chosen to discuss at some length have undeniable documentary value in illustrating conditions in the region over the past quarter century or so, but far more important is the undeniable literary quality that deserves the attention and applause of readers throughout the world.

1

Very Different
Central European and American Poets

Scott Fitzgerald began a story with the line, "The very rich are different from you and me." Later, his sometime friend Ernest Hemingway countered, "Yes, they have more money."

In explaining the difference between American and Central European writers, one might say of the latter, "Yes, they have more history. And less geography."

First geography, which is simpler. Most Central European writers are quite conscious of the literature and culture of other countries, including America, but they focus initially on their immediate language community. This means a limited audience and small circulation of their work, but the limitations have some advantages. Take, for example, the position of small publishers. In Slovenia, publishers like Brane Mozetič have a definite niche and can expect to exercise some influence within the community, and outside that community can, in translation, have a prestige of exoticism. But when Susan Smith Nash ran texture press from Norman, Oklahoma, she was almost unknown within the state, which has almost twice the population and nine times the area, and had no local influence. Instead, she addressed the avant garde audience in the whole United States — and in that context her books were buried by sheer numbers. And no one has ever thought Oklahoma exotic.

Then there is history. American writers have always had an uneasy relationship to the idea and sometimes to the fact of European history and culture. The critic Philip Rahv classified American writers up to, say, 1950 as either Palefaces or Redskins. Palefaces turned to the east — not just to the

Atlantic coast of America but to Europe, conscious of inheriting European themes and forms, including forms of language. Redskins faced west, toward frontiers of language, form, and theme.

The distinction is perfectly illustrated by the novelists Henry James and Mark Twain. James spent much of his life in Europe, first in France and then in England, where he became a citizen not long before he died. He thought that the American novelist labored under enormous handicaps because America had

> No State, in the European sense of the word.... No sovereign, no court, no personal loyalty, no aristocracy, no clergy, no army, no diplomatic service, no country gentlemen, no palaces, nor manors, nor old country houses, nor parsonages, nor thatched cottages, nor ivied ruins; no cathedrals, nor abbeys, nor little Norman churches; no great Universities nor public schools — no Oxford, nor Eton, nor Harrow; no literature, no novels, no museums, no pictures, no political society, no sporting class ... [*Hawthorne*, 1879].

Then he made a career, on the other side of the ocean, of writing about those handicaps in a language that became in the course of time too convoluted for most Englishmen to understand. Things may have changed since then, as some boosters of American culture and education would insist, but the general view is held by many Europeans and some Americans.

Mark Twain would have regarded most of these absences cited by James as giving the advantage to America. He traveled a good deal — in fact, he came to national attention by writing about a trip to Europe in *The Innocents Abroad*. This sounds like the title of a Henry James novel, but the tone and style are very different. Twain wrote, and talked, in Southwestern vernacular (the Southwest of his time, before Oklahoma, Arizona, and New Mexico were settled or even much thought of), and his values and language looked deceptively straightforward and folksy. His response to Europe was very much *nil admirari*—he wouldn't have used the Latin — and it can be encapsulated in the remark about the Balkans, which, he said, "produces more history than can be consumed locally."

He could well have said this about the American South in the nineteenth century, but like James, he turned away, both physically and metaphorically, from the tragedy of our Civil War. And neither of these writers, however different in most respects, had much historical consciousness.

Central European poets, in contrast, seem to the American eye and ear to have little else. This struck me when, in a visit to Slovenia to gather material for an article on the current literary situation, I read a number of poems in translation and talked to various writers. It would be difficult to find a region that produces more history than the uncertain border between the

Balkans and Central Europe, and Slovenian poets from France Prešeren to Aleš Debeljak have responded to the challenge. Historically, major Slovene writers, like their colleagues in Slovakia and in different ways in Hungary, were acutely conscious of their importance to national identity for a people who did not have their own state and who endured various invasions and occupations, political and linguistic as well as military. This sense of mission required a language, especially in poetry, that was sometimes more distinguished for exhortation than lyricism. Sándor Petőfi read from the steps of the National Museum in Budapest the poem that announced the beginning of the 1848 revolution. Prešeren wrote the poem that became the Slovene national anthem. Both are pictured on the currencies of their countries. In the twentieth century, Edvard Kocbek's "The Lippizaners" is a similar, if ironic, call to national consciousness, and Debeljak's "Bosnian Elegy" is one of many poems in the volume *The Muses Were Not Silent*, about the recent Balkan wars. Éva Tóth's "Memorial Poem" is personal rather than national, but in focusing on her life, family, and friends, she encapsulates Hungarian history since 1944.

Even when Central European poets are not consciously writing of these issues, history is like atmospheric pressure. They may not be conscious of it, but it pervades everything they do, including their response to current events. Perhaps as a result, they very much want literature to matter. At the Vilenica conference in 2001, I participated in a round-table on the ultimate PEN topic, "Can Literature Save the World?" My answer, which seemed to disappoint some of the audience, was not only that it couldn't but that, given the dubious political opinions of some modernist writers and the quirky indifference of some of their postmodern successors, it shouldn't even try. Still, a Lithuanian editor was interested enough to ask if he could publish a translation — only to back out when, less than a week after the conference, the terrorist attack took place on September 11. My conclusion, he felt, was too bleak. The implication was that something should at least try to save the world. And if not literature, what? A month or so later, I ran across Gerald Vizenor, a contemporary and former colleague, who had been asked for a comment, in literary or ordinary language, about 9-11. He had refused on the grounds that the best thing to say about the event, now and maybe ever, was nothing. At that point, I hadn't heard Czesław Miłosz's comment to the effect that large subjects made for bad writing, but Vizenor and I had already agreed.

American writers may not feel as uneasy about making large claims for literature as I do, but they seem to be uncomfortable, or at least self-conscious, in writing about history and current large events. There were many poems about Vietnam — but how many do readers remember at all, or remember without embarrassment at the forced rhetoric and largely unearned moral superiority?

One insight into the difference between American — and West European — writers and their colleagues to the east came to me in Bucharest in 2000 at a symposium on postmodernism. In the course of the discussions, I made the distinction between witnesses, including the writers from countries newly independent from Soviet control and writers from the former Yugoslavia, and spectators, including not just Americans but an Englishman and a Dutchman. The latter had seen the political and physical consequences in the media. To know what it was really like, you had, as Americans put it, to have been there.

And Americans and West Europeans hadn't been "there." Instead, it could be argued, most of our generations too young for the Depression and World War II looked to personal rather than to political experience.

Take, for example, what is arguably one of the most intensely personal subjects for a male poet: the relationship with his father. I found several poems by Slovene writers, and, looking for something from a younger generation, I asked Debeljak, born in 1961, if he had a poem about his father. He replied that his father is still alive — as if the father had to be dead for the son to write about him. This seemed odd until I thought about it — and shows, as I shall demonstrate, that Central Europeans and Americans are not, perhaps, all that different.

The difficulty of addressing a father directly when he is alive is illustrated in the prose piece, "Remembering an Unshared Narrative," by my friend and contemporary George Economou. Going to visit his father for the last time, he enters the hospital room, greets his father, and hears him say, "Who is this?" Economou tries to dismiss the lapse, until "his death restored it to a definitive standing in my memories of our relationship" and "introduced grounds for questioning all of my self-assured assumptions about how well I had known him.... My special images of us together were no longer secure, now that I realized it was only blind faith in my own feelings about them that led me to believe I knew anything concerning his feelings about them." At the end, Economou knows that "the memories, instead of behaving like simple acts of preservation, sustained the truth that I had indeed not known him as well as I thought I had and that I would spend the rest of my life trying to know him in memoriam under the same conditions as I had when he was alive, only now with all illusions eluded" (*Century Dead Center* [Left Hand Books, 1997]).

A few years ago, my son, in his early thirties, asked me, "What kind of father was grandpa?" I'd written a book of which, I discovered, my father was the central figure, and my son had read it. And still had to ask the question I fumbled to answer. I didn't want to ask him what kind of father I was — because, though I couldn't say it to him, I didn't think I was finished with the job. But I finally tried to answer his question in an essay, "Fathers and Sons," published in *The Ornamental Hermit: People and Places of the New West* (Texas Tech, 2004).

For Central European sons, the relationship seems to be remoter and more connected to history than it is to Americans. I haven't found a translation of a poem about his father by the Hungarian poet Ottó Orbán, but he once said, "My mother's relatives killed my father" — in a labor battalion in the second World War, because he was Jewish.

My near-contemporary Veno Taufer, born in 1933, dedicated his "Melancholy of the Second Echelon I — V" to his father, killed in 1943 during the second world war. However, this can hardly be seen as a personal poem. It begins not with a person or situation but with an indeterminate setting and an unspecified time:

> for long now the evenings
> the wax-dripped hands
> of our forebearers have been
>
> on columns of souls

and it goes on, three stanzas later, to speak not of a father but of "fathers." There is not even a single speaker, but a "we" who may, autobiographically considered, speak for Taufer's generation, but nothing in the poem limits the poem to a specific time. In fact, the language, stern, remote in tone, almost abstract, prevents identification with the reader and the situation. It is as impersonal as a requiem, ending

> with earthen eyes
> we will wait for
> the coup de grace
> and keep silent keep silent
>   [*Veno Taufer*, trans. Michael Biggins]

Iztok Osojnik's "Father" has first-person singular speaker in a specific room talking to what seems to be the memory of an actual father:

> You never said a thing
> and I didn't hear a thing,
> yet it is clear:
> my poet's apartment
> powerfully shines in
> the twilight of your
> silence.

But before very long, he moves from the personal, or personally impersonal relationship to a generalized natural setting and then, inevitably, to "fingers of world history [which] seeped through, and touched the shoulders." Not anyone's shoulders in particular and no real fingers at all — here I am anticipating images in poems by American writers. Born in 1951, he is, like his older contemporaries, aware that "History kept coming on like floods." Then, like Taufer, he speaks in first person plural:

> We are all marked,
> we all have, with centered foreheads, recorded what
> we have not always understood.

Finally, he returns to a definite historical time and place, "the vineyard cottage / which got nationalized after the war along with the rest / of the estate, making wine that received an award / that still hangs on the wall I'm looking at." At the end, he returns to the time and place in which the poem began ("Father," *The Fire Under the Moon*, trans. Mia Dintinjana).

Not all poems are this steeped in history, but even an apparently personal poem like Kajetan Kovič's "Mon père" focuses on a generalized, though moving and perfectly recognizable, sense of the uneasy relationship between son and father. Although they talked, the subjects are not mentioned, and the poem gives no sense of what the father was like, and there is not even a metaphorical finger or shoulder. At the end, the son speaks, but the father cannot listen: "There was no one like you / So alone, / So mine, So father, / Lost in the world / Like me" (*Poems*, trans. Igor Maver).

Poems by three American writers I have selected feature sons speaking to a father who is dead and silent. They seem, in contrast to their Central European counterparts, almost innocent of history or indeed of any context outside a hospital room. This is not due to innocence or lack of experience. All three have lived outside the United States; all have doctorates in literature from major universities and began as students of literature and scholars publishing on it. One is a combat veteran.

But the anxiety in these poems is not political, like that in Taufer and Osojnik, but deals with questions of personal survival and continuity rather than national concerns. Alvin Greenberg's "my father had connections" deals with the son's attempt to live by and gradual estrangement from the father's hopes and ideals. They work together in an office, and

> some days we even shared a desk, where under his dark eyes
> i wondered whose life he saw me living now. it wasn't mine,
> i knew: i couldn't wait to take it off when i got home,
> though daily i did the things i knew this stranger's life
> had me connected to: worked, lunched, joined the JCs,

married, golfed, home owned, drank a little ... more,
broke from the depths of dreams in dark and sudden terror.
*
but then one night it happens: the ballet master in your
head steps from the dark wings and orders you to make

an impossible lift....
though you've never danced before, and this odd outfit...
where did it come from? how does it fit? where can you go

like this that your father wouldn't turn away? and who,
exactly — as if you didn't know — are you supposed to lift?

In Greenberg's "in the examining room," the anxiety turns the other way. The fist is a simile for the lump on the father's spine that turns at the end into a metaphor, but the knot, spine, father, and speaker are very particular and almost unbearably real. And finally the pain is translated from the physical to the metaphysical, the only legacy the son can claim.

               in the examining room
my father said he felt no pain, though the doctor
thumped his back so hard it made me wince.

a knot at the base of his spine as big as a fist
that wouldn't let go pulled him further down each day.

the world grew short. my father said he felt no pain
but suddenly couldn't decide what he wanted to eat

and looked, all day, for the keys he didn't own.
the knot at the base of his spine as big as a fist

squeezed hard on the world it held in its grip.
names and keys and appetites got crushed. i winced

to hear my father say he felt no pain every time
the doctor thumped his back. however small it's

grown, a world needs more than that: the pain not
felt, lost keys and names, indifferent appetite

tighten their grip each day: a panicked swimmer,
absence grabs us all and pulls us down. the knot

as big as a fist at the base of his spine held on
to me, although my father said he felt no pain.

My "Lines of Descent" doesn't have a setting, but I conceived it while watching my father's drug-induced slumber in an intensive care unit. Like Greenberg's poem, it attempts to find some continuity across the generations, but here body parts have no obvious metaphorical weight except to show the differences between father and son. But in the final stanza there is both identification and metaphor, which may be a mistake:

> Looked at the other way, I am your son:
> legs built short to lever from the ground,
> weight of shoulder, torso's length,
> long spine stiff against the strain
> the world and we put on it [*Oklawaha Review*, 1989].

The third American poet, Walt McDonald, is a real Texan and a real cowboy, at least third generation in both cases, and an Air Force pilot who saw a great deal of combat in Vietnam and wrote about it—or, as in the poems in *After the Noise of Saigon*, about its effect on his view of the world. But in "Never in My Life," McDonald stands at the hospital bed on which his father lies dying, thinks of his father's service in Flanders and his own in Vietnam. But the two wars are biographical facts rather than determining factors in the relationship, in which neither has ever used the word "love." At the end, the poet says it, hears the old man gasp, and thinks "I've killed him." But the breathing continues, the father's eyes wander, and finally

> ... the drugs drowned him again
> in sleep. It was enough,
> was all I could receive or ever give
> to him. Even in that glaze
> that stared toward death,
> I had seen him take me in,
> been blessed by what I needed all my life
>   [*Whatever the Wind Delivers*].

In this poem, it is not too late to mention love. But mostly, as in Greenberg's "in the examining room," it is. I never said it to my father, but when my sister showed him "Lines of Descent," he said, "He certainly has a way with words." D. H. Lawrence wrote that "The essential American soul is hard, isolate, stoic, and a killer" ("Fenimore Cooper's Leatherstocking Novels"). These poems prove that at least we aren't all that hard or stoic. But our chief emotion is pathos, not tragedy. And what we mourn is loss of energy, motion.

The differences between the European and American poets I have mentioned are obvious. But how to account for them? It is easier for me to explain Americans. Very few of us are conscious of wanting to be poets from an early age. Writers my age probably saw poetry only in school anthologies, and dreary enough that was. As my first teaching mentor said in 1955, "If there's one thing that the average American boy hates more than Communism, it's poetry." Until I went to college in a fairly large city, I did not even know that magazines existed to publish living writers, and even then I saw them only in bound library volumes. American education may produce (mostly would-be) athletes — Greenberg and I held on to the fantasy that we were really baseball players well into middle age — or businessmen or consumers of popular culture and a great deal else. Mostly it teaches middle-class values when it teaches anything at all. But with rare exceptions the system does not encourage or even allow for the kind of passion that makes a young person with verbal skills burn, and train, to be a poet. Greenberg's experience in "my father had connections" differs only in details, not in spirit, from that of most American poets. We come to the practice of poetry, and for that matter reading it, relatively late. And we don't, except for periods like the Vietnam War and the occasional poem attacking ecological stupidity or a social injustice, seem to feel that poetry has much chance of changing anything. Ottó Orbán and some younger Slovene poets have come to the same conclusion, but they had to overcome decades or centuries of belief that poetry could be a powerful instrument of change.

Another possible reason: because we lack a culture in the European sense, we are much more closely bound to the specific heritage of our families — and, as my examples have shown, the death and absence of the father unsettles us into a doubt that is fertile even if it cannot be resolved.

Therefore, our poetry tends, as I've argued, to have a narrower focus than European writing. And because the traditional language of poetry does not seem natural even to poets, American poets tend to use vernacular rather than literary language, even if, as adults, they have been steeped in that language. To use myself as an example, when I was young, I regarded literature as a kind of magic carpet to a world different from anything I could see around me. For a long time, I didn't think of writers as people who, as our athletes say, put on their pants one leg at a time. Not until I was in my teens did it occur to me that I might be able to write myself, though I had no idea of how to go about it. As an undergraduate, I wrote a few poems, mostly doggerel, but still had no sense of writing, except perhaps journalism, as a vocation. Later, while studying for a doctorate in English, I discovered that writers were at least as human as other people, and sometimes moreso. Still later, after years of reading poetry for courses and exams, all the way through the Ph.D., teaching it as seldom as possible, and writing it not at all, I was driving from Lubbock, Texas, to Oklahoma when a rhythm came into my mind. At the next town, I pulled over and jotted some notes on a napkin and later published my first poem in thirty years.

The poem itself was full of literary allusions, but the voice and tone came from nothing and nowhere I could recognize from my schooling. Later, when I turned back to informal prose after an even longer hiatus and in a quite different style, I realized that both voices came less from academic training than from real voices echoing in my head—my father's and my maternal grandfather's. Grandfather Murray told wild, tall tales, and some of his rhythms show up in prose and prose poems, with some of the timing due to the oral style of mid-Missouri, where I grew up. But most of the poetry is in a voice a lot like my father's. I don't know if that would have pleased him, but it probably would have surprised him — though he wouldn't have shown it.

At any rate, my rhythms are based as much as possible on oral traditions. I'm more interested in the way the lines fall from the tongue than the way they look on the page. And that's obviously true of Greenberg and McDonald as well. And not so obviously true of Taufer's poem, though Osojnik's and Kovič's have, at least in translation, some oral qualities. Furthermore, many of the themes and images from my poems, and from Al's and Walt's, come from the ethos, values, and settings of my past. The training to become a writer was a way of riding the magic carpet away from where I began, but it is clear that many of my poems are a way of preserving and celebrating that past.

Another major contrast between Americans and Europeans is that Americans tended, at least before September 11, 2001, to act as though they think that history is over — or enough of them did to make Francis Fukuyama's *The End of History* a best-seller. Or, if it isn't over, that it took place somewhere else. Mark Twain's remark, quoted earlier, implies this view, and even Walt McDonald, in the uncollected poem "Fathers Who Fought in Flanders" as well as in lines about returning from Southeast Asia, implies that though war, and history, can affect Americans, it cannot within our shores directly touch us. Or could not. It is too soon to read poems written as a result of 9/11, though it is safe to say that, because American poets are not well versed in the language of public pronouncement, most of them will be bad, the rhetoric forced and the emotions escalated. And it remains to be seen whether one event can shatter any American myth.

The only American poets who really lack this aura of invulnerability are minority writers: African Americans, American Indians, some Asian-Americans, some Hispanics. Many of these writers draw energy from their situation and that of their people, so that the Spokane-Coeur d'Alene writer Sherman Alexie can posit the formula "Poetry = Anger × Imagination." And though they can risk bathos, they can sometimes go beyond pathos into tragedy. A white male poet not only risks bathos; he cannot escape it.

But the general image of America, for most Americans as well as Europeans, comes from the sheer concrete physical presence of America and Americans. I can spot a countryman anywhere in Europe because we look, move, and shape our words differently from any European. Those Europeans, especially Central Europeans, who contemplate the American scene must look at us as the earthbound looked at the televised scenes of the astronauts on the moon. How high they bounce, unweighted by gravity or history; how oddly they are dressed, protected by technology against danger and even inconvenience.

At some level, some Europeans would like to be able to do that. Orbán cannot resist thinking "what if"? Living in America forces him out onto a tightrope between Hungarian and English, aware that he could have emigrated and lived differently but content in the knowledge that "of all places my birthplace was the best where I could be I, / where whatever the pressure, since clamped in the vise of language and bad luck, / after every malarial onslaught of style I remained who I was" ("The Tightrope Walker Takes a Bow," *The Journey of Barbarus*, trans. Bruce Berlind).

Who he is is European. And though, unlike my colleagues at the 2000 PEN conference in Slovenia, he does not insist on talking about Literature with a capital L or its role in bringing about world peace, he is steeped in that tradition. And because of his experience under Nazis, Russians, and Hungarian communists, he can talk about Liberty without embarrassing anyone, least of all himself. No American writer has been able to do that since Whitman or perhaps since the beginning of the nineteenth century.

American poets may envy the high seriousness of the Europeans and long for the influence they had, especially under various repressive regimes when they were the sole voice of aspirations for freedom. But it would be a mistake for Americans to try to appropriate the language, themes, and tones of European poets. And it would be the deadliest kind of sin to envy the misfortunes which give weight to their work.

We can respect their work and perhaps flavor our own with what we learn from them. They can — and writers as various as Orbán, Debeljak, and Tomaž Šalamun have — learned from American writers that intense emotion can be conveyed in language that is the very reverse of rhetorical.

But all of us can do serious work only if we follow Orbán's implied advice to be true to ourselves — not just our vision, which can be forced and fraudulent, but what is most deeply felt in our lived experience. All of us can be better, but none of us can be other than what we are. We should remember, and adapt as best we can, the words of the very American F. Scott Fitzgerald: "Begin with an individual, and before you know it you find that you have created a type; begin with a type, and you find that you have created — nothing."

A Postscript

During a trip to Slovenia in 2003, I encountered the work of several poets who made me question my conclusion. In "Psalm — Magnolia in the April Snow," Uroš Zupan's speaker speaks to his father

> of the world that you will
> never enter, of heaven and hell,
> of ecstasies that take possession over me and of the fall of Icarus.

And so on, condemning his father for conventionality and hoping to free the older man to see

> Some piece of the moon above us and some bright moments
> which open to us like the magnolias
> of my dreams, magnolias opening in the April snow
> [*Ten Slovenian Poets of the Nineties*].

Zupan is in his early forties as I write; Peter Semolič is four years younger. In "Hatchet in a Knot," the speaker accepts the coldness between him and his father and asks him to admit that the sharp edge exists "So death will be easier for you / and life less of a burden for me" (*Ten*). Neither historicizes the father-son situation. Rather, they see the conflict in terms of cultural values familiar to anyone in America who grew up after World War II. And, of course, they are much younger than any of the poets, Slovene or American, whom I have mentioned.

Still, even Iztok Osojnik seems, in his collection *Mister Today*, to undercut my argument. In "Truth," the speaker's father is in a hospital, fading in and out of coma, the speaker absent when he did awaken. In "Son Meeting His Father," the poet looks at his infant son, aware that his own father is dying, "and between the two worlds incomprehensible chasms gape" (21). And in "A Sensitive Cold of Music Playing," the poet writes that

> For almost a year now my father has struggled
> on the border
> of life and death
> and I am getting fat. Who am I?

Without minimizing Central European and American differences, I can admit that age has something to do with attitudes toward the father. Osojnik apparently wrote the "Mister Today" poems in his late forties. McDonald, Greenberg, and I were all in our fifties when we wrote the poems I quoted, and all were fathers of grown children, in two cases grandfathers, and conscious of our position in a sequence that was beginning to seem like a chain.

In contrast, Aleš Šteger, who is younger than Orbán's and my children, offers in his poem "Europe" an interesting corrective to the simultaneous sentiments and rejections of those born before World War II.

EUROPE

Even now you're peddling the story that the Turks
Dismantling their tents at the gates of Vienna was just a ruse.
That in the clothing of shish-kebab vendors
They're only biding their time for the right moment
To leap out of the kiosks and slice your gizzard,
Though your tribes are lost forever
In the swamps of your barbaric designs
And you yourself can no longer tell the skull of a Goth
From the skull of a Slav from the skull of an Angle from the skull of a Frank,
Still you believe that only the death of your sons makes you young again.
You still think you'll fool us all.
Closing my tired eyes, I see you appear
In the image of a fat, hairy woman giving birth while snoring,
And a man, who in the dark beside her secretly masturbates,
Fantasizing about America [*Ten*].

2

Out of the Shadows
Slovene Writing After Independence

The flight path into Ljubljana from Western Europe comes over the Swiss or the Julian Alps, an impressive and indeed forbidding sight. But on the approach, evergreen forests slope into fields and down to Brnik Airport with its one-story terminal, rolling stairs descending to the tarmac and a waiting bus. As a German fellow passenger on his first visit remarked, "It's so quiet!"

Like everything in Slovenia, the airport is built to a very human scale. The country stretches, if that is the right term, from its Adriatic coastline of less than thirty miles east and up to the Italian border to Hungary and north and south between the Austrian border at the crest of the Alps and its longest border, with Croatia.

Even by European standards, it is a small country: the Lonely Planet guide, the only one devoted entirely to Slovenia, compares it "with Wales, Israel, or half of Switzerland." Yet it is remarkably varied. As a Slovenian folktale puts it, when God finished creating the rest of the world, He put everything left over into Slovenia.

Ljubljana, the capitol and largest city, is smaller and more compact than most European cities of comparable national importance. In the city center, within a radius of a few blocks, one can find Parliament, the opera house, the National Gallery, the Modern Art museum, the National Museum, Parliament, Presin theater, Prešern Square (named after the national poet, under whose statue most people choose to meet), the Slovenian Writers' Association, two gorgeous baroque churches and the cathedral, the cafes and boutiques which line the small, thoroughly tamed and photogenic Ljubljanica River, and excellent bookshops and restaurants, where in warm weather the inhabitants line the riverfront's outdoor cafes. The city is safe enough that a friend confidently sent his sons, four and six, down the crowded walkway to get ice cream—a shock to an American familiar with child abduction. The castle, not impossibly high above the city, is a stiff walk or short taxi ride from the center. In short, Ljubljana is a user- or at least tourist-friendly city, and the inhabitants seem less harried than in other capitols. A Dutch friend writes appreciatively of Slovenia and its people, in contrast to Austria, though he expects to see gnomes coming out of the forest.

Slovenia appears to have an enviable position among the recently independent states of southern and central Europe. For one thing, the guidebook insists that it is not really Balkan because the Balkans begin at the Kolpa River, part of the boundary with Croatia. But until 1991 it was tied more closely to the Balkans than many Slovenes found comfortable, and since then they have been struggling to escape the rest of former Yugoslavia and the rest of the Balkans, rather like the unfortunate cat trying to wriggle loose from the embraces of the amorous skunk Pepe le Peu in the cartoon.

Demographically, Slovenia has been fortunate. Until very recently, with Orthodox and Muslim immigration from more troubled areas of the former Yugoslavia, it had a population remarkably homogeneous compared to the rest of the region. And it enjoys great publicity in the West: the day the Slovenian government signed the agreement to enter the European Union, in April, 2003, the BBC carried a very favorable story, illustrated with clips from Prešeren Square, Lake Bled, and the Adriatic port Koper, about its current stability and bright economic future.

Of course, while Slovenia is undeniably picturesque and friendly, it has not been immune from the tremors of the past two centuries. The Austrian yoke seems in retrospect lighter than those of later regimes, but it was not easy to bear. Slovenians suffered during both World Wars, and every town has a memorial to the struggle against the Nazis. The Communist regime was to some degree less oppressive than Stalinism, but a Slovenian born in 1940, not a writer, speaks with only a little bitterness of conditions "as long as Tito was alive." And though Slovenia won independence from Yugoslavia within ten days and sixty-six fatalities, Slovenes watched with horror the anguish of former countrymen in Croatia, Bosnia-Hercegovina, and Kosovo.

Within its borders, however, the transition to capitalism and democracy went more smoothly than in other Slavic states. Slovenia was the most modern and prosperous of the Yugoslav republics (8 percent of the population produced 20 percent of the GNP and, according to one Slovenian, 30 percent of the federal tax revenue, of which, he says, about 10 percent was returned). In 2000, in Euromoney's ranking for country risk, Slovenia placed ahead of the Czech Republic, Poland, and Hungary, thirty-third to Austria's ninth. It was on the fastest track for NATO and EU membership, which came in 2004, and is systematically shifting its orientation and its public image from the Balkans to Central Europe. Better still, except for some Serbs, who call the Slovenes Western lackeys, there seems to be no animosity toward Slovenians on the part of other countries, even those who constitute minorities in the Trieste region in Italy and in Austria — though some Slovenes think that the Italians take every opportunity to remind them of their occupation of the Littoral, and Miran Košuta gives a gloomier picture from a Slovene in Italy in "Dzevad's Prophecy: Essay About the Minority Question" (*Slovenian Essay*). Some border problems with Italy and Croatia remain to be worked out, but these disputes do not appear to be heated.

There are also some unresolved issues with the Catholic Church. In Slovenia, as in other Central and Eastern European countries recovering from a half-century of communist domination, both church and state are still learning to function in a democratic society where at least seventy percent of the two million Slovenes are Catholic. A modus operandi or vivendi, let alone a tradition, cannot be established in a decade.

The cultures and institutions of the Hapsburgs and the Communists are gone, but they have a half-life that explains the conflict between Catholics determined to regain the position of the Church before World War II and liberals who speak darkly of the Church as a danger to individual freedom and even to the political future of the nation. For example, Marjan Rožanc thought the Counter-Reformation responsible for the fact that Slovenia accepted not only clericalism but also "our principal religious, cultural and political structure of life, which since then we would never get rid of again" (*Terra Incognita*). As a result, Slovenia never had a Renaissance, so that "our souls are distinctly subjected to clericalism and totalitarianism or, in a word, to servitude."

Rožanc goes back to the Reformation for historical and theoretical justification of anticlericalism, but there are more recent explanations. For example, many liberals are former communists, like president Milan Kučan and the Liberal Democrats who until recently were the dominant force in Parliament. They may not remember the Kingdom of Yugoslavia, but they were taught that the Church was not only the enemy of the people but had actively collaborated with German and Italian invaders.

On the other hand, until Church property was confiscated by the Tito regime in 1945, it maintained a broad network of educational, medical, and charitable institutions that was supported by extensive holdings, especially in the forest lands of Slovenia. Perhaps more significant was the fact that, under the Hapsburgs, the Church provided the major career opportunities for bright, ambitious Slovene boys. In many parishes, the priest was the only person who could have been called an intellectual, and thus the Church had enormous influence in social and cultural as well as religious matters—a distinction that few people observed then or—as some liberals insist—even now. And many Slovene Catholics would like to recover some of the influence lost in 1945.

Losses of all kinds were significant. About 250 priests were imprisoned; another 200 fled to the West. Many Catholics, including most lay intellectuals, were executed or went into exile, and the loss affects the Church and the political parties allied to it even now. Both clerics and anti-clericals agree that the conservatives suffer from the loss of a generation of potential leaders.

The Church labored under other restrictions. Church property was confiscated; Church publications were suppressed. The archdiocese had no formal leadership, and the vicar of Ljubljana (the bishop in exile was not replaced for political reasons obvious to anyone who lived through the Cold War) had to report nightly to the police. Nuns were forbidden to work in hospitals—many went to Macedonia and Montenegro—and teachers were forbidden on pain of dismissal to be affiliated with the Church. Priests had no access to hospitals, prisons, or homes for the aged. All religious education was banned from schools. Christmas was a working day.

Restoration of church rights and privileges followed a piecemeal pattern. After Slovenia gained independence, Archbishop Alojzij Šuštar moved with characteristic moderation. He told Christopher Merrill that "we distinguish between the country's politics and spiritual mission" and that "we are not connected to any political parties. We support the freedom of Catholics to choose their parties." (Of course, the hierarchy appears to hope that Catholics will choose the Peoples' Party and the Christian Democrats.) This moderation offended some conservative Catholics, and though Archbishop Šuštar joined well-known writers and intellectuals in signing what Sabrina Petra Ramet regards as a right-wing attack on supposed communist survivals in government, she reports that Šuštar was regarded as a "red archbishop."

His successor, Archbishop France Rode, was been far more outspoken, demanding that religious instruction be reintroduced into public schools and speaking against abortion before he assumed the Vatican post that Cardinal Ratzinger vacated when he became Pope Benedict XVI. Thus far, the Church has made little headway on the second issue, and in fact a 1995 poll indicated that two-thirds of those surveyed opposed the first measure. But by 2003, courses in religion had become optional—though not many students seemed to be exercising the option.

The Church is clearly eager to regain social influence, and this is stated most clearly in a pamphlet about the Church in Slovenia: "The Church is faced with the task of the restoration of the Spirit and moral values among the Slovene nation." Liberals see this as an attempt to limit personal freedom and return to the conditions of 1939, if not 1539.

But this controversy seems not to affect new social trends, positive or negative. On the streets of Ljubljana and Kočevje, where I have spent most time, there are numerous signs of individual and public prosperity. Near Kočevje, villages of German settlements established in the Fourteenth Century were emptied during and largely destroyed after the Axis occupation in World War II, but they are being rebuilt with solid new houses and repopulated, partly by immigrants displaced from Bosnia, Kosovo, and Croatia who have brought sheep-raising to the economy and a more problematic mixture of Orthodox and Muslim practices to the culture. Kočevje has a large and sparkling new library and a new grade school going up on the edge of town near the house of a surveyor who has just finished a large new house at a cost that in Ljubljana would buy a one-bedroom place. This raises some questions about Iztok Osojnik's quotable remark that the country may be poor, but the people are not.

Of course, there are no Edens left. The restrooms at the new library are kept locked because people as young as ten or eleven are using them to do drugs, and substance abuse is even more of a problem in Ljubljana. Aleš Šteger, a writer-musician just over thirty, comments that his generation was too young to participate in the changes in 1991 and therefore could not get the positions opening up. But people even younger seem to him aimless. "They're bored with everything. They think about Ecstasy and want to go to Paris and London. They drink, or smoke their joints, listen to techno music, hang out" (*Neue Zürcher Zeitung*, January 8, 2002).

But older writers do not seem to complain as much as their colleagues in Slovakia and Hungary, though when told this they seem disconcerted and perhaps a little offended. But their situation is different from that of writers in Hungary and Romania, though it is analogous to that of Slovakia. From the eighth century until 1991, Slovenes were a nation rather than a state, held together by language and culture rather than by self-generated political structures. This feeling is so strong that, in a country perhaps 80 percent Catholic, the door of Ljubljana's cathedral features the first three books printed in Slovene — all Protestant. From the nineteenth century on, writers like France Prešeren, Ivan Cankar, and Edvard Kocbek served as creators, conservators, and transmitters of Slovene identity, and their names and likenesses are prominent on street signs, public monuments, and currency. Slovenia not only has a high literacy rate, but the people actually read — in 1999, libraries circulated eight to ten million books to a total population of two million, and a person who reads fewer than ten books a year is not regarded as a serious reader. For example, the library in Kočevje has a steady stream of patrons of all ages. To be sure, some are there to use the Internet, like a group of teenagers doing a search on Evel Knevel.

Literature has continued to be important politically. After 1945, and especially in the decade before independence, writers continued to serve as the conscience of the Slovene people. They were in the forefront of movements for a free and democratic Slovenia, like the founders of the soon-suppressed magazine *Oder 57* (*Theater 57*). The Committee for Freedom of Speech and Writing, associated with the Slovenian Writers' Association, sponsored a group whose members wrote a draft that was the basis of the present Slovenian constitution; and a number of writers served in the first democratic government. And *Nova Revija* (New Review, founded 1982) was enormously influential. Aleš Debeljak noted that the organizations and initiatives "represented a kind of umbrella institution. Under its precarious protection sought and found refuge astoundingly varied ideological groups, individuals, tendencies, programs, and agendas. Because of its licentia poetica, the cultural sphere, vaguely defined as it always was, more or less successfully bypassed the communist control" (Debeljak, "Haven").

This activity was perhaps less dangerous than it would have been in the Soviet Bloc, for repression under Tito and his successors, though not to be minimized, was less severe. In fact, Aleš Berger was able to reject Party membership and even a position in theater. When he declined, "I didn't get beaten, I was even given as much fruit juice as I could drink," though there was some shouting ("Notes from Gmajna," *Slovenian Essay*). True, several collections of poems and rather more fiction and nonfiction had to appear in samizdat and many writers were arrested and tried and some convicted or, like Edvard Kocbek, officially silenced. This side of the communist era was memorialized in the exhibition and book, *The Dark Side of the Moon*, organized by Vasko Simoniti and Drago Jančar, which has not been translated. However, according to a writer who refused to participate in the project, many writers managed to survive official disapproval and even to become part of the nomenklatura. Now it is a mark of distinction to have been jailed. The fact that the sentence might have been for drunkenness is delicately avoided. Writers whose sole theme was dissidence now have difficulty coming up with new subjects.

For a variety of reasons, the government of independent Slovenia, whether liberal or conservative, has been inclined to foster what Iztok Osojnik terms the level of genuine creativity in language and culture. Although in 2003 there were complaints about diminishing support, and in 2004 a nationalist-conservative government was apparently purging liberals in the organizations they could not starve out by shifting resources, cultural funding has continued to a far greater extent than in the former Soviet satellites and in greater numbers than it did before 1991. For example, one survival from the Tito era is the program of the free artist which provides to about a thousand artists in all media minimal social and medical benefits and an automatic deduction of forty percent of income as costs of production. (There is discussion of abolishing the last benefit, and the liberals are regarded as most likely to push for that.) The government gives some support to the Slovenian Writers' Association, founded under the Hapsburgs, with three hundred members and a very active program. Unlike Slovakia, the Association is unified (though there was an attempted coup by younger writers beaten back by the older), with one rather than six organizations seeking funds. Unlike its Hungarian counterpart, the Association seems to be in fairly healthy condition.

There is some concern about increased bureaucratization in the Ministry of Culture, which according to one report has grown from forty to 120 employees, many of whom seem to be busy constructing forms so complicated that eighty percent of proposals have been rejected, with no appeal possible, purely on administrative grounds because publishers and writers can't figure them out. And one writer was told to comply with new directives by reducing his work week from forty-two to forty hours. The exact text of his reply has not been and probably cannot be published.

On the positive side, the Ministry of Culture subsidizes publication of books in many genres, including about 200 original works a year, forty to fifty of them literary works, about twenty translations of Slovene writers into other languages, seventy or so technical and cultural publications, and some translations, including William S. Burroughs' *Naked Lunch*, of foreign work into Slovenian. It also supports magazines like *Literatura* and nine theaters, three of them in Ljubljana, though some dramatists complain that translated popular work has all but driven out new Slovenian drama.

In fact, the number of books published each year has increased markedly since independence. To some extent, this is a result of independence: the need to catch up with the basic Western canon and also to publish in Slovene reference books that had, in Yugoslavia, appeared in Serbo-Croatian. But more original works are also being published.

Given a population of two million, editions tended to be small even under Communist rule. As a result, Slovenia did not experience as precipitous a drop in edition sizes as Hungary and Slovakia. With rare exceptions,

3,000 copies was a standard edition for a first novel before independence, and it sold out in six months. Now, even for books likely to be popular, 2,000 is a high number, with perhaps 500 for poetry. Andrej Blatnik, author of *Skinswaps* (Evanston, Ill.: Northwestern University Press, 1998) and other fiction and an editor at Cankarjeva publishing house, says that anything selling over five to seven hundred copies is regarded as a best-seller. Their biggest hit was a travel book about Burkina Faso which sold 2200 copies—why, he is not sure. And in "The Future of Literature..." he adds that "the difference in the sales of a genre best-seller and a hermetic collection of poems is some four hundred copies" (*Slovenian Essay*). Cankarjeva is a general publishing house, using cookbooks and other popular titles to finance creative work. Or it was until a bigger publishing house, now dominant in the market, bought it. Cankareva is still able to publish quality books, but there is increased pressure to consider profits, a situation familiar in American publishing.

Financial arrangements for writers are simple if not very remunerative. Instead of royalties, they receive a flat fee, usually ranging from $1,000 to $4,000, and magazines still pay for contributions. *Nova Revija* continues to be very important; *Literatura* and *Apokolipsa* (which includes some foreign writers in translation) are influential; and many other newspapers and magazines serve as outlets. However, in order to survive, writers have to be willing to write in all genres of journalism as well as literature, to teach, to translate, to edit, and to work as cultural managers of associations and institutions. But as Aleš Debeljak says, he and others write in non-literary genres not so much for money as to maintain their positions as public intellectuals.

But finding someone to listen is becoming more difficult. Debeljak says that "As individuals who struggled for freedom and against totalitarian limits to the human spirit, [writers] were defeated by their own success. Freedom of choice also implies a freedom not to choose to listen to the writers' voices any longer" (Debeljak, "Ethics"). Perhaps more important, nascent capitalism, farther advanced at the beginning of independence than in the Soviet Bloc, has given the potential audience a wider range of positive choice. Evald Flisar, former president of the Writers' Association and now a free-lance writer, notes that in free market the number of publishers mushroomed. Matej Bogataj counted 150 in 1999, with 2500 titles per year (*Mosaic*). Moreover, translations of popular psychology and New Age books, never before available, are bought by the kilo. (However, one does not see on the streets of Ljubljana, as in Budapest, the stalls lined with Harold Robbins, Barbara Cartland, and other writers of disposable books. Iztok Osojnik attributes the difference not to the superiority of Slovene taste but to the fact that other merchandise is much more profitable.)

As a result, the average book buyer—lower middle class—not only has more choice but has trouble paying the new prices. Besides, newly available consumer goods, the Internet, and other options have cut into the book market. And books are expensive. The paperback edition of *Naked Lunch* was priced at just over $18, the hardback now available $30, and a bookstore clerk was appalled at the $20 price of a very slim volume. One editor speculates that publishers know that a core audience of perhaps 500 will continue to buy books and do not think it worthwhile to lower prices to attract another hundred or so readers.

Nevertheless, writers of all generations continue to be productive, though the subject matter and sense of mission have gone through obvious changes. Historically, major Slovene writers were acutely conscious of their importance to Slovene identity, and this sense of mission required a language, especially in poetry, that was sometimes more distinguished for exhortation than lyricism. France Prešeren (1800–1849) is Slovenia's universally honored poet; his "A Toast to Freedom," which became the Slovenian national anthem, has lines like "Let thunder out of heaven / Strike down and smite our wanton foe!" A century later, Edvard Kocbek (1904–1981) wrote "The Lippizaners," which can be seen as an ironic complement to "Toast," though it too calls for all men, or Slovenians, to ride a horse that is not just a Lippizaner but perhaps Pegasus or another form of inspired aid, because

> motors tend to break down
> elephants eat too much,
> our road is a long one,
> and it is too far to walk [*Terra Incognita*].

His "Slovenian Hymn" contains lines like "Disowned, you endure, great mother, quietly calling us, you have been ravaged, fertile body, and your children put to shame," but it ends with imagery of intoxication in "the ageless secret" (*Terra Incognita*). And Kocbek's essay "On Poetry" (*Afterwards*) is full of vatic utterances like "poetry is divination on the border of the world of dreams and the world of reality...."

Kocbek was also a politician, and one of the founders of the Slovenian Liberation Front. Independent as poet and political thinker, he was discredited by the Tito regime, his work denied publication for more than a decade. Now that work is readily available—even, with a little trouble, in English. *Na vratih zvecer/At the Door at Evening*, published in Canada, I have not seen; *Edvard Kocbek*, published in Ljubljana, I acquired in Europe. Neither is likely to be familiar to most speakers of English. The third volume, *Embers in the House of Night* (Santa Fe, NM: Lumen, 1999, trans. Sonja Kravanja), was the most accessible, both physically and poetically, to the American reader until

Princeton University Press's publication in 2004 of *Nothing Is Lost: Selected Poems*.

Although neither volume dates the poems, Biggins' selection appears to present early, lyric poems dealing with traditional Slovene life in the natural world and those with long, Whitmanesque lines like "Song about Man," "Lesser Psalm," and "Slovene Hymn." Kravanja features poems addressed to women, invocations, vatic pronouncements, and apocalyptic visions of violence in nature, many of them with long series of clauses, and a love of abstractions like "history," "essence," "mystery," "ineffable." Her Kocbek is farther out on the edge of emotion.

American readers may find the short-lined, direct poems most sympathetic. ("The Lippizaners" has neither of these qualities, but it is not only a major poem but also an oblique survey of Slovenian history and statement of Kocbek's vision and method.) "In a Torched Village," "Hands," and "Fishnet" resist the tendency to leap to the cosmic and either imply or earn their generalizations, and "Standing by a Vessel" offers a corrective to Wallace Stevens' "Anecdote of the Jar" or for that matter Keats' "Ode on a Grecian Urn." Kocbek's vessel is a jug; the speaker drinks from it; it has been decorated and used by real human beings—and it is related to the world rather than dominating it: "you stand firm, staring tranquil, / with wide-open eyes, / into uncertainty."

As this indicates, Kocbek sees art as fragile but also as transforming, and again and again he asserts the primacy of the individual voice and vision. It is clear from this brief selection from a large body of work that he embodied the ideal expressed in the refrain of William Butler Yeats' "In Memory of Major Robert Gregory": "Soldier, scholar, statesman, he / Loved human liberty."

Jože Udovič (1912–1962) fought with the Partisans, but he was more heavily influenced by the modernists than by traditional Slovenian rhetoric, and his poems have appeared in English only in anthologies. This is a pity, because on the evidence of poems like "Leaden, Slanting Rain," he writes as least as well as any of his contemporaries, regardless of language or nationality. The poem is an ironic commentary on the Odysseus legend, only this time the landscape is scorched, there is no magic, and as Charon rows the protagonist to the other shore,

> In the distance he saw it:
> bare trees, a low horizon
> and falling on these a leaden,
> slanting rain [*Terra Incognita*].

However, Udovič's nature is not uniformly bleak. Even in ruins and ashes,

> somewhere a shelter is hidden, as yet unknown,
> a gentle womb of poems and feathers,
> of azure moss and breath
> which may give rise
> to an unheard-of harmony ["And Yet," *Terra Incognita*].

Moreover, there, as in poems like "The Life of a Captive," the speaker suggests that the natural world offers not only refuge from oppression, political or psychological or both, but a means of triumphing over it. The poem begins,

> I have been held captive
> beneath an arch of frigid shadows,
> and yet not a day has passed
> but that I've seized morning by the shoulders
> and walked through locked doors
> toward the forbidden light.

And it ends,

> My heart is made of light and desire,
> I cannot remain captive [*Terra Incognita*].

The shadows that inhabit the story "Silence," by Lojze Kovačič (1928) are harder to escape. The unnamed narrator returns after the end of World War II with a maimed trigger finger, to the hut left by his dead mother. Like Hemingway's Nick Adams in "Big Two-Hearted River," he longs "To be alone in the world and obedient to no-one" (*Terra Incognita*). But his demons are more concrete than Nick's, and in effect he has to enter the swamp and confront them. Completing simple tasks, he encounters the specter of his mother and shadows who seem to threaten, or promise, death and also with beings with "hairy bodies and glittering cat's eyes, which in a dumb and dissolute language conferred among themselves in the darkness." Then he sees a photograph of his father, who had never been to the hut. Although his father was weak, not a fighter, the narrator feels that "wherever we went together, it was always a man's world." In the last paragraph, the narrator realizes that "There is nothing to keep you here.... This room is alien and will not help me; it will forsake me. This is not my home."

The story may illustrate, in an extreme way, what many commentators point to as a central theme in Slovenian literature: the hold of the mother on the son. Here, in bitter and compelling fashion, that hold is broken.

Not even this much consolation is to be found in the poems of Dane Zajc (1929–2006) who also draws from the natural world, but in ways that would make the American Robinson Jeffers seem almost optimistic. According to Boris A. Novak, "Zajc was obliged to publish his first collection of poems, *The Burnt Grass*, at his own expense because his poetry had been condemned as being "too somber and pessimistic" (*Left Curve*, no. 22). Zajc's measured tone and bleak message take some getting used to, but after a while one can see why he is referred to as "the Nestor of modern poets."

Zajc maintains that "A poem has no measurable function" and "the only payment is in the act of giving that which we have received without having earned it, that is, in the giving away of our talent" (*Terra Incognita*).

His poem "Ransom" illustrates this bleak view even more eloquently, maintaining that there is neither redemption nor forgiveness and that the price of ransom is one's life. And "Bells of New Day," traditionally a sign of hope, ends with

> You are alone in this world.
> Like a rock is alone,
> sighs the wind
> past the mountain's craggy face.
> And with this solace, the broken bells
> of a herd of sheep
> ring in the new day [*Terra Incognita*].

However, the alternative to writing "is not to give freely of our gifts, to carry them inside us, unused and intact, to the grave. This goes against the ethic of life although in no way does life indicate that our presence is necessary to it. The necessity of our presence is obtained by force or perhaps we merely imagine it" (*Terra Incognita*).

The 2004 publication of *Barren Harvest: Selected Poems* gives American readers the opportunity to see Zajc's work in greater depth and scope. In the introduction, Zajc's younger colleague Aleš Debeljak uses the framework of a meeting on a café terrace to humanize Zajc as well as to give details about the wartime sufferings of his family, his difficulties with the Communist party as "a 'verbal delinquent'" (15), his characteristic themes and attitudes, and his emergence as a — some would argue, the — leading poet of his generation.

As Debeljak points out, Zajc's aesthetic was formed not by Anglo-American work, from which his generation was barred, but by the Russians. This may account for some of the rapid shifts in imagery, as in "Eyes," where, in the fourth of five stanzas, "Bulls rush across your mouth" (51) without foreshadowing or other preparation, or in "Offering," where after images of silver, birds, flowers, the poem concludes "And we lick the mouth of the green wolf / we suck the poison fungus from obsolete coins." These and other images seem melodramatic, and some readers may prefer early, terse work like the title poem, which records without consolation or mitigation the decay of the poet's brother's "beautiful brown eyes, / the barren harvest / of the unfeeling earth" (28).

These forty-three poems are drawn from volumes published over forty years, and it is possible to see some development from work like "Gothic Windows," from a collection of 1961, where eyes stare at the speaker, "Narrow. Empty. Dead. / Sad" (41) to the longer lines and more lyric imagery of poems nearly a quarter-century later, as in "Animals," in which "animals drink the shining water / from the passing clouds" and themselves are inhaled by the moon (87).

This kind of doubling, inversion, mirroring — the figure varies — recurs, and in most cases it is less consoling than in "Animals," since the promise of hope and peace are often withdrawn in a poem's final lines. Most often, the double or other is used in almost gothic fashion, settings and characters, including animals (often goats), in fairly generalized and symbolic terms.

Zajc's vision is consistent, if disturbing, and he will appeal most to those who respond to his attempt, in "Lump of Ashes," to "make a new language from the soil. / A tongue that speaks with words of clay" (*Terra*). At his best and, I think, his simplest, he succeeds in ways approached by no other poet.

The life as much as the work of Zajc's near-contemporary Veno Taufer (1933) leaves no doubt about his political purpose. Taufer is a member of what he calls the Critical Generation, whose ideas were formulated in the late 1940s and early 1950s. Like Kocbek, though from a different set of circumstances in his youth, he has been acutely aware of the relationship between literature and politics. His father was killed in 1943, and he sees himself as an heir to the resistance ideas. For readers of English, this is most clearly evident in his sequence "Melancholy of the Second Echelon, In memory of my father, killed in 1943." Though it seems without ideology, it was rejected on the grounds that it was "ideologically problematic" and published in samizdat. It seems innocent enough, talking of "the happiness / of a loyal death" at the end of one section and beginning another with

> when we die
> with our last respects
> and our last gaze
> of admiration
> at our forbearers' immortality
> we will not know
> that they are
> dying with us [*Veno Taufer*].

Taufer was also translating — Eliot, Yeats, Hughes, Pound, and currently Wallace Stevens as well as French, Russian, Macedonian, Serb, and Croat poets of his generation and younger — and, like Niko Grafenauer, Tomaž Šalamun, and others, writing modernist poems when, at least until the early 1960s, modernism was a political statement.

Taufer was also making more overt statements. As one of the founders of *Oder 57*, banned after a year and a half, and a theatrical group which lasted for eight years, he was imprisoned and interrogated for eighteen hours a day. In 1985, he was one of the architects and first chair of the Committee for Freedom of Speech and Writing; a year later, he converted the Vilenica conference into an international literary and cultural forum; and he was one of the authors of the draft constitution and a founder of the opposition party Slovenian Democratic Union and stood for election to the first freely elected parliament. Since then, he has given up politics—which, he said, played no part in his poetry except as a feeling and general source of experience, largely rage and disillusionment—though he is now president of Slovenian PEN.

In "Sarajevo," he mourns the destruction as only a writer can:

> two thousand years in the library books maps
> in flames the wind carries leaves away from memory
> blood sticks letters and pages in stiff fingers

Eleven lines later, the poem ends

> surviving scribes blinded by the seasons' explosion
>
> scrabble for shards of letters and scraps of parchment
> to write down in brief what the ancients already
> repeated in the terrible mystery of their fragments
>
> the word couples with mortal flesh to survive
> the age pursuing the shot to the heart struck by the echo in Sarajevo
> sinks with one of those ships in that list in the poem [*Veno Taufer*].

Niko Grafenauer (1940) is from Taufer's generation, but his work resembles Udovič's in its subdued tone and almost claustrophobic atmosphere. Characteristic are lines from "The House" (*Terra Incognita*):

> In the narrow crack of permitted consciousness
> projecting itself like a beam into dusk,
> moths quiver.

And in "The Walk,"

> Slowly
> as if veiled
> by a dying urge,
> I walk among somber winds that bar my way.

The reader could not tell from Grafenauer's translated poems that he had ever heard of Prešeren or Kocbek. Tomaž Šalamun clearly has, and for a time rebelled against that heritage. As he wrote in "Poker," "I grew tired of the image of my tribe and moved out"—though only after he had been imprisoned for rewriting "canonized patriotic poems" (*Terra Incognita*). He spent a good deal of time in the U.S.—which may help to account for the fact that he is probably the Slovenian writer most widely translated in America—as a Fulbright fellow, as a member of the Iowa Writers Workshop, and, after independence, as cultural attaché in New York.

Much of his poetry is highly idiosyncratic and often associational in ways that are difficult to follow logically, like a William S. Burroughs fold-in passage, as in

> In the fire we saved
> the sizzle of your tennis shoe. I pasted you up
> with resin, with tokens, so you could breathe
> only through your rhomboids ["Who's Standing," *Terra Incognita*].

But like Ezra Pound, who confessed in the poem to Walt Whitman that he had hated him long enough, Šalamun became aware of his debt to Kocbek.

> I have avoided you, great poet
> and thinker, because you were too heavy
> a burden. Fiercely I drew a line behind me,
> in order to be at ease, light,
>
> agile. An infinitesimal mote of sunlight,
> dancing as it crunches the muses' host
> for a joke....

Now, on Kocbek's seventieth birthday, he toasts "the shaper of our freedom." Still,

> Precisely because it's
> a holiday I must continue
> with my crunching. I sense that
> joy strengthens with every moment [*Terra Incognita*].

And in "Arrival in Saint-Nazaire," he goes beyond Prešeren and Kocbek, who helped to create Slovenia, praying

> ... for the day to come when I
> can mold the world with my Slovenianness
> Able to play strong, dense games [*Mosaic*].

Some of those games and crunchings play with the idea of the poet as master and creator of all in poems like "History," which begins

> Tomaž Šalamun is a monster.
> Tomaž Šalamun is a sphere rushing through the air...
> Maybe he is punishment from the gods,
> the boundary stone of the world.

The speaker is as amazed at the wonder of "Tomaž Šalamun" as the other spectators are. At the end, the mythologized Tomaž Šalamun goes to the store with his wife to buy milk. "He will drink it and this is history" (*Mosaic*). It is tempting to see this last line as deflating exaggerated claims for the poet. But it is also possible to see it as celebrating the wonder in what most of us dismiss as ordinary.

Few post-war poets are as playful as Šalamun. If the selections by fifty-five poets in *The Fire Under the Moon: Contemporary Slovene Poetry* are at all representative, being a poet is a very serious business.

Although the birth-dates of the poets range from 1885 (Lily Novy) to 1973 (Aleš Šteger and Miklavž Komelj), just over two-thirds were born between 1940 and 1970, five after that, six in the 1930s, another six before that. The heart of Taufer's "Orpheus" "is a bird of prey / it pecks his eyes out, inhabits his skull...." Esad Babačič's "The Lying Poet" is loved by readers who "won't do anything / when I am opening your wounds...." In Marko Pavček's "Flawless," it is the poet who "scrape[s] myself into a poem" until, without flesh or bone or heart, "I will have become absolutely flawless."

Darkness, death, silence, solitude are key words in many of the poems. The decks of Aldo Žerjal's boats in "The Old Water" are "unredeemed, for there is no light." When there is light, enough to create Svetlana Makarovič's "Shadow," where "The weary voice of the cuckoo is heard from afar. / No one is here to return its cry." Boris A. Novak's ballad "South-East of Memory" begins "Cruel is the crystal of memory," and the refrain is "leave the dead in the dusk!" Only Kocbek's "In a Torched Village," which grew out of his experiences as a Partisan in World War II, offers a specific cause for the pervasive sense of dread, and that is intensified by images of the recurrence of natural rhythms until the speaker "see[s] over / the shoulder of all horror."

Irena Zorko Novak's "Who?" begins with a similar sense of apprehension about an unknown being blocking her vision and movements, but in the last two lines swerves into "And who, each morning, / who is filling my empty milk bottles in front of my door?" This sudden swerve into a totally new mood is also found in Matjaž Pikalo's final lines, which have nothing whatever to do with "What's Lara Gerstein Doing?" and Erika Vouk's "Water the Horses," which ends "Bread is warm."

There is also a surreal strain in many of these poems, including those by Šalamun and Šteger and especially Gregor Strniša's "Evening Fairytale," which is very like a verbal transcription of a Dalí painting.

Examined closely, this and other collections indicate some of the contrasts between the modernist generation, who grew up under communism, and their successors, who never knew any other system. The latter is exemplified by novelist-playwright Drago Jančar (1948), novelist-travel writer-dramatist Evald Flisar (1945), the scarifying poet Ifegenija Zagoričnick (1953), and novelist-poet Iztok Osojnik (1951). Some believe that the generation born between 1945 and 1960 has been ignored, but there are signs that it is gaining recognition. Flisar was president of the Slovene Writers' Association; Osojnik ran the Vilenica festival for four years. They grew up in the hippie generation, and during the 1980s, when the struggles for democracy and independence (not, in the early stages, the same thing) were greatest, they had very different roles.

Jančar has been one of the most eloquent analysts of the transition to Slovenian independence. His "Memories of Yugoslavia" (*Terra Incognita*), written in January 1991, before Slovenia's final move to independence, was unhappily prophetic about the direction that would be taken by the Yugoslav army, communist-dominated and dedicated to the elimination of all kinds of dissent and even difference. It is not only a masterful analysis of the entire history of the formation, metamorphosis, and incipient disintegration of Yugoslavia but at times a compelling dramatic account of particular scenes. As he points out, Yugoslavia could sustain the illusion of viability only by contrast with countries — those under Soviet domination — that were doing worse. When they won independence, Yugoslavia's hollowness was exposed.

Jančar was no easier on Slovenians than he was on the Serb military and writers who supported the idea of Greater Serbia or the Western powers who supported Tito and Ceaușescu because they had distanced themselves, however slightly, from the USSR. "No longer," he writes,

> will anyone be able to argue that someone else is to blame for our lack of success, or that some unpleasant qualities in the Slovenian character are the consequences of ceaseless suppression or that ... society cannot develop completely because someone else is inhibiting this—once Vienna, then Rome, thirdly Belgrade, fourthly Moscow. No longer will Central European depression and a tendency to suicide be ascribable to external servitude.

He was no happier in an independent Slovenia, signing with other intellectuals, writers, and academics the 1997 manifesto "What Is to Be Done?" that called for full implementation of democratic institutions and procedures that the signatories thought were stifled by former communists who were not former enough.

Mocking Desire (Northwestern, 1998), a novel, deals with a Central European serving as visiting professor at an American university and could have been written by any number of people, but his story "Augsburg" (*Terra Incognita*) could probably not have been written by anyone else. Categorized as fiction, it is written in the first person, and like material in almost all of the anthologies from various countries, is maddeningly undated. The content indicates that it might be roughly contemporary with "Memories of Yugoslavia," for though the speaker is supposedly on a journey to the fabled city of Augsburg, the largest in Germany, in 1580, many of the perfectly real events took place in Jančar's lifetime.

Early in the story, he tells of a play in which actors kill a chicken in "'the poetics of sacrificial ritual.'" (This was Dušan Jovanović's play *Pupilija, Papa Pupilo Plus Pupilettes*, with a cast of poets. Jovanović notes the fate of the fowl: "Milan Jesih, the author of magnificent sonnets, would take the unfortunate animal home to his mother to cook" [*Slovenian Essay*]). Earlier some Austrian actors had killed cattle in the "'politics of ritual slaughter.'" That, Jančar's narrator says, was seven years ago, when these subjects could be debated. Then, back to the journey, he tells of a former border guard who is turning barbed wire into souvenirs. More animals are slaughtered, some for food, some in ritual, some, like a herd of Lippizaners, without apparent reason.

This act, rather than the slaughter of humans, enrages the Viennese press. Another Westerner is concerned not with the destruction of Vukovar but with its reconstruction in the proper style. "And at once everything became clear; of course, the important thing there is literature, drama, the literary vision." Here the false naiveté turns to the most scarifying irony. Finally attained, Augsburg is a questionable Eden, making the immigrant confront obstacles and having armed men in the cellars in case of trouble.

"Augsburg" is fiction in much the same way that Donald Barthelme's stories are fiction. Both use postmodern fantasy riffs on real places and events; both shift tone; both employ bemused narrators, often on quests, to emphasize their themes. But although Barthleme was engaged in some public issues as a person, his fiction comments only glancingly on political questions, and as he demonstrates in "Kierkegaard Unfair to Schlegel," he is an ironist who worries about the validity and quality of his irony. Jančar is postmodernist enough to use the techniques, Central European enough not to have a moment's doubt about the usefulness of his irony, and committed enough to reject postmodern corollaries of distance and undecidability.

In contrast to Jančar, Evald Flisar was living in London when he was not traveling to 70 other countries. A good deal of his work reflects his travel, and Matej Bogataj claims that he has "honed the skill of travel writing to the degree which warranted its acceptance as a literary genre" (*From the Heart of Europe*). Although Flisar had established himself as perhaps the first Slovenian metafictionist, as the later discussion of *My Father's Dreams* will show, the aptly titled collection *Tales of Wandering* draws more upon the tradition of W. Somerset Maugham, Rudyard Kipling, and even O. Henry.

In twenty-two tales, the longest some fifteen pages, most shorter, Flisar uses material from his extensive travels to give portraits of people and places that he refuses to term exotic. The places range from Australia to India to Africa to London. Most are narrated by a first-person narrator traveling with a rather shadowy wife; many begin with some variation of "I met" an unusual person whose situation and fate are the subject of the story.

Many of the stories are capped by ironies: "The Price of Heaven," an assignation with a beautiful young woman, is not just two hundred rupees but a sexually transmitted disease. In "Lord of the train," the narrator laments his Western ungenerosity towards India and its people but discovers that the man whom he refused to aid is a thief. "End of Innocence," about an American couple in Bali, even has an explicit moral at the end.

Although the book is labeled as fiction, the pieces can more properly be called sketches because they devote less attention to character and plot, in keeping with the brief contacts which travelers establish, than they do to sharply defined impressions of the countries, as of the night train across India in "Lord of the train" and the African savanna in "Robbers" and other stories, and of the inhabitants, not so much as characters but as physical and often intrusive presences.

Flisar neither romanticizes nor debunks. Instead, he displays, in prose that is often eloquent, in contrast to the rather seedy people and places it describes, the irremediable otherness, and at the same time the common frailties, of places and people.

Flisar's only novel in English, *My Father's Dreams: A Tale of Innocence Abused*, may not be quite metafictional, but it is complicated and disturbing enough to gain at least a cult following. Near the end, the narrator, Adam, prays: "God, if this is a dream, I want to wake up," and then, "God, if this is real, I want to start dreaming." In fact, the narrator, son of Joseph (a doctor) and Mary (a bookkeeper), is never sure whether or not he is dreaming—with details that might embarrass Freud—about his father's sexual relationship with the fifteen-year-old Eve (whom Adam twice fails to penetrate when interrupted by authority figures) and his desire to dispose of his mother.

To make some sense of his life, or at least to keep a record, he writes his dreams in diaries that he reads to Abortus, the fetus of his brother kept in a jar, to whom he feels an obligation "to live part of my life for him" and who, though of course mute, becomes his only confidant.

The narrative shifts back and forth from realistic, if overcharged, scenery to phantasmagoric, bleak landscape and from solo dreams to those shared with his father, which turn out more badly than anyone can believe. The image of Abortus grown into a baby with a frog's head recurs, at one point reading the book "My Father's Dreams" with the name of the author obscured. The act of displacement is clear enough; the meaning is never made any clearer.

Although Adam quotes several psychologists, including Jung (once to the effect that "dreams were messages from the hidden parts of ourselves to which no access could ever be gained"), the key to the novel's method, as opposed to the narrator's psyche, seems to lie in a young doctor's analysis of two paintings, one Hendrick Sorgh's realistic scene, the other Juan Miró's use of Sorgh's detail, "but broken up into color fragments" in which "reality ... had evaded the rules of ordinary perception and moved into the realm of imagination and dreams," so that Adam's perception of "shapes and meanings and events slightly out of focus or in double focus" becomes a way of dealing with shocking reality.

Near the end, the mother (apparently) dead by Adam's hand, his father confesses to the old sailor Grandpa Dominic, the sage who rescues and takes in Adam, that "It wasn't my son who was dreaming. I was the one who lost his grip on reality, dreaming that my actions were one thing, and I as a person another."

In this reading, Adam is not dreaming at all, though some things he records, like turning into a giant rooster followed by millions of hens sowing eggs over the earth, clearly have no real basis. At the end of the novel, years after the main action (or fantasy), he hopes to see once more the mythical Morsi, who cleanse the sea and whose touch frees one from loneliness. And in the final lines he seems to accept his experience as superior to that of people "who have not left the shallows of the known."

Perhaps the strangest thing about the novel—whose oddities are outlined in two brief introductions—is that, during the reading, it seems, if not normal, almost natural.

Iztok Osojnik (1951) has not equaled Flisar's range as a traveler, but he has ranged widely and recalls the Sixties and Seventies as an ideal time to be a Yugoslav because one could travel both east and west. Perhaps in consequence, they shared the political sentiments of their elders without their degree of engagement. But things changed. In the early days, he told me, someone would say, "Let's go to India," and in ten days they would be there. Later it took twenty days because of complications. Still later they couldn't go at all because of wars in the region. And then they couldn't even go to Zagreb....

In his youth, Osojnik was perhaps the closest a Slovene could come to being a Dadaist. He and two friends conducted a series of hoaxes, dumbfounding not the bourgeoisie, which is too easy, but those who wanted to be in on the latest thing. For example, they applied for and got government funding for a philosophical conference at which the speakers spouted gibberish, and at the end let the audience in on the joke. They were not amused. Nor were those who attended a so-called experimental rock concert at which Osojnik appeared in drag. Now, he says, he doesn't have to do anything outrageous; he simply has to appear at a cultural gathering to make people nervous.

Perhaps as a result, he has only recently been able to publish manuscripts that he wrote sixteen to eighteen years ago and that were paid for and then refused not, or not so much, because of ideological reasons but because the audience, including editors who had themselves been censored, were not ready for his tone and subject matter. His fiction has not been translated, but his poems are as measured and somber as those as many of his elders.

This is obvious from his first long work published in English. *And Things Happen for the First Time: Selected Poems* reveals him as a poet who blends aesthetic theory and philosophy with a sharp appreciation of the physical world. As Richard Jackson notes in the introduction, the poems "are aimed at two projects: transcending the self, and creating some sense of presence and fullness to fill the 'empty sky' of all that lies beyond the self."

One might add, as Jackson does, that the two projects are often interlinked and with the sense of emptying and renewing. The book's title comes from the last stanza of "Li Po I."

> The silver ribbon of the day vanishes to the bottom of thoughts.
> It blows chestnut leaves away, leaving no trace of
> cormorants in the air. But someone is not blown away
> and things happen for the first time.

This motif is picked up in later poems, which note "the restless power of creation" and assert that the speaker "moved into my own absence." The theme of possession by another who may or may not be the self carries through a number of the poems.

English readers will recognize echoes of T. S. Eliot in the meditation on time in "Antigone" and of Wallace Stevens in "An Afternoon in Bolzano," but Osojnik echoes rather than imitates. Contemplating Antigone's fate, the speaker does not retreat into eternity but insists on the living paradoxes of shame and honor and at the end of the poem, by far the book's longest, insists that

> In the light of such awakening
> the poetry reveals itself
> as an open door to the beyond
> and as the essential spine of the world.

In "An Afternoon," the speaker stands, like Stevens's, beside the sea, whose "immense substance tenses with / the density of the round horizon," thinking of von der Vogelweide's song. But unlike the singer in "Idea of Order at Key West," the words do not order the sea, and Osojnik's speaker "knows who sang, and why," and also what he did not say, and who inspired his song.

In his best poems, Osojnik comes back to the particular, which may or may not be symbolic but leaves the reader with a sense of the physical world, fog and rain on a mountain, "bushes rustling in mistral," and most notably in "Schumann, Bucharest 1985," where, after the description of an apartment full of smoke and music, separate from "the fascism outside," and a meditation on "unfinished paintings, unspoken / sentences, untold stories ... and meanings, hints and distorted fragments of he past," the poem ends with three fragments: "The piano concerto. The vermilion trees. In September."

In Osojnik's second North American volume, his persona Mister Today writes in a somewhat more relaxed and whimsical style than the speaker in Osojnik's *And Things Happen for the First Time*. The nature of the self, the cosmos, and the nature of poetry still pervade the poems, but Mister Today is far more aware of the *blague* surrounding bad translations by famous people, interviews, launchings, and readings, since "If you write, you have to think of its sound / in a smoky bar under the scaffolding of a Thursday, / when autumn spreads its wet towel on Beethoven Street."

Even in writing about philosophy, he can descend from the existential to the herbal: "Deep inside man there is an enormous abyss / of nothingness and parsley." Many of the poems sound less like angst than kvetching, but more often the cosmic and the commonplace are placed in surprising and not always comic juxtaposition.

Occasionally, Mister Today allows himself to indulge in the purely lyrical, as when "a tree in the wind ... shivers, scratching itself, stretching and cuddling, / it flakes and airs its veins." Even here the poet uses the wind as the traditional figure for inspiration, "swishing through your circulation like an avalanche...."

Perhaps, in middle age, Mister Today and his creator are more aware of necessities like mowing the lawn, caring for an infant son and dying father, and learning to play with words, ideas, and pictures, "to write one anyway.... Even if no one bothers to read it" because "The world is seven /times bigger than everything one could possibly grasp, / and Mister Today knows his human nature...."

In the work of Boris A. Novak (1953) that I have seen, he seems consistently serious and impatient with fragments. His "Coronation" is a sequence of fourteen sonnets, the end of one furnishing the first line of the next, and the concluding "Sonnet of Sonnets" is composed of the first lines of all fourteen. Yet this is not an empty exercise in formalism. Novak weaves a highly complex web of motifs and variations on themes of poetic creation, human gestation and birth, death and renewal, and the ways in which memory is both created from the past and created for the future. "Word is a womb of the human world" (*Terra Incognita*), and the speaker, in effacing or destroying himself, creates the poem which is a legacy of "all the wonders," for "The poem is a body of the body," so that when the child grows up, he—or she—should "whisper to this poem: You are mine." Novak has genuine political commitment, evident in his work for Bosnian relief and for the PEN Peace Committee. This is not obvious in the poems I have read, but Aleš Debeljak gives a broader view of his career in "Boris A. Novak and the Poetry of Insomnia."

The next generation of writers was born between 1955 and 1965, according to Aleš Debeljak (1961; see "Visions"), and never experienced Stalinist-style repression. Therefore, he says, "the external need to write Aesopian tales and in coded metaphors vanished..." (*Twilight*), as did the tendency to see good and evil as merely a matter of communist/noncommunist. "In this way," he adds, "Central and Eastern Europe witnessed a shift in the use of poetry, which too often had been fraught with an exalted political or moral 'noble mind' which has, as Czesław Miłosz once shrewdly observed, no place in poems." Therefore, this generation was even less involved with politics than that of 1945–60 and more inclined to write about ordinary people and events.

Andre Blatnik (1963) and Debeljak are quite aware of their generation. Blatnik writes that it "has frequently been accused of careerism, cosmopolitanism, conformity, lack of personal experience, insufficient personal involvement in protesting against the society, and the like," charges leveled not just against writers but the whole generation. True enough, he says, if standards from the past are used, but he wonders "whether today (and our time is today) any other way is at all possible. In other words: our stance may not be so much a matter of personal choice as the only possible way." In short, perhaps it is the case that "We think of literature the way we've learned to, and write it the way we feel, as an idealist might say" (*Slovenian Essay*).

There is no official roster of members of this generation, but Debeljak mentions Jure Potokar (1956), Maja Haderlap (1961), and Alojz Ihan (1961) among the poets of his generation—writers he included in the Slovenian section of *Shifting Borders*, and Potokar, Ihan, Debeljak, and Brane Mozetič (1958) in Richard Jackson's *Double Vision*. Blatnik and Lela Bajda Njatin (1963) can be mentioned as fiction writers allied with this generation. Blatnik and Debeljak were editors of Aleph, a small independent press, and Blatnik edits *Literatura*, one of the important literary magazines. As Blatnik says, this post-hippie generation is characterized by some as being much more interested in organizations and institutions than their predecessors, and in fact Debeljak began his career as editor of *Tribune*, a fortnightly student newspaper (not, he hastens to add, like American student papers) that was suppressed, and Debeljak was forced to resign. To the question, which he raised himself, of why he didn't become a politician, Debeljak says that his first book of poems came out and that he became interested in pan–Yugoslav culture. These contacts were, of course, interrupted and in many cases destroyed by the war.

The war may also have put an end to nascent interest in postmodernism, which never gained a significant foothold in Slovenia and is now disparaged by every writer I spoke to. Blatnik's generation was, falsely, he thinks, identified with Western post-modernism, and though he tries to develop unusual formal and narrative patterns in his fiction, he claims little influence from Robert Coover and Thomas Pynchon.

In fact, some of his fiction seems to reveal older influences. "Billie Holiday" (*Terra Incognita*) records a conversation between a man who is trying to leave one woman and intermittently talking on the phone to another. To an American reader, the flat rhythms sound like Hemingway in "The End of Something" and "Hills Like White Elephants" or even Dorothy Parker, and Blatnik's story only gains by the comparisons. "Thin Red Line" (*From the Heart of Europe*) is like one of Flisar's travel tales, in deadpan third person, about a displaced terrorist who comes to believe his leader's maxim, "If you can't change the fate of the majority, you must share it," and dies in a ritual to bring rain to an African village. Blatnik clearly learned something from translating Paul Bowles.

Jani Virk (1962) is consciously less literary than some of his contemporaries. For example, he is unable to think of himself "as a true Slovene writer" because

> I have never had any difficulties with the blank page before the author's troubled computer-paled face, nor with the tangled erotic commitment to literature and similar fashionable ailments.... Whenever I return home from abroad ... and then stroll round the streets of Ljubljana, my eyes do not shine with the clear recognition that I am a poetic seer amongst the mass of pitiful worms. If my mother comes to visit, to look after my children for a while, I do not burst out at her *Oh mother, you have born a poet*. The end of history, of literature, of the subject, and similar concepts, has never either pained or frightened me [Virk].

However, his stories are much more recognizably Central European than these remarks might indicate. Those I have seen in English all feature a first-person narrator who feels separate from ordinary society. Those of "A View of Tycho Brahe" and "The Door" immerse themselves in cosmological issues, the speaker of the second floating "in space with an open mind" and attending cosmology lectures before meeting and making love to a mysterious woman and stepping through a hitherto unused door into the void. The narrator of the first, speaking randomly into a Dictaphone in a Copenhagen hotel, knows that his words might be erased even as he speaks, but there are too many words, too inaccurate anyway. He fears "being torn off Earth and carried behind the edge of the Cosmos, where there's nothing at all," outside the scope of God's eye. Closing his eyes, he sees lights, knowing "this is how stars emerged in God's eye." His body, his very existence, is fluid, and he feels that "my life's been lost since the beginning of time" (Virk; the other three stories can be found in *The Day Tito Died*).

All of Virk's narrators have troubles with women. That of "Tycho Brahe" can't approach them; that of "The Door" finds a soul-mate who leads him to nothingness; that of "Rošlin and Verjanko" gives up the study of philosophy (he has written an essay, "God's Insomnia and Loss of the Penultimate Hope") to enjoy the favors of his friend's mother, is imprisoned in a maze, and realizes, in the last sentence, "I'm already dead." The narrator of "Regatta" isolates himself on a beach, rejects the favors of two naked girls, crews on a boat, and steps onto an isolated island.

Virk himself either does not share this angst or has gotten over it. He has been a newspaper editor, a filmmaker, and, in the most recent listing I can find, editor of cultural and arts programs for Slovenian public television.

In Alojz Ihan's (1961) interview with Richard Jackson, he says that "My ambition is to make a story, and that story has at least two levels, a realistic story and a picture of the private inner life. There must be a balance between these two" (*Double Vision*). His essay "The Reservation of Reality" offers a more complex approach. Meditating on the internet's "fascinating electronic images," he says that "reality is that faint trail, that image of the world which is the hardest to catch." And when one does, the problem is "how to preserve the pale and mostly blurred image out of all the colourful images of electronic kitsch." Unfortunately, "in actual life ... reality could not survive for a minute. Reservations are the only alternative of reality. There it can survive and preserve its genes for different times that will need reality outside reservations as well." That is the job of art, and despite the fact that postmodern intellectuals "have swapped reality for fanciful playrooms full of glittering, plastic utopias" and "need art no more," art and human reality remain the same. Artists are the only defenders of reality, and "despite their loneliness, this is not such a bad position" (*The Slovenian Essay*).

Ihan's poetry looks at a reality beneath the surface in some interesting ways, as in an untitled seduction poem:

> First I unhook your skirt and you languish
> like a bird and shake your name off amid cries,
> then, with precision, I go about forgetting your face
> and finally
> we pulsate evenly
> like protozoa or algae in our slimy, warm juices,
> under whose deaf surface we quietly degrade
> to molecules and atoms, all the way to the first day
> and the beginning and end of all tales [*Double Vision*].

In "Lover," the woman gives herself to the "eternal lover," to wake next to the physical man whom she leaves for the bath. And in "The Knifethrower," the artist and his woman target know that, beyond all chance, "only murder is possible between them" and rather than return for a bow, they lock themselves away "and make love and make love and make love."

Some poems, like "The Seasons" and "Girl, Young Girl," are more obviously tender, but others have a harsher edge. American readers will be reminded of Tom Sawyer's showing up for his own funeral in "The Boy in the Tree (for Edvard Kocbek)," but after observing the searchers, Ihan's boy

> will slide stealthily down from his tree
> and, comforted now, head for
> the precipice.

"Of Human Flesh," in which the speaker is told that eating a dead child will help feed others, goes beyond Swift's "Modest Proposal," for the speaker, convinced, says "From / that day on, I have been eating human flesh."

Ihan can have fun at his own expense, as in "The Festival of Poetry," where, awakened at two-thirty a.m. to receive poetic code like a ham radio operator in "the odd brotherhood" which

> preys on sounds, on codes, and
> is forever writing them down with a bureaucratic insistence

in the hope that someone can make sense out of what he transcribes. Meanwhile, he longs for American poets to wake and relieve him, but they may be asleep, hung over, watching television, or blown up by an atomic disaster, "you can't ever really rely on American, can you..." (*Double Vision*).

Suzana Tratnik (1963) cannot, as a lesbian activist, be called postmodern, and the stories I have seen (see www.ljudmila.org/litcenter) are rather flat in tone and preserve unities of time and place. The most direct of these, and in many ways the most effective is "Berlin-Metelkova," which presents the aftermath of a panel discussion on homosexuality. The narrator finishes speaking and is approached by a younger woman, new to the scene, who asks her if she feels discriminated against.

> Do I feel discriminated against? I lit a cigarette and tried to give the question some serious thought. "Sure," I said after a short pause, "sure I feel discriminated against."—"I thought so," Anita was visibly encouraged, as though she'd found we had something in common. "And—in what way? How do you feel discriminated against?" Now I no longer needed to think long or particularly hard. In addition to having beautiful teeth she also had lovely hands and I liked what she was wearing. "Well, in several ways." Anita nodded eagerly. "I can't get a scholarship because I'm too old. I don't have the right kind of relatives. I never get to meet the right people, or if I do, I find them uninteresting. I can't smoke pot in bars and other public places because it's not legalized here. I'm not a homeowner."

Anita moves away, and the narrator describes to her friend a dream woman and, just in case, a backup dream woman—whom she uses, when Anita returns, to brush off her sexual offer. But then the narrator relents and agrees to go to Anita's apartment, thinking "maybe I will tell you about discrimination after all, and perhaps also something about ideal women."

"Games with Greta" deals with a narrator's first awareness of attraction to a cousin and at the same time an attraction to blood and violence, which is barely curbed. "Trip Is on Sale Too," the only third-person narrative of these stories, presents a painful reunion of two women, one constantly unsettled, the other enjoying feeling sorry for herself. Both women are very annoying, and even more annoying is the apparently happy ending—unless it is too quickly ironic—in which nothing ever goes wrong between them again. The other two stories end with the narrator pleased with the outcome, but one feels that those endings have been earned.

Lela B. Njatin is willing to have more or less happy endings in her fairy tales, but in her novel *Intolerance* (1987) does not relent from excruciating and oppressive detail. She has claimed, at least in the past, common ground with "the retroavantgarde Neue Slowenische Kunst movement which includes the music group Laibach and art group Irwin" (*Mosaic*; see also *Veiled*). Only fragments of *Intolerance* have appeared in English, but they reveal a phantasmagoric intensity. In one episode (*From the Heart of Europe*), soldiers chase the narrator, who holds them off when she stops at a manure pile. "I strip off the upper layer and grab a handful of worms burrowing into the putrefaction. I start stuffing myself with them." Horror follows horror, but since the episodes, related in a matter-of-fact tone, do not connect, the reader becomes as dissociated as the narrator.

The poet Maja Vidmar (1961) allows no dissociation from the possibility of pain, but, though the word "death" recurs in her poems, as for Cleopatra in Shakespeare's play, death is like a lover's pinch, that hurts and is desired. This politically very incorrect theme is explicit in poems like "The Shape of Death," where—the syntax is obscure—the poet calls for

> A few more hands,
> male hands,
> to draw me again
> towards death [*From the Heart of Europe*].

The connection between sex and death is even more clearly Shakespearean in "Erotic Position":

> I am kneeling
> before you,
> ready for death,
> if you want to murder,
> but ready to leap,
> if you don't mean it [*Heart*].

Only a little of Vidmar's work seems to have been translated into English, perhaps because she is not likely to be a favorite of the feminists, but it would be interesting to know if she has written explicitly about the esthetic and broadly political bases of her work.

Barbara Korun (1963) makes Vidmar look like a radical feminist, and an inhibited one at that. "Stag" and "The Wolf," the poems translated in *Ten Slovenian Poets of the Nineties*, are physiologically explicit, as in "I wake up to a warm stag's tongue between my legs" (*Ten* 17) and becomes more detailed. But the violent sensuality in both poems causes her to flower and heal:

> ... I do not trust the wolf, but it will be all right, this
> force in me is more potent than he, it transforms him,
> heals him, it heals me, heals the wound [*Ten*].

Bridgette Bates believes that ever since Prešern women have been confined to the roles of "strictly lover or muse" and argues that despite the equality of women (at least legal and formal) under communism, women have been underrepresented, receiving only ten percent of literary awards and financing seventy-five percent of self-published books in Slovenia. But of the seven women she includes in the *New Letters* selection, only Taja Kramberger, in her miniature epic about her father's service in war and return home, displays much vitality of feeling or language. And Bates notes that Svetlana Makarovič, "widely considered to be the most important Slovene poet for the past 30 years," refuses to be included in anthologies of women's poetry.

A broader and in most ways more revealing selection of *The Voice in the Body: Three Slovenian Women Poets*— Erika Vouk, Meta Kušar, and Maja Vidmar in Slovene and French as well as English. Perhaps the translations are to blame, but the poems often seem little better than truncated prose. However, the bio-biographical notes and Stanislava Chrobáková Repar's twenty-page commentary, mostly descriptive, provide a welcome context in which these and perhaps other women poets can be seen.

There is clearly room for progress. In 2001, only about ten percent of the 280 members of the Slovenian Writers Association were women, but at least five women were on the twelve-member board of the magazine *Literatura* (McLaughlin).

Aleš Debeljak is more philosophical and less detailed than these two women poets, and indeed than most of his contemporaries, and he is as prolific an essayist, cultural theorist, and anthologist as he is as poet. Born in 1961, he spent several years in the U.S., receiving a Ph.D. at Syracuse University, and he has exhibited not only wide range but also one of the most interesting patterns of development. In the late 1980s Debeljak edited collected translations of John Barth, Donald Barthelme, Coover, and Pynchon. In the early 1990s, he seemed to value some of his contemporaries' attempt "to seize another [than socio-political] reality, that of mental homelessness and human indifference" ("Visions"). Now he realizes what he had in common with other so-called postmodernists was negative: none wanted explicitly political engagement. He has since argued in *Reluctant Modernity: The Institution of Art and Its Historical Forms* that unfettered subjectivity failed to account for the Balkan wars and that aesthetic standards are impossible without ethics. Therefore, he has addressed the issue of the war in various genres.

But even in his earliest poetry, Debeljak seemed to arrive fully formed as a poet. No reader, unaided by the biographical note, would guess that *The Dictionary of Silence*, which appeared in translation in 1999, was in fact written early in his career, published in Slovenia in 1987, by a poet in his mid-twenties. Nor, without being told, would she be able to tell from the seamless language of Sonja Kravanja's translation of these poems that they were not originally in English. At the same time, the sensibility is clearly not that of a native speaker of English. It is melancholy without giving way to despair, conscious that "Today will not be different from any other day" without succumbing to ennui, committed to silence but uttering, grudgingly, "An everyday phrase / from a conversation that lasts forever. And consists of four, / five words."

Debeljak uses a few more words, but synonyms for "alone," "nothing," "silent," "useless," "shudder," "wandering" echo throughout the seven sequences, each with seven poems consisting of three four-line stanzas, roughly sixteen syllables, mostly one per word, to a line. These are followed by the final "Essay on Melancholy" in which the speaker is "vanishing into the text / to bring the poetics of this hallucination to light" and has "no more words left. / Even these are not necessary. Hi ho." (The last sentence indicates that he read Donald Barthelme's *Snow White* to some advantage.) Only repeated reading of the poems themselves can give a real sense of the remarkable tension between the strain of the content and the assuredness of the poetic voice.

Unlike some youthful wonders, Debeljak has continued to be productive as poet and critic: this is his fifth book in English, through of course out of sequence in his career. Some of the poems in *The Imagination of Terra Incognita* and *Mosaic* (three are in both) show the effect of Yugoslavia's collapse on his work. "Bosnian Elegy," addressed to Miljenko Jergović, indicate that he came to believe that words are not only necessary but crucial. "Elegy" begins in the vocative: "Sing, young poet," not of death and destruction but of "what's left," which includes the sound of birds, novels, "the downy blond fuzz on the earlobes of babes that disappears so suddenly." And the poem ends with another command to the poet to "Sing, as you sang before you turned gray" (*Terra Incognita* 284). And in "The Imperfect Passion of a Word," the speaker concludes

> I can only say:
> silence interests me less than the imperfect passion of a word,
>
> from which a seed explodes into flower. Channeling the delirious
> vows of strangers, the century's bodies and souls, into the aqueduct
> of language: In my blood I know that this is not in vain [*Mosaic*].

Less widely translated and less internationally active than Debeljak, Brane Mozetič (1958), had until 2004 appeared in English only in anthologies of poetry and fiction. But he has had an active career, translating a number of gay French writers, founding a small press, and editing the gay magazine *Revolver*. His poems deal with emotional and physical longings and failures in unillusioned language perfectly understandable to heterosexuals, as in the first stanza of the untitled

> each time different lips bending down to meet you
> and bodies to explore, unending repertoire of stories
> for you to hear, and you repeat the tired phrases
> awake the same old hopes when morning comes
> and time to leave—all loves,
> all loves are the same, they always show themselves
> too late, when you've long since given up, applied the
> last brushstroke,
> and all efforts are in vain [*Terra Incognita*].

Something of the same tone pervades *Butterflies*. The vision of a world at once feared and desired pervades this impressive sequence of ninety-four unrhymed quatrains and a ninety-fifth poem which begins with a quatrain and adds thirty-six lines obliquely answering the question "then what?" (still more disorientation). Throughout, Mozetič interweaves disturbingly surreal images of death, pain, and dislocated consciousness and spatial orientation with lyric, almost idyllic moments of peace and joy. Many of the poems are addressed to "you," at times possibly a muse, for the most part probably a lover whom the speaker alternately desires and rejects. Butterflies leave "havoc in their wake"; in contrast, a painting full of images of blood and horror is capped, "right at the top" by "a blue butterfly." The collection will repay further study, as will Mozetič's debt to the edgier French authors, from Rimbaud to Foucault, whom he has translated. His persona would like to be anywhere out of this world but returns at the end to Ljubljana,

> a refuge for psychos,
> you can't miss it on the map:
> on one side an Austrian waiting room,
> on the other an Italian nursing home,
> underneath only isolation wards:
> b wing for those who think they are heroes....

The "you" has turned green, like the dragons flanking one of the bridges and, like the speaker, does not know where to turn.

The cover photo of Mozetič's collection of stories, *Passion*, features boots, chains, and belt buckles and indicates clearly that he is not writing about the kind of sanitized homosexuals like those on TV's "Will and Grace," virginal as housewives in a 1950s sitcom. Perhaps that is why an anonymous caller says, "We hate it how you keep writing and shooting your mouth off about gays." In fact, the traditional sense of "gay" hardly applies to responses by any of the characters in the collection's thirty-five pieces.

The title is more accurate, although the narrator's major passions are rage at his lack of options; fear of and desire for death (AIDS, violence), often simultaneously; savage indignation at the pretense or whining of those he encounters; sadistic or masochistic glee at pain inflicted or endured.

The longest of the sketches covers only six pages, most only four. The narrator begins with a sense of his own desiccation, unable to feel or remember or to join in a parody of Communion since it's "as if I did not belong there." He rages at straights who "don't have to mind the looks, they don't live in constant terror of where the sperm will squirt, the drop of blood fall, or how deep they can sink their teeth into skin."

He is no kinder to the "flashy nonentity" in "Disco" who seems "the right victim" in whom he can find "a showdown" in order "to cleanse myself, to gather new strength." As his victim climaxes, he wonders "Is that what death is like? When you hurt bad enough to go crazy.... Was I giving him this kind of death, was it already inside him?" And in "The Reader" he meets a young man excited by his sadistic story who wants to be in a book, has sex with him, strangles him, and returns home "to write, in order to fulfill the boy's expectations completely." But most encounters infuriate him because of "this absolute impossibility of finding in a guy a person capable of feeling for another."

As the collection progresses, however, the narrator's obsession with the "you" to whom most of the stories are addressed becomes more central to the stories and to his consciousness. After another violent encounter, he realizes "that the sum total [of all his lovers] amounted to zero, to some sort of void, a state of no value at all." Here the narrator begins to reveal his longing, even tenderness, and in the lower depths of an orgiastic disco scene, "I wished I could be with you, and that they would leave me alone. That you'd be with me, forever." In "You," the final story, blood and sperm mingle as the narrator imagines pulling the lover's knife to his own throat.

Mozetič's fictional world is harsh and disquieting, but his simultaneous refusal to sentimentalize and his willingness to reveal genuine, if seemingly unattainable, desire are more valuable than sunnier depictions of gay life.

Mozetič's press is an individual effort. Some of the youngest generation of writers, born about 1970, are associated with the Students' Publishing House, sponsored in part by the student organizations of the University of Ljubljana and the University of Maribor, about 60,000 students in all. The umbrella organization has existed for twenty-five years, but since 1996 it has attracted more and more people more interested in literature than in money—though some are paid—who for the past five or six years have formed a stable group. This organization sponsors various series which publish forty to fifty books a year, including a series in literary theory, one of critiques of media culture, and one in classics of philosophy. It also publishes translations, mostly of living authors, and in the Beletrina series, eight to ten books by some of the best younger Slovenian writers. It also issues recordings of authors, from Dane Zajc, one of the best performers of his own and others' work, to the newest writers, reading their own work. (See the website, www.studentskazalozba.com.)

In 1999, Beletrina authors won most of the literary prizes, and the editors try to keep writers on their list to reinforce name recognition of publisher and author. According to Aleš Šteger, this is not the usual practice; authors tend to move to different houses from one book to another. A nonprofit organization—and the only one, according to some older writers, subsidized by the government—it has to spend everything it earns on publishing and other projects like readings and discussions in order to foster a literary atmosphere throughout Slovenia.

Much newer, but equally ambitious, is Littera, sponsored by the Student Organization of the University of Maribor. Founded in 2001, it publishes anthologies of Slovenian literature as well as individual writers, of whom Šalamun is the best known to American readers.

In Šteger's view, many writers of this generation feel free from the earlier necessity to create and further Slovene identity and ideology and from the role of the poet as seer. They are also less hermetic than older writers—perhaps Šalamun is an example, though his name was not mentioned—and more interested in making contact with the reader. While not discounting form, in other words, they want to say something.

These reactions to the poet's inflated self-conception to statements like the concluding lines of Šalamun's "The Fish":

> I slide headfirst into people's
> mouths and kill and give birth,
> kill and give birth, because I write [*From the Heart of Europe*].

Or he may be thinking of more extreme claims, like those of Uroš Zupan (1963) in "Cosmology of the Birth of a Poet":

> From the red-hot magma, its already congealed layers,
> from the great emptiness of silence on the ocean bed,
>   from the submerged temples of Atlantis, from the
> petrified forests of sea grass, the stillness of the Arctic
>
> ice, from the immeasurable depths of thought,
>   its invisible hands,
> roaming through space like burning comets, from the
>   Tibetan
> Book of the Dead, from long breaths of life recreated,
>
> I ascend [*Terra Incognita*].

And so on for many lines and aeons, up at least through Hiroshima.

This poem illustrates what Peter Kolšek calls Zupan's Whitmanesque side, which is sometimes combined with "the revolt of the Beatnik generation" (*Ten*). That shows most clearly in "Psalm—Magnolias in the April Snow," where he sounds rather like the American poet who railed about the sons of bitches in their Brooks Brothers suits who killed Dylan Thomas (though in fact Thomas didn't need any help). This is addressed to his father, whom he hopes to encounter when the father is as smart and free as the poet is.

However, in "Hölderlin Tower" he has begun to reject the anguished isolation of the German poet, rollerskating,

> Living undercover. Reading
> theological treatises in conjunction with sports

> pages. Half and hour of Grace and Gravity
> followed by half an hour of World Soccer.
> The order is not important and the effects
> Are already surprisingly visible [*Ten*].

And in "The Horizontal Sun" Zupan pays tribute to a different kind of father, Jože Udovič, whose "Leaden, Slanting Rain" serves as a motif in a love poem in which the poet confesses that

> I don't get along very well with my former
> self. He was too savage, innocent,
>
> trusting the grace of heights.

The poem ends,

> No one knows which one of us will be the first to hand a coin to
>   the somber
> boatman. But long before, we'll live in a house with gay balconies.
> Your flowers will bloom and drop, will drop and bloom.
>
> And outside will fall the slanting rain.
> And outside will shine the horizontal sun [*Ten*].

Some writers seem better able to stay out on the edge. A contrast can be drawn, cautiously because only fragments are available in English, between a mid-generation novelist like Berta Bojetu-Boeta (1946–1997) in *Filo Is Not at Home* (1990; see *Afterwards* and *Veiled*) and Dušan Šarotar (1968) in *Island of the Dead*. Both have an air of hallucination, but *Filo*, in what seem to be fragments from a journal, has clear allegorical references to the island prisons under the communist regime. The second, visionary rather than allegorical, relies on closely observed detail that wavers between dream and reality. In an introduction to the chapbook, Šarotar says that he is "writing now that the urgent tasks every individual faces [as opposed to political struggles?] have finally got underway again. Naturally, we should always ask ourselves what these urgent tasks are and what time is right for them but we are probably unlikely to ever get an answer."

Of course, these and other writers like the novelists Aleš Čar and Nina Kokelj and poets Peter Semolič, Primož Čučnik, and Esad Babačič are difficult to assess for non–Slovenes because little of their work has been translated, but clearly there is a good deal of energy in this literary generation, and just as clearly they are still formulating an aesthetic or rather a series of individual aesthetics.

Of course, some are more equal than others, and some individual works are clearly better than others in the developing canon. Even a friendly anthologist-critic can come to this conclusion. In *The Key Witnesses: The*

Younger Slovene Prose at the Turn of the Millennia, twenty-three stories by thirteen writers born between 1960 and 1974, Mitja Čander's appended essay is far more pointed and comprehensive than the genre usually allows. Most of the stories present a reality "which seems too dense and even neurotic," often in the form of "extended anecdotes in a bar" set in a world which "escapes [the characters'] field of vision."

Indeed, most of these stories portray characters who have no sense of their social, political, professional, or even personal contexts, and the first-person or extremely limited narrative focus prevents the reader from seeing or inferring any.

An exception to this sense of limitation can be found in the work of Andrej Blatnik, perhaps, in American eyes, the best-established writer in the collection. In "The Day of Independence," the first-person narrator tells of his conception from the vantage point of the womb, and Blatnik's "Electric Guitar," in third person, deals with an abused boy confined to a single room who accidentally electrocutes his father. In both, the central figure is released into a wide, frightening, and unknown world.

There is no such release for the sado-masochistic narrator of Aleš Čar's (1971) "The Floors" or for the sexually abused child of "Hansel and Gretel" who not only endure but crave the abuse by which they are defined. Mohor Hudej's (1968) "To Serve or Not to Serve," Tomaž Kosmač's (1965) "To see Žiri and Die," and Mart Lenardič's (1963) "The Fighter" are narrated by unpleasant, aimless, lumpen males in or from bars. Characters in Andrej Morovič's (1963) "In the Evening We Go Out Together" and Čar's "Out of Order" find satisfaction in their partner's sexual encounters with other men. On the whole, sex is not equated with love, and love itself is expressed in strange, even twisted, fashion.

Some of the stories do attempt to rise above banality and severely limited horizons. Jani Virk's (1962) "On the Border" achieves something like the tone of folk tale or opera in telling the tale of an unexplained feud almost removed from a wider social context, and Maja Novak's (1960) "This Story Should Have Been Written by Simenon" enlivens a banal story with her intertextual wit. These stories deal with more than the "shit" that, as item of vocabulary and as metaphor, pervades many of the other stories.

The real problem with this collection, which Čander does not address, is that in conjunction the stories are so similar in tone and subject matter that the total effect is monotonous. Readers may agree with Čander's view that the writers present the world they have to work with. But we are not obliged to find that world, as presented, very interesting or to refrain from wishing that, as in the cases of Virk, Blatnik, and Dušan Čater, they were told with more leaven of imagination.

Beletrina pamphlets excerpting the work of Aleš Čar and Nina Kokelj (1972) exhibit extremes. Čar's *Dog's Tango* seems, in these eleven pages tracing the central character's move from his former girlfriend's flat to a basement apartment in the suburbs, contains observations about people and settings, but the central character, a kind of picaro who doesn't go anywhere, makes Lucky Jim seem like a real go-getter. In contrast, Kokelj's *Grace* seems to have almost too much imagination, rather like a late D. H. Lawrence story without any plot, at least in the present. Čar says in his blurb "Too much of everything flows through the words not to detect in writing an immediate smell of blood." One can agree without regarding this as praise. Like late Lawrence, the setting is rather vague, the time indeterminate, though there is a reference to Mao. A not uncharacteristic paragraph, in length and style, reads:

> They stopped and the air began moaning. He moved his legs and with greedy fingers at which she stared fixedly, he caressed the lantern. His dark eyes narrowed to unrecognizable slits.

And compare Lawrence's *St. Mawr* to this memory, actually a memory of a memory remembered on

> the orange couch on which she had sulked and sobbed for the horse that flung itself into the abyss, preferring death to life as a hireling. She could see it, the horse, with sweat belly, plunging with tempestuous mane into the blue [Kokelj].

Other passages, like the central character's awareness of "loneliness, despair and approaching mental derangement," read like parodies of 1950s American Southern Gothic fiction.

Feri Lainšček's *Instead of Whom Does the Flower Bloom* is the most recent Slovenian fiction in English that I have seen, and though the author is roughly contemporary with Blatnik and Debeljak, he can be placed here because this novel, his seventh, shows not only a proper balance of detail and imagination but also a strain of Slovenian fiction unique in the translations I have seen.

Although the novel is set in Tito's Yugoslavia, the world of Halgato, the central character, is much like that of a folk tale. Halgato is a Gypsy, and the world of his village is premodern in its housing and implements and in its social structure. Halgato's father, who bequeaths him a legendary violin, is killed by the secret police; his stepfather kills the man who impregnates his two daughters and is imprisoned. The stepfather's son, Pišti, wants to escape Gypsy life by getting an education. The difference between the friends is that Pišti "would die if I stopped wondering" about new things, hopes to get clear out not only of the Gypsy village but of the country, and is impatient because

Halgato, content in autumn, cannot foresee that winter will come. Halgato accepts cycles: sure, winter will come, but it won't be as bad as last winter. "The world is like the weather," always changing.

Pišti falls in love with a "white" girl, takes the blame for her car accident (he's been reading *The Great Gatsby*), and goes to prison. Halgato has been jealous of the new relationship, and in a fugue rapes the girl, who retreats to a convent. The novel begins with Halgato isolated even from his village and Pišti's return after twenty-three years, now rich, with a grand new house in Big Village. The body of the novel begins with Halgato's growing consciousness and ends with his retreat from humanity. In the final section, Halgato goes with Pišti to his new house, warns him that he cannot steal the girl from God, and exits the house to the sound of a gunshot.

The novel seems to endorse Halgato's notion of fate, especially gypsy fate: "God allows Gypsies only humility.... And if a Gypsy, haughty or naive, should lift his head, he is sure to get his." Pišti does; Halgato, who has sacrificed almost everything for his friend, is desolate at losing him and racked with guilt at the rape. His friend is dead; he is left in a void, suspended by the narrator without further motion.

I said that the novel is in many ways like a folk tale. That is true of the matter-of-factness with which horrifying details are rendered. But it is also operatic in the scope of the passions, in the personal, even lyric, confrontations between the characters. *Instead of Whom* is not comfortable reading, but it is more satisfying than the work of many younger fiction writers because it has a consistent and uncompromising vision. It has been translated to film as *Halgato* and then to television.

Aleš Šteger is, like his contemporaries and most of his elders, a very different kind of writer than Lainšček. His work is just beginning to appear in English, most recently in on-line versions of little magazines. Some of his work seems quite accessible. "Being a Child" ("When I Was a Child" in another venue) describes the speaker's childhood reading about two ways that stars die, both taking eons and awing the young mind. But then,

> When the child disappeared
> Each birth became just an imitation of
> One of these two kinds of death.
> The origin of civilisation. The birth of poetry.
> Twice was I born and twice my father despaired of me.
> You stare too much at books,
> He said, it's bad for your health.
> You'd do much better to learn
> How to hold the racket properly
> And hit the ball further than the net.

And in "Coming Home," the speaker, though at first alienated, finds that

> The look on the face in the bathroom mirror
> From which I fled such distances,
> Did not, not even for a moment, let me out of its sight [*Ten*].

In other poems, Šteger seems quite aware of literary traditions he sometimes parodies or twists. In "The Romantic and the Realist School," he describes a river "bearing away the dead angels, that had been asleep under the snow. How beautiful they are, we said, how even in this dirty river, their broken wings stay white, their faces untouched." The romantics dream of more angels while the realists "ran to get their fishing tackle and began an angel fishing derby.... These were the realists, people who loved angels from up close and would later burn at the stake. Nor did we fare much better. The whiteness in which we died was swept away, and all at once we felt the hooks that tied us, while we were still alive to this only, this therefore best of all worlds" (*Ten*).

Elsewhere, Šteger treads the line between the poet as magician and as trickster. In "For You," the reader is instructed to blow up a condom and draw eyes and a mouth on it. Then something odd happens:

> I understand: you would like to draw me
> And thus become my master, but you haven't really
> Got me right and now you're angry. You're mad.
> But — what's this? It seems that behind my smile,
> Where there is nothing except the air you breathed out,
> There is something.

The speaker knows that listener grows more and more apprehensive and is finally told,

> Now there is no
> Doubt any more. In the emptiness of the condom
> There is someone, and you know bloody well that
> Only God can be where there is no one [*Ten*].

When the listener tries to cut the condom with a razor blade, he cannot be sure that "I" will disappear. The poet may or may not have become God, but the listener is caught in the web of words that have been spun. In this and in poems like "Walnut" and "Anti-Cyclone," the listener is caught, encapsulated, unable to escape the spell of the poet. This, like Šteger's "Europe," quoted in an earlier chapter, counters one tendency in Slovenian poetry: to expand, take in the universe, open possibility to the reader. Other poets have concentrated on natural images, which may console or oppress the reader, but none have, like Steger, put the reader inside the poem and closed the box.

Now some poets regard Šteger as a member of the elite. What, or who, is next? Some indications were evident at a literary salon in Novo Mesto, a town of about 25,000 southeast of Ljubljana, hosted by Marjanca Kočevar over some thirty meetings since 1999. The core of the salon is a group of poets from the cities of Kočevje and Novo Mesto, but the meetings have involved some hundred and sixty artists, including painters, photographers, poets and prose writers, one clown, and more than three hundred guests, mostly poets, from as far away as Mexico. Besides reading their own work and that of favorite writers, the members share information about publishing houses and magazines and generally encourage each other's work.

The night I attended, the youngest writer was twenty-three-year-old, Katja Plut, described as an "Adrenalin girl writing adrenalin poetry," who has published three books of poetry. Stanka Hrastelj, twenty-eight, a theology student and icon painter, has just had a book of poems accepted by Beletrina. Jože Guardijančič, thirty, places his poems in photography exhibits on the theory that more people will see them than they would in literary magazines. All of the members, ranging in age into the mid-fifties, continue to publish. David Šušel got funding from more than three dozen sponsors and donors in Kočevje to publish a handsome anthology of work by local writers.

Some of these writers feel that their counterparts in the capitol have an advantage and envy writers like Šteger and Zupan who only have to submit a poem once. And one complains that his day job keeps him from writing more.

This is a common complaint now that Slovenia and its people are free from outside oppression. A Ljubljana writer in his early forties, wildly successful by any standards, laments that when he has finished teaching and dealing with his very attractive and obviously cherished wife and children, he has little time to write. But in fact, he does continue to write. So Andrej Blatnik's conclusion that "The future of literature is literature" should be emended to "The future of literature is writers — and readers."

All of the writers I spoke to read avidly, and not just Slovenian literature. Writers from all postwar generations seem to take for granted the inevitability of interacting with the literatures of other countries, and many of them are translators. Before independence, the most important literary as well as well as commercial and political contacts were with the other republics of Yugoslavia. In fact, Boris A. Novak was born in Belgrade; Šalamun was born in Zagreb; Debeljak speaks Serbo-Croatian without an accent. The generations seem to differ on the question of the former Yugoslavia. Dušan Jovanović, who is part German and part Serb and a tangle of ethnicities and cultural connections that would baffle William Faulkner and that Jovanović could only describe as "Yugoslavian," wrote in 1996 that "Our biographies and our lives are thus hacked in half: the first half belonging to the past, the second devoid of a future. What is easily discernible is the distortions and deformities, some sort of paraphenomena: parahuman, paraworld, parahistory" (*Slovenian Essay*).

Andrej Blatnik thinks that in general the older generation of Slovenians welcomes the split but that those in their twenties have a kind of pop-cult nostalgia for Balkan food and music. And in 2003, a popular bar in Ljubljana was called "Tito." On a more informed level, Debeljak regrets the loss of the time when Yugoslav "linguistic, artistic, national, and religious differences converged in productive synthesis" (*Twilight*). Now, he feels, he has lost one of the three forces — "Slovenian tradition, the tradition of worldwide mass culture, and finally the unique experience of Yugoslavia's cultural weaving" (*Twilight*) — that formed his cultural and artistic identity. Even Miran Košuta, writing from the perspective of the Slovenian minority in Italy, believes, perhaps because he has to, that "A Slovenia of cultural, economic and political dialogues with Belgrade, Zagreb, Priština or Novi Sad is not some past utopia but a future certainty" (*Slovenian Essay*).

But most current effort concentrates on creating the sense that Slovenia is a free-standing country and not *terra incognita* for the rest of the world. One of the problems with sudden independence, according to Iztok Osojnik, is the lack of a tradition in international relations, diplomacy, and cultural ties. And it is clear that in all areas Slovenes are working hard to escape from being labeled Balkan and emphasizing their ties with Central Europe and the West.

One initiative tries to bring the rest of the world to Slovenia. A young vineyard owner, Aleš Klinec, wanted to do something for culture, and he and others, with the help of the Beletrina Student Publishing House, began a wine and poetry festival to bring together younger poets from various countries. The Student Publishing House has used its contacts and published anthologies of work by the participants. Poets can come only once to read, though some return to listen, and participants stay in the houses of local people. Readings, which have drawn as many as 400 people from Venice and Austria as well as Slovenia, held each evening under a mulberry tree that was the subject of a poem by a local writer.

Longer running is the annual Vilenica conference, which began in 1986 and which Veno Taufer developed from a poetry festival into a venue for reestablishing Central European identity. In some ways, this is parallel to the Visegradi group, but it is spiritual and cultural rather than political and commercial, and it includes Germany and northern Italy in the unique culture that differs from West, East, and Mediterranean. In recent years, the conference, held each September in and around the Vilenica cave, has extended its range and purpose to include writers from the Far East and North and South America in order to make the world aware of the Central European idea — and the writers of work in each others' countries. The Council of Admissions, composed of writers from the Central European countries, proposes a list of future guests and nominates writers for an award of $10,000, which cannot go to a Slovene writer, to be given to a Central European writer for a life's work. The Slovenian jury cuts the list to five people, reads their work, and votes. There is also a crystal prize—a trophy; no money—awarded to one of their number by each year's participants, and work by the participants is published, translated into several languages, in the annual volume, which in future will be issued on CD.

A complementary effort is being made to bring Slovene writing to the rest of the world. A relatively new organization, the Center for Slovenian Literature, has had, with government support, the mission of bringing Slovenian writing to an international audience through reading tours, publication programs, and publicity services. However, as I said earlier, state funding has been shifted to another organization. In 2003, the Center instituted a Creative Residence for writers and translators interested in Slovenian literature, but funding did not continue. A non-governmental organization, it seeks private funds and cooperates with Slovenian PEN and the Slovene Writers' Association in the Trubar Foundation, which subsidizes foreign publication of translations with funds from the Ministry of Culture. (For a list of authors, translations, and organizations, see *Key* in the Works Cited.)

In recent years, small American publishing houses like Lumen Books, White Pine Press and Richard Jackson's Poetry Miscellany chapbook series have issued more and more anthologies of Slovene literature and volumes by individual authors like Kocbek, Šalamun, and Debeljak. Slovene writing is increasingly available in French, Spanish Portuguese, Russian, and several Central European languages. Aleš Debeljak has been very active in collecting, editing, and promoting Slovene writing abroad, especially in England and America. Translators based in America, like Sonja Kravanja, Michael Biggins, Christopher Merrill, Andrew Zawacki, and Richard Jackson, have the linguistic expertise and literary network to make still more work available. Of course, translation cannot indicate the full range of these writers. Most of them have written numerous stage and radio plays and film scripts, and many have written children's books as well as novels and essays that have not been translated even in fragments. But these works continue to be published and produced in Slovenia, so the literary culture is even healthier than it seems from the outside.

Therefore, the concern of a German-speaking writer, voiced at the 2000 PEN conference, that small literatures like Slovenian might not survive in the multi-national culture seems misplaced. True, Aleš Debeljak worries about Slovene writers being merely European, though he by no means advocates ostrich-nationalism. Rather, he insists on the preservation of "a cultural narrative about the symbolic and material value of the language, ethical values, the fateful burden of history and the mythic tradition" in order to make Slovenes "see our lives against the broader background of the national condition" and "preserve our national culture and language in the era of the current European integration that, openly or not, considers smaller nations an unnecessary inconvenience" (Debeljak, "Cosmopolitanism and National Tradition").

There are signs that some Slovenian writers see larger nations in the same way. The International Gathering of Writers at Vilenica has, under a new director, become conspicuously less international since I attended in 2001 and in the most recent meeting was limited to writers in or near Slovenia. More ominously, the new head of the Slovenian Writers Association is reported by at least four reliable sources to have said, in his welcoming remarks, "Europe is our enemy."

Mataj Bogotaj sees the enemy as internal "primitive neoliberalism" which seems, in the present government, responsible for gradually choking off cultural funding and in the culture at large for consolidation of publishing houses into a monopoly. While he praises writers' tolerance for all styles and schools, he gloomily notes that "As the space to maneuver shrinks, the notion unfortunately seems to be surfacing that only a part will survive, so now a part of the community of writers is jostling to ensure their survival ... at the expense of all those kept at bay" ("A Cohabitation, in Principle, of Styles and Generations," in *Winged Words*).

Even under these circumstances, older writers like Iztok Osojnik are more hopeful than defiant. He sees Slovenia as the new geographical center of Europe and implies that, through the Vilenica conference and other cultural means, it can be as important culturally as it is geographically. This seems very ambitious prophecy, but for a country and a language that have survived against the odds of Austrian and then Serb domination, perhaps it is not impossible.

Works Cited

Afterwards: Slovenian Writing 1945–1995. Ed. Andrew Zawacki. Buffalo, NY: White Pine Press, 1999.
Bates, Bridgette. "New Slovenian Women's Poetry." *New Letters*, vol. 71, no. 1. Introductory essay and poems, 47–72.
Čar, Aleš. *Dog's Tango*. Trans. Ana Jelnikar. Ljubljana: Beletrina, n.d. Full text published in Slovenian, 1999.
The Day Tito Died: Contemporary Slovenian Short Stories. Boston and London: Forest Books, 1993.
Debeljak, Aleš. "Boris A. Novak and the Poetry of Insomnia." *World Literature Today*, 80:4 (July–August 2006), 46–49.
———. "Cosmopolitanism and National Tradition." *International Journal of Politics, Culture, and Society—Special Issue: Studies in the Social History of Destruction: The Case of Yugoslavia*. Eds. Aleš Debeljak and Srdja Pavlovič. Vol. 17, No. 1, Fall 2003.
———. *The Dictionary of Silence*. Trans. Sonja Kravanja. Santa Fe, NM: Lumen Books, 1999.
———. "A Haven of Free Speech: The Story of Nova revija in Slovenia." *Budapest Review of Books*, 6:3 (Fall 1996), 149–152.
———. *The Hidden Handshake: National Identity and Europe in the Post-Communist World*. Trans. Aleš Debeljak and Rawley Grau. New York and Oxford: Roman & Littlefield, 2004.
———. *Twilight of the Idols: Recollections of a Lost Yugoslavia*. Fredonia, NY: White Pine Press, 1994. The book has also been published in German, Croatian, Hungarian, Polish, Czech, and other languages.
———. "Visions of Despair and Hope Against Hope: Poetry in Yugoslavia in the Eighties." *World Literature Today*, 66:3 (Summer 1992), 427–431.
Double Vision: Four Slovenian Poets. Ed. Richard Jackson. Ljubljana, Slovenia, and Chattanooga, TN: Aleph; Poetry Miscellany Books, 1993.
The Fire Under the Moon: Contemporary Slovene Poetry. Ed. Richard Jackson and Rachel Morgan, 2nd revised edition. Chattanooga, TN, and Elgin, IL: PM Books and Black Dirt Press, 1999.
Flisar, Evald. *My Father's Dreams: A Tale of Innocence Abused*. Trans. Evald Flisar and Alan McConnell-Duff. Norman, OK: Texture Press, 2002
———. *Tales of Wandering*. Trans. Evald Flisar and Alan McConnell-Duff. Norman, OK: Texture Press, 2001.
From the Heart of Europe: Walkabout of Five Slovenian Writers Down Under. Ed. Evald Flisar and Alan McConnell-Duff. Ljubljana: Center for Slovenian Literature, 2001.
The Imagination of Terra Incognita: Slovenian Writing 1945–1995. Ed. Aleš Debeljak. Fredonia, NY: White Pine Press, [1997?].
Key: Slovenia. Contemporary Slovenian Literature in Translation. Ljubljana, Ministry of Culture. Trans. Lili Potpara. Ljubljana: Študentska založba, 2002. Updated 2004, trans. Ante Bračič. Lists "the [seventy] living authors whose works have already been translated," gives brief biographical sketches of and postal and e-mail addresses for each.
The Key Witnesses: The Younger Slovene Prose at the Turn of the Millennia. Ljubljana: Slovene Writers' Association, 2003.
Kokelj, Nina. *Grace*. Trans. Alasdair McKinnon. Ljubljana: Beletrina, n.d. Published in Slovenian in 1998.
Lainšček, Feri. *Instead of Whom Does the Flower Bloom*. Trans. Irena Zorko Novak. Ljubljana: Slovene Writers' Association, 2002. Originally published 1991.
McLaughlin, Donal. "1000 Ljubljana," *Edinburgh Review*, 108 (2001), 123–135.
Mosaic of Seven Pebbles: Insight into Contemporary Slovenian Literature. Ed. Lela B. Njatin.

Ljubljana: Center for Slovenian Literature, 1999. Includes work by and brief biographical notes about Svetlana Maraković, Tomaž Šalamun, Aleš Debeljak, Brane Mozetič, Evald Flisar, Lela B. Njatin, and Maja Novak.

Mozetič, Brane. *Butterflies*. Trans. Ana Jelnikar. New York: Spuyten Duyvil, 2004.

———. *Passion*. Trans. Tamara Soban. Jersey City, NJ. Talisman Publishers, 2005.

Osojnik, Iztok. *And Things Happen for the First Time: Selected Poems*. Trans. Sonja Kravanja. Mississauga, Ontario, Canada: Modry Peter Publishers, 2001.

———. *Mister Today*. Trans. Ana Jelnikar. San Jose, CA: Jacaranda Press, 2003.

Prisoners of Freedom: Contemporary Slovenian Poetry. Ed. Aleš Debeljak. Santa Fe, NM: Pedernal Press, 1994.

Šarotar, Dušan. *Island of the Dead*. Ljubljana: Beletrina, 1999.

The Slovenian Essay of the Nineties. Ed. Matevž Kos. Ljubljana: Slovene Writers' Association, 2000.

Šteger, Aleš. "Being a Child." Translated by the author, Nikolai Jeffs, Richard George and Brian Henry. http://au.geocities.com/masthead_2/current/child.html.

"A Symposium of Slovenian Poetry and Prose in Translation." *Third Coast*, no. 22, Spring 2006 (edited and introduced by Erica Johnson Debeljak). Includes works by Drago Jancar, Barbara Korun, Tomaz Salamun, Uroš Zupan and Ales Debeljak.

Taufer, Veno. *Veno Taufer: Poems*. Ljubljana: Slovene Writers' Association, 1999.

Ten Slovenian Poets of the Nineties. Ed. Aleš Berger. Ljubljana: Slovene Writers' Association, 2002.

The Veiled Landscape: Slovenian Women Writing. Ed. Zdravko Dusa. Trans. Sonja Kravanja. Ljubljana: Slovenian Office for Women's Policy, 1995.

Virk, Jani. *A View of Tycho Brahe* (excerpt). Trans Lili Potpara. Ljubljana: Beletrina, 1998.

The Voice in the Body: Three Slovenian Women Poets. Ed. Barbara Pognačnik. Ljubljana: Slovene Writers' Association, 2005.

Winged Words: 9 Authors from Slovenia. Ed. Barbara Šubert. Ljubljana: Slovenian Writers Association, 2006.

Zajc, Dane. *Barren Harvest: Selected Poems*. Trans. Erica Johnson Debeljak. Buffalo, NY: White Pine Press. 2004.

———. "Ransom." Trans. Sonja Kravanja. www.poetryinternational.org/cwolk/view/18093.

BIBLIOGRAPHICAL ADDENDA

For a web site giving brief biographies, photos, bibliographies, and brief selections from the work of writers on the Brazilian and Frankfurt tours, see www.ljudmila.org/lit center.

For a list of Slovene writing available in English, see Miran Hladnik's web site, www.ijs.si/lit/slov_lit.html. Hladnik notes that Slovene books may be ordered by e-mail from Slovenska knjiga (http://www.slo-knjiga.si/knjigarna/).

For some of the books published in the USA, check http://www.utc.edu/~engl dept/pm/pmhp.html or Poetry Miscellany Chapbooks ($3 each), ed. Richard Jackson. See also "Contemporary Slovenian Literature in Translation," *Litterae Slovenicae/Slovenian Literary Magazine*, 2 (1993) [31:82]. This indicates translations available for publication as well as those in print.

Meta Klinar has done work on Slovene prose in French translation.

Earlier bibliographies of Slovene works translated into other languages were reportedly published in 1975 and 1984 in *Le livre Slovene*, which I have not seen.

3

Desperate but Not Serious
Hungarian Writing After 1989

> *"All this to illustrate how tough it is to be Hungarian. And that is not going to get any easier, even if, as they promise, the Russians leave...."* Péter Eszterházy, *"The Miraculous Life of Prince Bluebeard,"* The Kiss.

If Eszterházy wrote this before 1991, he was not just indulging in the national sport of complaining wittily about Hungary's situations but was a prophet. Even if he had the benefit of hindsight, he is more accurate than those Hungarians, and not just writers, who expected that after the end of communism, as one critic puts it, the West would come in and turn all the Central European countries into Denmark overnight, or at least in not more than four years. Of course, the Russians have been gone for a while and had stopped paying much attention to Hungarian intransigence even before 1989.

Although Hungary became fashionable about that time, not many people have a clear sense even now of what it was and is like. For example, in 1996 a young American behind me in the line for the Jewish Museum at the Dohány Street synagogue in Budapest was disgusted at having to go through a metal detector in order to be admitted. I tried to explain that Jews in Central Europe had good reasons for being cautious. "I'm Jewish," he said, "and I'm from Miami. And we don't have to do that."

Perhaps the only real disadvantage of going to Hungary, especially to Budapest, is that one runs into tourists, especially in the five-star hotels on the Pest bank of the Danube and the Hilton on Castle Hill, patched together from a thirteenth century monastery and the latest, or latest 1970s, glass-front architecture. (This accords with Budapest style: the locals call the Pest parish church "The Mule" because it combines styles from many centuries.)

Perhaps the best place to get away from tourists, and certainly the best place to get an even more spectacular view than from the balustrade of the Castle is the Citadel at the top of Gellért Hill, named after the bishop who was martyred by being rolled down it in a barrel by recalcitrant nobles who resented his political influence even more than they did his proselytizing. As with many Hungarian sites and institutions, Hungarians have, as the character in Joseph Heller's *Catch-22* puts it, acted as though they were proud of something they ought to be ashamed of. The Austrians built the Citadel after the Revolution of 1848 to overlook the city and cow it with artillery. After the Austrians left and the Hungarians decommissioned it, a statue of a female figure holding a wing aloft was designed as a memorial to the aviator son of Admiral Horthy, the de facto ruler of Hungary from the end of World War I until the Germans deposed him for not being enthusiastic enough about the Axis cause and the Final Solution. Then it was erected as a memorial to the heroic Soviet liberators of Hungary, though many Budapesters called it "Natasha with the fish." Now the Cyrillic characters have been removed from the foot of Independence Monument.

Looking up-river, one can see the Castle in its latest of many reconstructions after a siege, the incredibly ornate Parliament building, and the bridges across the Danube as it sweeps past Margaret Island. The Chain Bridge was the first across the Danube in Budapest and has been regarded, before and after the young lawyer crossed it on his way to Castle Dracula, as the link between East and West. Downstream are the University of Economics, formerly Karl Marx University, the Technical University, and, still further down, the heavy industry of Csepel Island.

But the layout of Buda and Pest, once separate cities, overturns stereotypes of Western order and Eastern confusion. Buda, the royal city, is hilly, and the street plan is accordingly confused. Pest was the bourgeois site of late nineteenth and early twentieth century commercial and literary energy, and it is laid out along concentric half-circles that link three different sets of bridges.

Pest is also the site of some of the most interesting, though not the oldest, architecture. Some of it was built by the Eiffel Company. Some of it is in incredibly ornate Secessionist style. (In the town of Kecskemét, one site is called the Ornate Building, which is as worthy of note as the sign on Telegraph Hill in San Francisco that says "Hill." If the Hungarians think it is ornate....) "Eclectic" is not a Hungarian word, but it should be. For example, the mustard-colored building that swings around the streets that join at

Deak Square has at least five decorative styles ranging from Classical to Ottoman and less identifiable ornamentation.

Erecting such a building, let alone letting it stand through so much accidental destruction, indicates a great deal of confidence. And despite one military defeat after another, Hungarians have never lacked confidence. The young women are taller, more beautiful, and better dressed than their counterparts in Vienna. Intellectuals and writers are confident not only that they are a part of Europe but that they are an indispensable part. In all these people and aspects, there is not just a sense of style but what, in American slang, is called styling—flaunting individuality and excess. Fortunately, this confidence is moderated with an irony applied to themselves as well as to the rest of the world and with a gloomy attitude typified by the joke about the difference between the optimist and the pessimist. The pessimist is better informed.

For people who don't know the joke or anything but tourist Budapest, Susan Rubin Suleiman's *Budapest Diary: In Search of the Motherbook* is an ideal guide to the ethos of the city and to many of its interesting writers, politicians, and intellectuals — not, as is common in America but not in Central Europe, necessarily distinct groups. In structure her book is a personal narrative, drawing upon three visits to Budapest beginning thirty-five years after she fled with her family, and "a tour guide to my own life." During her longest visit, she kept a diary of which the plot becomes "the gradual move ... to a feeling of 'at homeness'" and the theme the recovery of documents from what is called in Hungarian "the motherbook" and a clearer sense of the histories of her parents.

But the book is far more valuable as a guide to Hungary after "the Change" of 1989. Because of Suleiman's Hungarian roots and growing recovery of the language, she has a deeper if not a wider view of the current situation, but on the whole her perspective is not markedly different from that of any monoglot Anglophone.

She visits the obligatory sights and monuments, though her descriptions of them are meager. She is told the stories about the 1956 uprising and about life under the Kádár regime that all Hungarians relate to sympathetic outsiders. She is attentive to the situation of the surviving Jews and their descendants, still the target of right-wing nationalists. It is, one says, always "dangerous to be a Jew in Hungary." She catches the tone and flavor of the conversation of Central European intellectuals — the sense of history, the irony, the fatalism, and, in the men, a distrust of American feminism, and the sense that, in Budapest, everyone knows everyone else. She notes seemingly minor cultural differences, down to the configuration of Hungarian toilets.

Most important, she becomes aware of the ambivalence towards "the

Change" which at some point surfaces in conversations with Hungarian intellectuals. On the surface, there is more freedom, to be sure, but there is also more uncertainty about the present and a widespread feeling that the country will not stabilize economically for twenty years and politically for at least that long. Perhaps that is the result of what she calls "the famous 'Hungarian melancholy'" which, any sensible observer will testify, is a real aspect of the national character.

A very different portrait of Budapest can be found in Arthur Phillips's novel *Prague*, which is in fact set in Budapest during the heady post–Communist period 1990–1991, but the expatriates at the center of the novel consider that Prague is where the real Central European action is taking place rather than, as one character calls it, "this God-forsaken paprika-stained Austrian test market."

The young Americans at the center of the novel are either on the make or are listless losers. There are several plots, but as in many antique galleries, the picture is less interesting than the frame. The novel presents a dead-accurate description of the physical appearance and atmosphere of a city struggling out of a forty-year coma. The roof of Keleti Station is "not quite transparent, dirty white, like the plastic top of an enormous, shabby garden shed." A sports jacket bears the legend "1972 FREE MY VALUE TIGERS." Sullen and indifferent waiters deny having any of the many palatable-sounding dishes on the menu. Hungarian hospitals are primitive. The lovely buildings are crumbling or have given way to holes in the ground in which hotels for the capitalists will be set. Hungarians, like the rest of Eastern Europe, know that "they were old-fashioned before they could do anything about it. Their politics, their culture, their technology, their lives were out-of-date, no problem as long as they didn't know it, but they knew."

At least that is one character's view. However, alone among the foreigners, he attempts to understand and appreciate Hungarians and their history. He intermittently admires Imre Horváth, imprisoned for publishing manifestoes in 1956, extremely conscious, or self-conscious, of his firm's place in Hungarian history, and insistent that "A life must make sense...." And he is fascinated by Nádja, an elderly pianist who claims to have been everywhere and experienced everything and offers him excellent advice about an American girl with whom he is obsessed. But Nádja dies, and Horváth, after a stroke, can communicate only by blinking his eyes, his family's publishing house and legacy sold to an Australian media magnate. And one by one the ex-pates flee or are driven out.

Of course, *Prague* is not social history, or not just social history. And it is a very good novel. The language is wicked in its ironic precision. The fertility of invention — writers and song lyrics and parodies of Greatest Generation rhetoric applied to the aimless slackers of the early 1990s and counterpoints of invented histories in widely different periods, among many other delights — is as exhilarating as anything since another first novel published more than forty years ago: Thomas Pynchon's *V.*

As counterpoint and complement of these books, I can offer testimony based on nine trips to Hungary beginning in 1981, the first of my family to go east across the Atlantic, as only the third Fulbright lecturer allowed into the country. The city did not seem wholly foreign, since any modern metropolis has the same general infrastructure, but the architecture, the culture, the life on the streets, the irony and quickness of the professors and intellectuals I met, and of course the fact that it was governed by a Communist regime made it seem very exotic to someone with middle-American tastes who had lived for thirty years in a town that did not exist in 1888. And since Americans were at that time fairly exotic to the Hungarians, they afforded me a new and enjoyable kind of attention. I enjoyed myself enough to think of Hungary as a second homeland, to value the friends I made, and to return briefly in 1983. This time people were less guarded about their views of the regime and their stories about 1956 and after — perhaps because no one who had spoken to me two years earlier had suffered any consequences. If I was a double agent, I was obviously incompetent enough to be reassuring.

When I returned in the exciting days of fall, 1989, the Communist Party was in the process of abolishing itself on television, the red stars came tumbling down, my older friends rejoiced in a sense of freedom they had not felt since the immediate post-war period, and my younger friends worried about what would happen in a political system of which they had no experience.

On my next visit to Hungary, in 1996, my friends wanted to know what differences I saw. "More McDonalds," I said. "More English. And more toilet paper." Viewed symbolically rather than literally, this represents a truth, if not the whole truth, about what has happened since "the change."

"McDonalds" is shorthand for the capitalist horde which has overrun the Hungarian marketplace and for the many new points of reference that, to an American, make Budapest and even provincial cities seem less foreign. In the stores, American brand names do not dominate, but they have a strong presence. Billboards carry familiar names: Burger King, Samsung, Kentucky Fried Chicken, Daewoo. On the streets, Russian Ladas and East German Trabants have not disappeared, but they are almost lost among the Citroens, Opels, Daihatsus, and other West European and Asian and even a few American cars. Suzuki has an assembly plant just south of Esztergom, the country's ecclesiastical capital.

In 1981, getting a new car was difficult. One had to deposit the full purchase price and then wait several years for delivery. Even then, as a friend at the American Embassy remarked, it was hard to imagine what Budapest would be like if it was easy to get a car. Now the only barrier is economic, and though Hungarians rightly complain about inflation and though a traffic jam is a traffic jam and hard to quantify, there is certainly no shortage of cars.

There are other indications that late capitalism has come to Hungary. Luxury goods have moved outside the boundaries of the tourist mecca, Váci Street, the Hungarian equivalent of Rodeo Drive. Casinos offer an alternative to Lotto, so that rich people — who exist in larger or more obvious numbers — can gamble too. A third television channel has been added, and cable service offers stations in English, German, Italian, and French. People complain about telephone service, but it is much more widely available and efficient than it was in 1981. And while some of the old heavy-cholesterol restaurants (Berlin, Sofia) have closed, new ones of all nations and ethnicities have sprung up. In 1989, the sudden availability of bananas was cause for excitement; now street stalls and supermarkets routinely offer foreign produce, so that diet does not depend solely on seasonal fruits and vegetables.

Diet and exercise play a much larger part in Hungarian life than they did in 1981 and even in 1989. At the beginning of the 1980s, another American remarked that if you saw someone running, it was probably a Marine from the American Embassy. Now joggers, bicyclists, skaters, runners, and even marathoners are not uncommon, and there is a gym called "Arnold." Smoking is still more common and less stigmatized than in the U.S., but Feri Takács, my first Hungarian friend, quit several years ago and reports that people no longer smoke in department meetings. He is more conscious of his diet and has taken to walking long distances to work and even paces less active friends in their circuit of a large park.

That is less pleasant than it used to be, he reports, because it is now a refuge for glue-sniffers. They would not have been tolerated under the Kádár regime, which would also have suppressed evidence of petty street criminals such as pickpockets and scam artists, the beginnings of gang warfare, and of what seems to be a whole new class of the destitute and even homeless. Many of the latter have been displaced by the collapse of Hungarian heavy industry, which, like that in most of the former Soviet Bloc, has been unable to make the transition to the free market.

Hungarians on fixed incomes or barely flexible incomes are only slightly better off because of inflation, and public sector workers are underpaid and demoralized. When Hungarian currency was fixed, the exchange rate was 33 forints to the dollar in 1981 and in 1989 only 40 forints. Now free-floating, it converted, in October, 1996, at just over 153 to the dollar, in June 2003 was 225 to the dollar, and at the end of 2006 is back down to 193 to the dollar. Prices have risen accordingly. At the most basic level, using a public toilet cost one forint in 1981 and into 1989, when the rate increased to five forints. In 1996 it was twenty forints, in 2003 not less than 50 and sometimes 100 forints. (The restrooms in McDonalds are, or until 2001 were, free, one reason not to repine at the advance of capitalism.) Tickets on public transportation, once a forint to a forint and a half, had risen to 50 forints in 1999 and are now at least 200 forints. Other prices have risen comparably, and while goods and services are not expensive by West European standards, the bargains of the 1980s are gone.

But on the whole Hungary is now more comfortable for Anglophones than it was twenty-five or even ten years ago, partly because of the official desire to increase tourism and partly because the Hungarians realize that English is the language of commerce and of the future. Departments of English and American Studies have more applicants than they can handle, and English language schools provide work in the secondary and tertiary economies for anyone with a reasonable facility in the language. Of course, many Hungarians have always been at least bilingual. In 1981, when I responded to a comment or question with my only Hungarian sentence, "Nem tudom Magyarul"—"I don't speak Hungarian"—people would try me in German, which I don't speak either but which is easier to fake than Hungarian. In 1989, at least in Budapest, there was an even chance that they would move to English. In 1996, especially in Budapest, people often began in English, and on several occasions when they didn't and I identified myself as American, they asked if I was Canadian. Since I've been asked the same thing in Nova Scotia, the question indicates linguistic sophistication enough to hear the oddity of my version of English. In 2001, they didn't bother with anything but English. Even in the provinces English is far more prevalent than it was even in 1989. The most startling evidence of this came at a restaurant in Eger, where my host at Károly Eszterházy College (through 1989 Ho Chi Min College) pointed out a party which included the mayor and his deputy and a delegation of businessmen from France—all speaking English.

While English is not yet universal, it is slowly advancing. In museums, broad explanatory signs are repeated in English, at least for the major exhibitions and on the first floor, but not the legends for individual items or on the upper levels. Most restaurants, even in the provinces, have menus in English that is sometimes not very appetizing, as in "Lard goose with steamed cabbage," and sometimes surreal, as in "Nisp duck." (My Hungarian friends and I decided that this meant "crisp," but we never did figure out the meaning of the popular billboard legend, "Stool your image.") On the railways, first class carriages have signs in English as well as Russian, German, and French; second class carriages do not.

Nor do they have toilet paper. This is noteworthy because most other toilets do, a condition that did not prevail in the 1980s. Paper for other uses is now a good deal slicker, and the kind and amount of tourist information, in 1996 featuring 1100 years of Magyar occupation of the region, is greater in quality and quantity. At the airport, where customs is far less forbidding than it was during the Kádár regime, the booth for tourists offers the Budapest Pocket Guide, which not only gives maps of the central city but guides to local and national transportation, suggestions about excursions and sights, advice about making telephone calls, weather data, and useful words and phrases, and a business directory. *Where Budapest*, distributed at hotels, is larger and more given to feature stories, to display and classified advertisements, and to spelled-out advice about public transportation and even religious services in English. Nothing like this was available before the change.

As for hard news and information about current happenings, monoglot Anglophones were almost entirely in the dark in the early 1980s. Then the only source of information, except for week-old copies of the *International Herald Tribune* at the Embassy Library, was the state-produced *Daily News*, four pages evenly divided between English and German and uninformative even by the standards of someone who grew up reading small-town American newspapers, partly because there was, by Western standards, no political news, but mostly because editorial policy seemed designed to prevent foreigners from learning anything about the country. As for the arts, the only way to find movies in English or anything else was to dodge back and forth between the pages of *Pesti Műsor* and a Hungarian-English dictionary.

In 1996 there were three independent English-language newspapers in Budapest: *Budapest Week* (since moved on-line), the *Budapest Sun* (which still exists), and *Budapest Business Journal* (which seems to have been supplanted by the Chamber of Commerce monthly). All were weeklies, in tabloid format; all began publication in the 1990s; all, though they acknowledge the needs of tourists, are directed primarily to the growing and, by Hungarian standards, affluent expatriate community. The first two resemble the down-scale *Village Voice* imitations published in many American cities — Phoenix, Albuquerque, Oklahoma City, for example — and though they devote a good deal of space to art and leisure, they seemed to take what my Hungarian friends seem to regard at least inoffensive and at best serious and responsible positions on Hungarian politics and culture, including stories about the many political parties in — and out — of Parliament. They seemed to pay little attention to American issues, though in the October 31, 1996, issue the *Sun* promised next-day coverage of the election and information about coverage on CNN International and a watch party at the Marriott to which all Americans were invited. Both carried devastatingly accurate reviews of the film "Independence Day"; both listed current movies playing in English — twice as many as in all other languages combined.

Budapest Business Journal, published by a company which has similar papers in Warsaw and Prague, was what one might expect: who's up, down, in, out at various companies; the effect of government policies; financial difficulties and scandals in and out of government; a list, instead of movies and restaurants, of "Investment Banks and Advisers Ranked by number of employees" (only one, the second smallest, founded before 1989).

To me the most interesting story was "Culture fund fights to keep state subsidy," partly for its effect on some of my friends and partly for what it reveals about the current climate in Hungary. The National Cultural Fund's largest source of revenue is a culture tax, "1–2 percent on cultural products and services such as theater tickets, books, museum admissions, video rentals and magazines. Items featuring sex and violence are taxed 20 percent." (This could account for the collapse of the Hungarian edition of *Playboy*, though the superiority of Hungarian pornography is more likely.) By now, "artificial flowers, copy machines and newspaper ads" are supposedly liable to tax. The Ministry of Culture and Education government had been granting up to $2 million a year, just under 15 percent of the total, but the subsidy ended in March, 1997.

The effect on cultural institutions could be severe. For example, the Petőfi Literary Museum in downtown Pest was until 1993 fully funded by the culture ministry. That body then gave only enough to pay utility bills; the National Cultural Fund contribution covered half of all other expenses.

This struck me because in 1996 the museum was the site of a conference sponsored by Hungarian PEN and the Friedrich-Naumann Foundation on the topic "In the Jungle of Freedom: The Fragility of Our Civilisation." Most of the speakers were from countries in the former Soviet Bloc or what used to be Yugoslavia; many had spent their most productive years under political and other constraints upon their freedom to express themselves. Their testimony was moving and, to someone who has never had to face conditions anything like this, humbling.

The younger writers, like those represented in Gustav Murín's collection *Central Europe Now! Almanac from Young Writers' Meeting*, and older ones, like my contemporaries Éva Tóth and Ottó Orbán, had an enviably detached view of and energetic approach to their circumstances. But some delegates, especially the ones who had suffered longest and might be expected to rejoice in the new openness, expressed openly the conference title's ambivalence about freedom. Yes, the undercurrent ran, Soviet repression was a terrible thing, and thank God it is over. On the other hand, for whatever motives and however grudgingly, the previous regimes did support culture and the arts, especially literature, especially the PEN clubs, especially....

Since 1989, American governmental and foundation support of Hungarians has also narrowed to a trickle. Ten years later, the number of Fulbright lecturers and scholars was down about 45 percent from the closing days of Cold War, when the struggle for the hearts and minds of the freedom-loving Hungarians was being pursued most vigorously. Funds for the program to send American lecturers abroad are drying up. *U.S.A.*, published by the State Department to show the beauties of our country and, more subtly, of its economic and political systems, died long enough ago that in 1999 the cultural attaché had never heard of it. The International Research and Exchanges Board no longer supports senior foreign scholars. Even the library at the American Embassy has been gutted (the cultural materials donated to Eötvös Loránd University and kept above the swimming pool in the complex that once belonged to the Communist Party) and turned into an information center, mostly on-line, to serve business interests. My friends laugh, though not heartily, when I tell them that what they need is another Cold War so that America will launch a second cultural crusade.

Hungary certainly needs new money and new business as badly as it needs to move old business out of the black and gray markets and the streets and metro stations, where the spirit of free enterprise is alive if not exactly well, into the tax-paying daylight of international commerce. And since the tourist industry is at least a palliative for what Hungarians hope is the temporary loss of heavy industry, one has to guard against the attitude I've seen in Santa Fe, New Mexico, where residents of a few years complain bitterly about the incursion of tourists and other newcomers. But to someone who walked the nearly empty streets of Szentendre, the picturesque art colony north of Budapest that is the Hungarian equivalent of Taos, it is rather jarring to return and have to edge between racks of mass-produced souvenirs and packs of German and Japanese tourists, to hear the grating, familiar accents of other Americans, and to hope in vain that one won't be regarded as being anything like them.

Fortunately, even in Szentendre the museums and the streets north of the shopping district are not crowded, and in towns like Esztergom, Eger, Veszprém, and Kecskemét, the inhabitants go reassuringly about their normal business as if no tourists were within a thousand miles.

Better still, my friends go on with their lives as teachers and writers, producing and transmitting work that even in translation is moving and funny and more finely crafted than anything in the tourist stalls or in the boutiques on Váci Street, pleased if I and my countrymen are interested but in no way dependent upon our approval.

My last full day in Budapest in 1999 was All Soul's Day, a Saturday on which intermittent clouds finally dispersed and the wind died. Feri and I took a leisurely walk in the city where he has lived all his life: through the City Park and the open-air flea market and back, after an ample lunch, past Embassy Row and his old neighborhood to what I still think of a Lenin körút, now Teréz körút, a segment of one of the boulevards in Pest that begins and ends at the Danube. The sidewalks were full of people, moving more leisurely than on a weekday, even stopping to look at the displays in the stores.

Feri is usually more sardonic than sanguine about political, economic, and all other conditions than most Hungarians, which is very sardonic indeed, but even he softened under the influence of the day. His countrymen, he reflected, were not such a shabby people after all, and it was good to see them enjoying themselves.

My impression is that the writers aren't enjoying themselves, but if they were, they wouldn't be Hungarians. And for a change there is some good news along with the bad news. The good news is that writers can say anything they want to. The bad news is that they have trouble getting it into print and even greater trouble getting paid. That is one reason why, speaking of the state of literature in Hungary, an editor in Budapest referred to the pre–1989 period as "the good old bad old days," and while no one else in the Hungarian literary community whom I spoke to used quite the same language, the sentiment was echoed by those who produce and publish creative work in print and on the air and with varying degrees of lesser strength by writers.

First some more bad news. Publishers went through a very rough period. For example, before "the changes," Corvina was a leading publisher of Hungarian literature in translation and also published other literatures in Hungarian as well as lavishly illustrated art books, guides, history books, cookbooks, and others related to Hungary. As many as a hundred and fifty staff members occupied fifteen offices in a modern building at the end of the most fashionable or at any rate most expensive street in Pest and produced two hundred and fifty titles a year.

Corvina and the other twenty or so state-approved publishing houses in Hungary — and in the rest of the Warsaw Pact countries, for that matter — didn't have to worry about the bottom line because they had no bottom line. As P. Hiemstra and L. Kúnos put it, "The government decided on volumes, printing costs, market discounts and salaries. In this way the whole sequence of publishing and selling of books could be seen as being in the hands of one single nation-sized company: an overstaffed, overregulated, slow and bureaucratic company" ("Restructuring of the publishing sector in Hungary," *The Change*). Print runs used to be artificially high. Júlia Lázár, who translated Sylvia Plath's *Journals*, said that the reader's report, made before the changes of 1989, recommended a printing of 50,000 copies, about average for the period. Now a print run even ten per cent of that is unusual. The Plath *Journals* were published in 1996 in an edition of not more than 2,000.

New, smaller publishers of original Hungarian writing may publish ten books a year, and sometimes they have a run as large as 1,500 copies, though most are smaller, perhaps 500 for poetry. And that is hardly profitable. Some small publishers use two or three different names for different lines, partly for tax purposes, and they sell out, regroup, and emerge under other names.

The good news in the old days was that books were carefully edited. As many as seven people saw a manuscript through production, checking textual quality as well as political orthodoxy. The bad news is that now an author is lucky if one person is responsible for checking the accuracy of the text. And books were (artificially) cheap and readily available — unless they sold out, in which case reprinting was impossible because of lock-step schedules set three to five years in advance. Now, under free market conditions, books are so expensive that the diminishing number of serious readers cannot afford them.

The most difficult year for publishers, according to one editor, was 1993 — another says 1996 — when privatization occurred through a long and complex process. Employees were encouraged to bid for their company, especially if there was not a large gap between management and staff, but anyone could bid, and in any case employees had to seek financing. In one publishing company, the three top managers got 51 percent of the stock and the other employees 49 percent, a lesson that it is not just socialism under which some animals are more equal than others. The system of privatization, and not just in publishing, was felt to benefit those who had been in power under the Communists.

This transition was less painful than the one in 1990, when the government decided to abandon control of publishing and nearly two thousand so-called publishing houses were founded. Some were get-rich-quick, one-book publishers, often of pornography which they sold on street corners, and even now there are many hurried and bad translations of very bad American genre fiction issued in hope of making a quick profit. Like the thirty or forty political parties which emerged in the fall of 1989, not all of these publishers survived the neo–Darwinian processes of the free market, but they radically altered the situation. Some of the old mammoth publishing houses like Gondolat, which had published several hundred books a year before the change, could not adjust under its Socialist Party managers and did not survive. A French publisher considered buying Gondolat but, after looking at its padded payroll and other problems, backed out. Publishing houses that did survive, László Kúnos says, "understood that unavoidable steps had to be taken."

In Corvina's case, this meant reducing staff and new titles per year by roughly two-thirds. And the nature of the list has changed. While Corvina still publishes illustrated and art books, they have become too expensive to produce without careful attention to the market, and far fewer are issued. Corvina now depends more heavily on upper-level textbooks for high schools, especially guides summarizing the subjects of the final examinations that all students take at the end of their schooling. Another line features handbooks and textbooks for university students, mostly in the humanities, and a third offers language teaching, especially English, German, and French.

As this summary indicates, publishers in the past had to be careful about ideology. Today they have to be careful about the balance sheet, and as a result are less inclined to take chances with quality work that might have high production costs. One press refused to consider issuing a translation of *Angela's Ashes* because it was twice as long as any novel they had published. Another asked Éva Tóth, a leading translator, to do something for them, but not poetry or drama. And when radio producer Márton Mesterházi tried to interest publishers in translations of three Yeats plays he had commissioned, he was at first laughed at.

This is not good news, but things are changing. Some of the best news can be found in the Balassi Bookshop near the Buda end of the Margaret Bridge. Founded in 1991, Balassi publishes, on average, eighty titles per year, most of them so academic as to be hopelessly uncommercial: classical Hungarian literature, art history, sociology, cultural history, reproductions of 18th and 19th century type faces and printers' and papermakers' watermarks, dual language editions of classic Chinese texts like Sun Tzu's *The Art of War*, catalogues of medieval and Renaissance libraries in Hungary. But with print runs between 500 and 3,000, publishers like Balassi and Argumentum cannot maintain this kind of list without subsidies.

Some funds have been available up through 1999, primarily but not exclusively for books that would not otherwise see print, but Gábor Csordás, head of Jelenkor publishing house, says that these are drying up. Major sources have been the National Cultural Fund and the Hungarian Book Foundation, both linked to the Ministry of Culture, which has some funds of its own; the Soros Foundation; the Attila József Foundation, run by the MSZP or Socialist Party; and, the newest and perhaps the largest, the Higher Education Textbook Foundation — which, out of its 400 million forint budget (about $170 million, using, as in all later conversions, the exchange rate of early May, 1999), could fund even books which might plausibly be used as supplementary texts.

The National Cultural Fund distributed about 2.7 billion forints ($14 million) in 1997, drawing funds from the "trash tax" on material in print and other media not judged to be of high quality and on "culture-related consumer-electronic goods" like TV sets, copying machines, floppy disks (not more than 1 percent each), and toy weapons (10 percent). Besides books and periodicals, it supports film, theater, music, visual and folk arts, and cultural institutions like libraries and museums.

Soros, which predates the change by five years, and has many programs that are not specifically cultural, has been a major supporter of publishers like Balassi. It put about 80 million forints a year ($350,000) into big publishing projects. Until the late 1990s, Soros's Hungarian branch, like other foundations, gave grants directly to publishers. Then, in a unique program, Soros money supported specific titles and was intended to benefit readers who would otherwise not buy books because of the cost. In effect, Soros prefinanced the production of quality manuscripts which, in the judgment of a board comprised of a literary historian and representatives of three major libraries, met the very broad criteria of reflecting the values of an open society. These include accessibility of ideas and equality of opportunity, which explains why a book on modern art led even *The Scenario of the Change of the Regime* in 1999's selections. Then, after surveying as many as four thousand librarians about the needs and desires of their clients, Soros bought and distributed, free, between two hundred and three thousand copies.

The Soros Foundation has had a number of smaller programs. One, in cooperation with the Open Society Institute (comprising thirty foundations in the area of the post–Soviet empire), selects ten to fifteen titles in the political and human sciences suggested by each foundation and arranges for their translation into the various national languages. In one program, which began before 1989, classic philosophical works in English are translated — so far about 350 titles. In another, East Translates East, important books from the human sciences in the past ten years are translated into the various languages. This is important because, as György Orbán of Balassi says, intellectuals in these countries almost certainly know what is going on in Paris, London, and New York, but someone in Budapest may not know what is going on in Bucharest or Warsaw. Now, however, with Hungary in NATO and the European Union, these and other activities have shifted to the south and east, notably to Bulgaria, where the Next Page Foundation has taken over translation projects, Romania, Croatia, and Yugoslavia.

All of these programs have been established to provide the reading audience with material that, because of slender or even negative margins between production cost and selling price, would otherwise be unavailable. In 1997, for example, Soros received 602 applications to produce original manuscripts and funded 162. Balassi received fourteen of these grants, Magvető, Ozirisz, and Seneca ten each. Nine of seventeen applications to translate foreign works were funded; Ozirisz and Balassi got three each. Of twenty-four applications to publish the first books of young writers, eight were accepted. And Soros had begun a competitive program to encourage the production of literary biography, until now not a significant Hungarian genre.

As the concentration of grants might suggest, some people in the literary world have the impression that the foundations, especially Soros and the National Cultural fund, are dominated by a clearly defined group of interests, with an unhealthy overlap between board members and people on the lists of editorial boards — either before or after grants are given. A controversy arose in 1999 because the current government included in its budget a line to subsidize, at a million forints per title, cheap new editions of 150 classics of Hungarian literature to celebrate the millennium. The publisher chosen was Ozirisz, which had very close ties to the administration. The decision was widely protested, and the word in 1999 was that five publishers would be chosen for the project, though it was not clear how the spoils would be divided. It is clear that Hungarians have embraced a certain strain of democratic behavior familiar to Americans.

These cheap editions and those subsidized by Soros may help a little to ease the pressure on libraries. The good news, one editor says, is that they are jammed with patrons. The bad news, a librarian counters, is that library budgets are shrinking, book prices, especially of foreign books, are growing, so that libraries can afford to buy fewer books for the use of patrons who now cannot afford to buy books they used to have in personal libraries. Another problem is the change in the book deposit law. Formerly, publishers were required to supply sixteen copies of each title issued, and these would be distributed to the country's important libraries. Now only six copies are required — and often not sent, either because new publishers don't know about the law or because they go out of business so rapidly that what enforcement there is cannot catch up with them.

The Soros Foundation realizes that these grants, even combined with others, will not solve publishers' problems, who are encouraged to pursue cross-financing — that is, find income from other sources. One publisher survives partly because of its very popular magazine on dogs. Balassi runs a chain of bookshops, including two at museums in the Buda Castle. But there are still cash flow problems, and Soros was lending money at half the national bank rate to publishers whose lists met open society standards. In 1997, Soros had thirty-one applications and made thirteen loans. Almost a quarter of the 60,500,000 forints (just under $300,000 at the rate then existing) went to Balassi. (Balassi also sponsors art exhibitions, but they are an attempt to recreate the coffee house culture of the past rather than to make money.)

Publishers clearly need this kind of help. As László Kúnos of Corvina says, patterns of incomes and finances have changed. Books now have to be priced realistically; inflation has cut discretionary income; the distribution system had to be reinvented; and the number of bookstores dropped by fifty per cent in the 1990s. Moreover, as university librarian Nóra Deák and various others agree, the younger generation doesn't read as much as its predecessors, perhaps because of television, disaffection, or other cultural shifts but at least partly because of the cost of books. At any rate, it is harder to move the product than it used to be.

And when people do read, it is clear that their tastes have changed. Some of the worst trash has disappeared, but it was probably true that Hungary had been, in András Török's words, "an over-cultured country," partly because government control had kept out Western genre trash. Now the street-corner booksellers have ten or twenty Heather Grahams, Harold Robbinses, and Wilbur Smiths to one Vonnegut, Mailer, or Rushdie.

In another kind of attempt to foster a culture based on quality literature, the National Cultural Fund and the Soros Foundation have supported literary and other journals — Soros, fifteen of what they consider the most important cultural journals with liberal attitudes towards free expression of opinion. Gabriella Szilárd, director of Cultural Programs in 1999, said that Hungary is a country of journals, that every town of more than forty or fifty thousand has a journal, and that new writers find in them a first way into print. In 1997, forty-five of 145 applications were funded.

Soros and other granting agencies apparently tried to be even-handed among competing ideologies — so much so that the editor of a nonpartisan magazine that has never received a subsidy was advised, perhaps partly in jest, to sell it to the Smallholders Party and get seven million forints in the next distribution.

Clearly there is not as much money to go around as there was in the good/bad old days or even in the 1990s, partly because, according to one source, there are now 140 literary journals, though only seventy-three are listed in *Magyar Irodalom*. Those that survive have had to learn to be at least as flexible and ingenious as the publishing houses. A case in point is *Nagyvilág* (Great World). It was first published, though planned earlier, in October, 1956, exact contemporary of the Revolution, to bring world literature, which had been ignored by Marxist critics, to the Hungarian audience. After the Revolution was suppressed, the Party allowed it to continue, at first freely and then under supervision. as one of the concessions to Hungarian intellectuals. It featured for the first time translations of work by Pasternak, Brecht, Sartre, and other writers more controversial, from the Party point of view, than the last two.

It became one of the most popular journals in Hungary, read by everyone who claimed to be an intellectual, publishing 30,000 copies a month. It had a staff of twenty full-time employees, including the ideological supervisor, many of whom showed up only to collect their salaries. It had the funds to subscribe to all the leading journals and many newspapers throughout the world.

When the change came, each new interest group wanted its own journal, and there was more conflict over shrinking subsidies. *Nagyvilág* and many other government-controlled journals had been under the direction of the parent company Pallas. When that went under, a smaller company, controlling twenty-two journals, was formed. That lasted two or three years, and when it sank, several journals went with it. *Nagyvilág* was close to sinking, and many of the staff left for other jobs. Those remaining formed a foundation for friends of the journal, invested a month's salary each, and sent letters inviting writers and writers to join the foundation. The journal survived — with a staff of four, all part-time, and a print run of 3,000.

Subscriptions and sales won't keep the journal going, so the editors have applied, with indifferent success, for foundation support. So they turned to special monographic issues devoted to individual writers and national literatures and received support (e.g., from Argentina for the Borges issue) from various embassies. And they began to publish books, beginning with three a year and currently nine, including a popular series of short stories from national literatures — American, Italian, Swedish, French, Japanese, British — which have previously appeared in the journal. They also publish, besides translations of books by writers like Camus, Hamsun, Silone, and Unamuno, original work by contemporary Hungarian poets and critics. This program has received support from Soros and other foundations, including foreign ones.

As a result of these efforts, *Nagyvilág* is surviving. But it is hardly thriving because, as editor Anikó Fázsy says, world literature is beyond or beneath everyday politics. To broaden its base, the magazine has begun to sponsor literary evenings in which writers confront critics or various sides debate issues like postmodernism, the crisis of values, or a new book like Győző Ferencz's *Where Is Poetry Now?* These meetings have drawn crowds which are not just standing room only but spill down the staircase—a situation that helps to account for Fázsy's optimism about the prospects for literature.

Of course, applying for subsidies means paperwork at both ends of the publishing process, the grant and the report, and the process and all the other shifts to raise money necessarily (in two senses) take time away from the real business of creating and producing real work.

Still, according to Miklós Vajda, editor of *Hungarian Quarterly*, quality publishing is making a comeback. An even more optimistic account of publishing and indeed the general cultural situation is András Török's in the *Budapest Review of Books*: taking everything into account, he says, "subsidies [in 1998] are as much as 160 percent higher than those of last year." It should be said that Török was secretary of state in the previous government's Ministry of Culture and may have been exaggerating its accomplishments. Other accounts are less rosy, and one should remember that the pessimist is better informed.

Some of the good news about publishing is, according to some critics, bad news because, as Török says, they think that, even under difficult circumstances, so many literary journals have sprung up "that it is too easy to get a manuscript published and that this is harmful to the intrinsic development of literature."

The poets I spoke to did not, naturally, share this view, though one of them, Győző Ferencz, agrees that it is easier to publish and that sheer volume may make it more difficult for readers to find the best work. But in the Eighties, he says, it was no easier to find the best writers because many could not get published at all. There were two monthly and one weekly outlets for poetry in Budapest and four or five in the provinces. All were government run, and all had the same political/aesthetic policies, so that if one rejected a poet, there was no chance with the others.

Furthermore, there was a kind of cronyism to which Americans are not strangers. If a new poet took a poem to a literary magazine, it would probably be rejected. Never, of course, on ideological grounds. Some other excuse would be given. Or the editors would simply lose it or make the poet wait years for rejection.

Now things are better—for poets. Dramatists are in worse shape. According to Márton Mesterházi, a drama editor at Hungarian Radio for thirty years, the largest and most important theaters have become almost purely commercial, producing West End and Broadway hits and musicals. New Hungarian plays are produced, if at all, in theaters with two to three hundred seats — or in the provinces.

András Török paints a characteristically rosy picture of provincial theater, where the "Young Turks" have established themselves as "the ruling elite in the current theater." And he points to a program of the National Cultural Fund "to pay repertory theater companies in the country that are willing to book (alternative) studio productions." However, his glowing report about the National Theater, supposedly under construction when he wrote in 1998, had had to be qualified several times over. In 1999 there was a very large hole next to the main bus station and the junction of the three metro lines in downtown Pest, but the government formed in the fall of 1998 decided to build it elsewhere. One man very active in the literary world asks, rather sourly, whether a national theater is a building or a company of players — and, he says, Hungary already has the latter. As of 2002, it has the former — near the southernmost bridge, Lágymányosi, across the Danube on the Pest side, part of the Millenium Center.

Mesterházi is no happier about the state of radio drama than of conventional productions. At one point, he worked on one hundred and thirty-five adaptations of classic drama from Aeschylus to Sean O'Casey, many put into Hungarian for the first time. Now, he says, all divisions of Hungarian Radio are bankrupt. No one in top management seems interested in the work itself or seems to have a sense of what good public radio should be. They want government subsidies for public radio while coveting the profits of commercial radio in "a euphoric state of marketing."

Marketing is an area not really open to writers, who have little control over the process. In the past, writers may not have had a great deal of power vis-à-vis the government, but at least they were organized — because everyone had to be organized. The Communists founded the Hungarian Writers Association, and in 1989 some argued that this Stalinist institution did not deserve to survive. Others argued that it did help to effect change and was a major force in the revolution of 1956. In any case, the argument continues, even a liberal government would channel funds through and at the suggestion of this and other organizations. The organization now has about six hundred members. And the prediction was correct: the Ministry of Culture asks for recommendations about the distribution of literary prizes. Several years ago a dozen or so writers founded another organization in order to have a voice. And there is a post-modernist organization on one end of the literary-political spectrum and the so-called Populists (or "Popular" or "Folk" group) on the other, with the Hungarian Writers Association somewhere in the middle. But none of the new organizations has much power or money or importance for the communication of ideas — which may amount to the same thing.

Győző Ferencz, who has belonged to several of these organizations but says he refuses to join new ones and is getting out of the old ones, says that he has found little advantage in them. He did get an invitation to a conference in Washington, D.C., that turned out to be sponsored by the followers of the Rev. Moon, and he has an occasional family vacation at Szigliget, the Art Fund's retreat on the north shore of Lake Balaton. Even that is open for shorter periods than in the past.

Hungarian writers may not have effective organizations, but that doesn't stop them from choosing sides. A number of people I spoke to were less interested in discussing organizations than in lamenting the factionalism that blights the literary landscape. The basic split is between what are called, respectively, rural and urban writers. Some call the rural camp Populists, but Miklós Vajda prefers the Hungarian word "népi," "of the people" or "of the village," as more accurate. He traces their heritage to Dezső Szabó, a novelist and essayist in the 1930s who responded to the effects of the Treaty of Trianon, which transferred huge slices of Hungarian territory and population to Slovakia, Romania, and Yugoslavia. Szabó was ultra-nationalist, anti–German, and anti–Semitic. The anti–German strain was also notable in the work of László Németh, who in *Witness*, a periodical he wrote single-handed, advocated a "revolution of quality," a return to Magyar roots.

At the beginning of the twenty-first century, Vajda says, the ideology is an anachronism, and in fact the népi are united by little more than a solidarity of background. Both Vajda and Éva Tóth, who describes herself as an urban populist, think that the key to understanding this group is Ferenc Juhász's long poem, "The Boy Changed to a Stag Cries Out at the Gate of Secrets," based, like poems by József Erdélyi and László Nagy, on a Transylvanian folk tale. The theme is like Thomas Wolfe's "you can't go home again" in that the provincial cannot return to the old way of life but does not fit in with the liberal intellectual world of Budapest. The népi tend not to orient themselves toward Budapest, tend not to know English, and tend to be ignored by translators, so that I was not able to talk to any of them.

Before 1989, Vajda says, there were groupings but no animosity. Then, with the rise of multi-party politics, rivalry and resentment have increased, breaking formal associations, friendships, even marriages. The népi regard the urbanites as arrogant because of their advantages in education, travel, and knowledge of languages — a gap that it will take a generation or more to close. Urban liberals think it unfair to label all népi as anti–Semitic, but they assume that the rural group is burdened by ideology and by an inferiority complex or complexes.

Mesterházi cites as typical his experience with Menyhért Tamás, with whom he had a long relationship at Hungarian Radio. Tamás writes short novels which he then turns into radio plays — or plays which he turns into novels. The last project the two men worked on was "Stations," dealing with Hungarians from Voivodina, Slovakia, the Ukraine, and Hungary proper. The four are confined to a railway carriage, and the windows are blocked and they must rely on station loudspeakers for information on their whereabouts. Each has his secrets and neuroses, and in the course of fifty-five minutes, these are explored in a kind of Hungarian "No Exit."

Mesterházi did none of the writing, but he cut, pushed, tried to curtail irrelevancy and didacticism and, as he said, hit Tamás with a ruler. The play was, he thought, quite successful in its 1995 production. A year later, he received a copy of the novel with a dedication. It had the same title and the core of the radio script. But on page three, Mesterházi says, Tamás started preaching and never stopped.

Clearly Tamás has different aesthetic views than his editor, who holds that the best Hungarian drama follows István Örkeny in employing irony and "radical contempt of pathos." Perhaps irony and detachment are primarily urban qualities; certainly they are not prominent in early stages of committed literature, as demonstrated by proletarian and early feminist writing in the United States. And obviously Tamás would not agree with Mesterházi's view of Hungarian drama. But at least Mesterházi and Tamás were for a time able to work together.

This is rare, and the factionalism affects every area of literary life. Győző Ferencz says that he never tries to write at Szigliget because of the atmosphere. The rural group drinks upstairs; the urbanites drink downstairs; and the Transylvanian Hungarians march up and down the staircase between the two. The same kind of self-segregation occurs on the beach.

A number of Hungarians in Western Europe and North America continue to write in their native language, but it is not clear how deeply involved they are in literary politics. George Szirtes may not be typical, since he began writing in English before he began to write in and translate from Hungarian, but he has published a number of books in England and is therefore more accessible than other emigrés. In 1956, at the age of eight, he walked into Austria with his parents and younger brother, learned English, and only after the death of his mother began seriously to examine his Hungarian roots. For the most part, Szirtes looks at Hungary in some poems "from the no-man's land of childhood memory"; in others, "a pretty desperate attempt on my part to discover bridges between my life in England and my history in Hungary"; in still others an attempt to create images of life in Hungary before he was born, from photographs and from imagination, as in the sequence METRO, in which picture frames

> hold names
> At an aesthetic distance, where, by willing,
> We can work them into fictions and animate
> The past, which remains forever another place.

Elsewhere, as in "The First, Second, Third, and Fourth Circles" and in "Transylvania," Szirtes presents images of contemporary Budapest (the circles are in part the boulevards that ring Pest) and of Romania, which he calls "a highly photo-journalistic poem" (*The Budapest File*).

Szirtes is clearly aware of Hungarian poetic tradition — several poems are addressed to major poets, and he has done a number of translations — but he seems not to be involved in the local literary scene and its conflicting aesthetic and political views.

As for Hungarian writers in regions cut off from Hungary by Trianon, one scholar/poet says that most of the Hungarian writers in Voivodina have moved north of the Yugoslav border. Transylvanian writers tend to get favorable reception because they were persecuted for years under the Ceaușescu regime and because, cut off from the shifts in language, they supposedly speak and write an older, purer Hungarian. Still, while the Hungarian government periodically protests the treatment of Hungarians in Slovakia, the situation of writers seems enviable by comparison with those in Transylvania and Voivodina. Lajos Grendel has been president of Slovak PEN and is currently chair of the Association of Slovak Writers; Kalligram publishes about seventy-five books a year. But Grendel came to Budapest to launch his latest novel for the obvious reason that the Hungarian national audience is crucial to his and others' success.

Lajos Grendel says that the rural-urban split isn't characteristic of the eighty to ninety Hungarian writers in Slovakia; rather, there is a generational disagreement about the nature and purpose of writing between older writers, who tend to write like nineteenth century realists and as socially responsible moralists, and most younger writers, who are post-modernists. This seems partly true of writers in Hungary proper. Béla Pomogáts, president of the Hungarian Writers' Association in 1999, admits that there are more traditional writers but is concerned that "the postmodern trend in Hungarian literature has started with the creative personality heeding no values outside literature and often replacing the traditional narrative with reflection, focusing mainly on language and modes of discourse."

Some of the division between older, fairly traditional writers and young post-modernists can be seen in the recent anthology, *Swimming in the Ground*.

As the translators note, much of the work "suggests the assimilation of impressionism, abstract arts, the surreal." Some of the poets, like Károly Bari, are hardliners, as in "The calmness deters from the adobe knot's hidden fire" and "memories lashed by lanky winds linger on the trees." Some, like Zsófia Balla, move from language like "You are here but you are not / A wet wire" to straightforward if ironic scenes from a writer's conference in "Oil Change."

These selections may indicate as much about the editors' taste as about the state of contemporary Hungarian poetry. For example, the two selections by Ottó Orbán are far more experimental than anything in the three volumes of his poems published in the U.S. And both Orbán and Ágnes Gergely, born in the 1930s, can sound almost as postmodern as some of the younger poets.

Not all of the poets are on the edge, of course. Győző Ferencz's "Light Metal Construction in Poetry," which contrasts the mechanism of a dismantled poem with "the supporting power / Where the process began," is a sonnet. And in "Drama Fragment," György Somlyó. the oldest poet in the collection, born in 1920, uses the structure of stanza, epode, anti-stanza, and dedication to describe the situation of a Central European Jew.

Only two poets, János Marno (silenced for thirteen years by the Kádár regime) and Tibor Zalán make even oblique references to the political situation. In "As If Right Now, "Zalán asserts that "The honey has melted / off those great slogans you waved on the barricades," and in "He Believed He Existed" he refers to the withdrawal of the conquerors and poverty staring with "a gaping mouth / at the public romping through the alleys"—clearly a reference to the transition from communism to democracy. Marno is more oblique in "Common Cold," which ends with the image of "A dark file cabinet" overlooking a hallway "where the elderly roam / under the nictating light tubes."

Since none of the poems in the anthology are dated, it may be a mistake to assume that poets who write in dissociated images and dislocated syntax were finding refuge from censors who could find nothing subversive in highly unconventional language. But the sense of isolation, loneliness, and dismemberment of the body or divesture of elements of the psyche appears over and over again in poems of all styles.

Some writers, like the novelist Ferenc Temesi, recognize the existence of the urban-népi, traditional-modernist-postmodernist splits but have grown impatient with labels. His most popular novel, the two-volume *Dust*, written in the form of a dictionary (A–K, L–Z) is obviously, as he claims, postmodern. But he also calls it "an historical, family, and autobiographical novel" covering six generations from 1833 to 1973, though not in chronological order. And being from Szeged, which one poet calls the most conservative city in

Hungary and Temesi calls the heart and real capital, he has affinities with the népi and has written the novel in the dialect of that city. It is therefore, he says, not really translatable. The mixture of elements is essentially Hungarian, like the mustard-colored building facing the Pest bus station. Both volumes of the novel were bestsellers; his father, after strong initial misgivings, helped to find material and was pleased with the result; and Temesi can go home to Szeged.

Now, however, Temesi says that he has stopped being a postmodernist and has decided that novels need plot, event, resolution. Some younger writers seem to feel the same way and are presumably post-postmodern or neo-traditionalists.

At any rate, divisions and schools still exist, and most of the people I interviewed think that the most important division is urban-populist. It is generally agreed that writers who publish in magazines of one faction don't even submit to opposition counterparts. Books by urban writers aren't reviewed by populists, and vice versa. And within the various camps, magazines have more or less prestige — a situation which of course changes. In 1989 two of the most influential magazines were *Kortársá* (Contemporary) and *Új Írs* (New Writing). The latter lost support under the new Minister of Culture and disappeared; the former survives. *Élet és Irodalom* (Life and Letters), referred to simply as "És" (And), was more influential before 1989 but survives as what some regard as an organ of the Free Democratic Party. Some literary people think it in the great tradition; others think it too neo-liberal. Its rival, *Magyar Napló* (Hungarian Journal) began as an urban, post-modern venue, then was taken over by the Writers Association and then by the Populists and has lost so many readers that it struggles to survive. Other magazines mentioned with varying degrees of enthusiasm are *2000*, *Parnassus*, edited by István Turczi and devoted to poetry, *Holmi* (Thing), edited by Szabolcz Várady, *Jelenkor*, from the publishing house of the same name, and *Kalligram*, another publishing house/magazine in Slovakia. County governments put money into journals: *Műhely* (Workshop) in Győr is a good example. Many of the newer magazines tend to be devoted to a particular kind of literary politics, and their life is precarious. *Orpheusz* reappeared in 1999 after a two-year hiatus due to financial difficulties; unlike *2000*, *És*, *Holmi*, *Jelenkor*, and *Kalligram*, it didn't get a Soros subsidy in 1997.

Speaking of financial difficulties, all but a few writers have almost given up expecting any financial reward for their work. There are some exceptions: Péter Eszterházy gets half a million forints per book from his publisher; Péter Nádas is able to live on his writing because of royalties from Germany. (Hungarian writing is currently popular in Germany and France — and writers translated into these languages are then accessible to publishers elsewhere.)

Most writers, however, are not fortunate enough to gain foreign attention and royalties. Győző Ferencz, described as a fine poet by people from three different generations, published two books of poems and two of essays in the 1990s—and has yet to receive a forint in royalties. László Kúnos of Corvina Publishers and Miklós Vajda of *The Hungarian Quarterly* testify that this is not unusual. Most writers make their living teaching, translating, or doing readers' reports—or all three and more. Some younger poets make a living writing soap opera scripts. Translators at least get paid—currently 20,000 to 25,000 forints (roughly $90–$110 for every twenty pages. That is more than the $63 equivalent in 1999, but of course other prices have risen. And there is a new system in which translators get paid by the letter—not counting spaces.

There are various grants and stipends for writers. The Soros Foundation has given non-competitive grants to writers at several stages of their careers: for a body of work; for mid-career writers; and for young writers. These varied from 1.4 million forints at the top to 40,000 forints. The Ministry of Culture has given direct grants of double the minimum wage to writers under thirty-five, about 60,000 forints (just over $250) per month for ten or eleven months. The National Cultural Fund has had grants and twenty to thirty annual prizes, and it has supported former Kossuth Prize Winners in return for electronic rights to all work, past and future. But one writer complained that, except for the Kossuth support, the same names keep appearing in different order in the various prize lists, and in any case, there is not and never will be enough money to go around.

Hungarian and Slovak and probably writers in other former Soviet Bloc countries regard this situation as unusual. Gustáv Murín is writing an article about pay for writers in Slovakia and says that his colleagues complain about lack of compensation and insist that "If I were in America…." Americans have in this case a rare opportunity to disillusion Central Europeans. Most American writers get very little from their work. And editors in the U.S. complain about the lack of time, personnel, and resources to do the kind of careful work that was characteristic of the good old days.

This and much other anecdotal evidence demonstrates that what my Central European friends regard as a post-apocalyptic situation is in fact nothing more than the normal operation of capitalism. (The obvious difference is that American academics are fairly well paid.) Or, as László Kúnos put it, the changes since 1989 have been a big shock for Hungarian writers and the literary public. They have had to get used to the idea that literature is less important to society and the general culture than it used to be. He referred primarily to the economic situation. Ferenc Temesi put it more bluntly: in Central and Eastern Europe, "literature, in one moment, lost its importance, its role."

Béla Pomogáts asked the more relevant question about what the writer is to do now. "Does literature ... still belong in part to the political sphere or is it solely art?" Should writers enter politics, or it is it possible that we don't need another Havel? Pomogáts does say that "the sense of importance rooted in [literature's] responsibility for public and national issues ... has been shattered" along with "the impoverishment of literary institutions and a perceivable loss of the prestige accorded to writers and their creative work."

One reason for this, Frederick Turner has argued, is that unlike Sándor Petőfi in the revolution of 1848 (and, Irén Kiss adds, many writers in 1956), the ideas and energy for the revolution of 1989 came not from writers but from bureaucrats, accountants, and other non-literary types who saw that the old system had failed and worked to modify and to change it. "How," Turner asks, "does one celebrate the patient growing of wealth and culture, the slow process of cultivation, virtuous discipline, democratic compromise, economic federalism, wide environmental management, the evolutionary chaos of the market?" All these are not only inconsistent with but antipathetic to much of Hungarian and indeed of other Western literature.

That may be arguable, but it is obvious that most of the stories in *Give or Take a Day* (Corvina, 1997) and *Thy Kingdom Come* (Noran/Palatinus, 1998) look backward, often in great and justifiable bitterness, rather than forward.

Perhaps, at the end of the twentieth century, the idea of a prophetic writer seems more than a little ridiculous. Think of the attitude towards Norman Mailer. But Irén Kiss calls for a return to the sense of the strength of the writer's personality and for the preservation and renewal of the roots of Hungarian language and culture—not in a racial or racist sense but in terms of their pan–European, pan–Asian connections. If, she says, writers are not able to take these risks, then they deserve to be marginalized. In her recent collection of plays, *Innocents, Heroes, Saints*, she turns to historical figures like Cardinal Mindszenty and St. Elizabeth of Hungary for inspiration. And Ferenc Temesi, after being a 1960s Hungarian Beatnik (rock and roll instead of progressive jazz, as in the American 1950s) and a postmodernist innovator, now says that a nation needs strong novels if it is to mature and hopes that his generation of writers has helped to create it.

Of course, even for writers of the older generation, there is unfinished business from the past. Some, like Imre Kertész, a recent Nobel Prize winner, are still dealing with the psychological/spiritual consequences of the Holocaust. *Kaddish for a Child Not Born* looks like the kind of novel that, critic and translator Ferenc Takács once said of another book, could have been written by any European intellectual in six weeks. This may not be true of *Kaddish*, but only a Central European intellectual could have written it.

The novel is difficult to describe: part meditation, part fictional memoir, part highly abstract and a chronic narrative in the first person, part transcriptions from drafts of earlier work, part a circling around a series of scenes, images, and issues that reaches no conclusion except the fact that it ends with a prayer to cease forever. In form and style, it resembles the classic depiction of obsessive-compulsive behavior of a being threatened by forces it cannot control and can barely comprehend: Franz Kafka's "The Burrow."

"No," the first word of the novel, answers a question posed four pages later: does the narrator have children? Repeated again and again, the negative comes to embrace the narrator's response to even the idea of having a child, of his marriage, of his Jewishness, of authority, of love, of life itself. What is left is work — which is either a way of not existing, of existing, or of using his pen as a spade to dig himself a grave in the air, a grave that has been being dug by others throughout his life. He works out of his pain, because of his pain, and only incidentally, because writing implies an audience, to sustain a dialogue.

In the course of ninety-five very dense pages — there are no divisions into sections or chapters, and one paragraph covers more than a fourth of the book, with some others not appreciably shorter — the reader learns that the narrator has survived Auschwitz, that his once and future wife was attracted to him because of his writing and his ability to free her from her obsessions and then left him because he could not escape his, and that his private boarding school and then his relationship with his father taught him that all authority led directly to Auschwitz. At the end, he senses the sewer lines beneath the street and announces that he has written this account "so that with the baggage of this life in my raised hands I may go and in the dark stream of the fast-flowing black warmth / I may drown / Lord God /let me drown / forever, / Amen."

Kaddish for a Child Not Born is both somber and exhilarating — somber because of the subject and the obsessive prose, exhilarating because of the creative energy. Ideally, like Marlow's accounts in Joseph Conrad's *Heart of Darkness* and *Lord Jim*, it should be read in one sitting, for like both novels, it condenses a lifetime into a story told in a single night.

As Kertész's example shows in a particular mind and *Contemporary Jewish Writing in Hungary: An Anthology* shows again and again, Hungarian Jews are still dealing with the effects of centuries of anti–Semitism. In two stories in the collection, characters say that the Holocaust "came about," as if the result was inexplicable and unconnected to any human agency.

As the editors explain in their lengthy, impressive introduction, the roots of the Holocaust, in Hungary at least, go back at least to the mid–nineteenth century. A large percentage of Hungarian Jews, especially in Budapest, gave up German and Yiddish for the Hungarian language, assumed Hungarian names, and tried to become good Hungarians. This became increasingly difficult between the two world wars, when radical Magyar nationalists denied that Jews could be Hungarians and passed discriminatory legislation. Then came the Holocaust. After that, Imre Kertész notes, the Communist Party tried "to smother [the memory], then to degrade it to some petty 'Jewish affair'..." and, as the editors note, being "'a good Jew' meant rejecting Jewish particularity." That silence ended as Communist domination eased and then disappeared, but freedom to discuss has also meant freedom to make anti-Semitic statements.

The two dozen writers in this anthology, in which about half the work is translated into English for the first time, fall roughly into four generations (the editors find three): those who came to maturity before World War II, those who endured the war as children or adolescents, those born during and just after the war who heard the official silence about the Holocaust, and those born after the silence ended.

Work from the first generation — Ernö Szép, Béla Zsolt, György Somlyó, István Örkény, György Kardos, Stefánia Mándy — tends toward the documentary even when experience is fictionalized. The prose is not obviously literary, but it is nonetheless brilliant, particularly Szép's understated account of life in the 1944 ghetto from *The Smell of Humans* (1945; in English translation, in Budapest, in 1994), a seminal book that deserves wider circulation. Not all are entirely grim. Kardos's "You Must Like Théophile Gautier," for example is a picaresque in which Bulgarians overwhelm the narrator with gifts out of their "huge surplus stock of tenderness" but leave him barefoot. And one can smile at the ragged, homeless trio in Somlyó's story who try to ferry across the still-bridgeless Danube manuscripts that will bring about "a fresh start in Hungarian literature."

Still, even Kardos and Somlyó achieve their effects by building up immediate detail. Writers like Kertész, György Konrád, and Ottó Orbán, who came to maturity after the war and are better known to Western audiences, provide various contexts in which the recent past can be understood, and their work is more clearly literary, even experimental. Mária Ember interpolates into her story of a young boy in a labor camp excerpts from official documents, including an invoice for materials used in fencing a small-town ghetto and post-war interrogation of an Austrian S.S. member denying his past. In the excerpt from *The Loser*, Konrád retreats from a visit to a cemetery to the comfortable past of the narrator's grandfather, a merchant who is prosperous but also gives a monitory Seder speech which ends, "We are no longer worthy of being chosen." For the most part, the flashbacks are given in the present tense, as if the narrator is trying to keep that happy and comfortable past alive.

Orbán and Ágnes Gergely look at their experience more obliquely, sometimes from the vantage point of the Iowa Writers Workshop, sometimes defining themselves more as European than Hungarian and at times, at least in these poems, only tangentially as Jewish. Orbán in particular sees himself as a poet, not quite with a capital P, who "peels roughly the apple called poetry / and is curious about the hidden kernel." He could stay in America but returns to Hungary because "only here in my home, the place I was born, could I be what I am ... the vice of misfortune and language would keep me in hand."

Younger writers tend to make dislocation a narrative rather than a personal strategy. Péter Lengyel moves back and forth from the sixteenth to the twentieth century, in which anti–Semitism is perhaps less virulent but no less present. Mihály Kornis distances the narrator from himself by shifting from first to third person, by interpolating surreal conversations with the dead in the bricks of the Death Wall, and by breaking the language into centered, poetic lines. And Lászlo Márton uses conscious fiction to manipulate the past so that his characters can survive, at least in imagination. One character is delighted to see that a friend has been sentenced to death. Why? Because that means that he survived the camps.

Most of these writers are acutely aware of being Jewish, even if some of the younger ones aren't always sure what that means or what it's worth. György Dalos's young narrator hopes to find a way of being Jewish, Hungarian, Communist, and somehow Christian. He isn't circumcised, and Kornis's narrator has no clear idea of who Jews are, either in practice or as an idea. Characters in work by some older writers are enjoined to stop being Jewish as soon as possible.

One of the most interesting questions is what anti–Semitism does not just to Jews but to Hungary. Szép sees "atrophy of reason, spirit, humor. When would we ever recover from the damage done to the mind and soul of this nation?" Péter Nádas's narrator in "The Lamb" is from a lower-class Christian family and is now a scientist struggling to understand the workings of a system that leads to mind-numbing conformity and repression of anything outside the system.

Perhaps still younger writers will be less subject to being singled out as aliens. "Budapest Analyses," subsidized by the Fidesz right-center party, reports that between 1993 and 2003 the percentage of people who said they disliked Jews had dropped from fourteen to six or seven percent, that overt incidents of anti–Semitism had disappeared, and that accusations of anti–Semitism were being used as a political tool to try to discredit Fidesz.

Perhaps. As Lengyel's narrator says of the higher figure, "I'm doing just fucking great. Better than burglars, rapists, desecrators of tombs, motherfuckers and patricides."

And perhaps not. As the youngest writer represented, Gábor Szántó, hints, Jews can never feel entirely safe. His narrator emerges from a derelict synagogue wearing a yarmulke, and a mother, seeing it, bends and whispers to her child. The situation is not just paranoid or fictional. In 1989, I left an old synagogue in eastern Hungary with a fellow Fulbrighter who spoke German. He attracted a crowd of curious, cheerful urchins, excited by a (then) rare glimpse of an American. He asked about the new synagogue being built and was told, "That's for the dirty Jews."

Orbán (1936–2002) has perhaps the widest distribution in America, and his themes extend beyond his Jewish heritage, from his father, and even beyond Hungary. Orbán's death was a personal as well as a poetic loss, but *Our Bearings at Sea: A Novel in Poems* serves as a fitting memorial poem. Except for the introductory self-interview of 2001 and the free verse poems from the early 1970s at the beginning and end, this is a translation of a volume that appeared in Hungarian in 1983. However, it presents to Orbán's growing audience in English a new aspect of his work.

That work has always drawn upon close observation of whatever scene lies before him, but here Orbán discusses explicitly the heritage of his early life: losing his father to the Holocaust; surviving the siege of Budapest and then an orphanage; turning to words to find "a means to think about my life"; realizing only later the dual heritage from his parents: "Sensitivity, perceptiveness, the cultured part of my talent comes from my father; but the stubborn, struggling, warrior-like drive for survival" comes from his mother.

Several poems scattered through the volume can be summarized in a kind of ars poetica. "The good poem," he says in "Poetry," is a nail into things as they are, and the starry sky hangs on it, a somber tapestry." Rejecting Parnassian idealization for "crucial details," his kind of poet shields a small flame that may, must, flare up. In "Keats," he writes, "'we remember' is in itself resurrection ... while that bodiless sewage, the first death and the hundredth, pours gurgling down the cosmic gutter." A better epitaph for Orbán himself could not be written.

The shifts from grotesque to sublime in this passage are even more emphatic not only in the images but in the attitudes of other poems. Standing in the National Gallery, he scorns pig-faced kings and their hangers-on.

Yet, in the end, he sees that "they won the new year, the new century, the chance to survive." In general, he is willing to forgive those who acted or those "Relatives," real or metaphorical, who, "Compared to the whorish rhetoric that trifles with infinity ... are the precise, the too-mortal Central European yardstick." Even "The General," who commits all sorts of professional horrors, is shown as harried paterfamilias. But he is unrelenting towards intellectuals who hunt rabbits (a recurring image) with "a club of abstraction" while the phenomenal, metaphoric big cat slaps away traps "and slips away unscathed into the trackless thicket of new generations."

The wide swings of attitude as well as image, not to speak of straining metaphor and the (by me) unaccountable reappearance of Columbus make these poems disconcerting reading. Indeed, as a whole the volume is even more unsettling. But it presents an accurate and eloquent picture not only of twentieth century Hungary but of the ways in which poetry can survive in an iron time and even, reluctantly and by indirection, console and elevate the spirit.

However, unlike some of his contemporaries and successors, Orbán does not simply look back or inward to Hungary. As translator into Hungarian of Allen Ginsberg and Robert Lowell, among others, Orbán had an intimate relationship with America long before he visited it. His poems "America I" and "II" in *The Journey of Barbarus* reveal Ginsberg's influence in theme and technique, while "Snowfall in Boston" refers directly to Lowell's "The Old South Boston Aquarium" and, as Bruce Berlind points out (in an introduction so good that one almost fears — needlessly — that the poems discussed will reveal less in the actual reading), Orbán borrows from Lowell the unrhymed sonnet form.

But Orbán's most eloquent testimony to American poetry is in "Canto," a meditation on Ezra Pound in the Pisan cage that leads Orbán to conclude that "it makes no difference that somebody isn't evil / if the stink of a carcass smells like violets to him" and, further, that behind all the tricks of poetry "one's curious to see the concealed core," which, finally, reveals that Liberty "is the only possible hero of every true poem." And because of Orbán's experience, he can give to "Liberty," even capitalized, a weight that no American could even attempt without embarrassment.

Moreover, he does not make the common American mistake of trying to naturalize the word. In fact, like many a European who "stare[s] at myself in the large, continent-sized mirror," he both hates the U.S. (especially cars all around him and airliners overhead) and finds many things to like — "nothing so much as / that I no longer envy them for anything."

Discovery of and fidelity to the self are central to Orbán's best poems in this collection. "Oklahoma Gold" does so with particular eloquence for me, not merely because it deals with a landscape, culture, and occasion (the deliberations of the Neustadt Prize jury) I know well. After eight years, the speaker returns to Oklahoma, wearier, more firmly in the grip of a physical paralysis, aware of "time vanishing from the depths of the well." After two days of discussing literature, including Sándor Weöres, whom he heard read as a child and now has nominated for the prize, he wonders if words are always distorted between speaker and audience. Then, in an abrupt shift to the present occasion and a landscape which has devoured Indians and land-rushers and will devour intellectuals, he has a vision of "a stifling peak, / where poem and reality secretly converge."

Then, in the last of four sixteen-line stanzas, he moves from the corruption of the oil gushing from Oklahoma's wells to the idea that poetry is nothing more than a tool for drilling and producing a "hissing column of joy and suffering" that mutates from "commemorative column" to pond, "from symbol to thermal energy," until, finally, "the flickering torch's poem on top of the pipe work / is proof: that, blazing with provocative madness, we exist!"

Like Orbán, Éva Tóth (b. 1939) concentrates on the complex history of her time and its effect on her, her family, and her contemporaries. Tóth's superb four-page *Memorial Poem* (see Appendix) traces personal, regional, and national history framed by the 1956 uprising and looking back to the Russian occupation in 1945 and forward to the poet's experience, marked by these events, ending with the funeral of a comrade who shared the experience. Written on the fortieth anniversary of the uprising, it has been translated into a dozen languages and published in a superb edition which, like the poem, has been awarded a major prize.

Tóth maintains that the poem is "simply a monologue, akin to the 'personal song' found in Finno-Ugrian folk-poetry," which "recounts her life story from birth to the very moment of the narration, including the small trivia of everyday life and momentous events alike."

Everyone familiar with Hungarian history knows about the momentous events, but the strength of the poem lies in the particulars of the geography and domestic arrangements of the town of Debrecen, seen from the point of view of a young girl and woman. The tone is deliberately undramatic, the events recounted one after another without surprise or comment, almost in documentary fashion.

The poem is prefaced by eloquent tributes from writers in many languages, but none seems to have noticed that it is also a tribute to Hungarian poetry. It begins with the purchase of a book of Kosztolányi poems, published in the year of her birth, and near the end, speaking of her impulse to emigrate in 1956, she lists the books she kept "in my small briefcase prepared for every eventuality." Finally, she speaks at the grave of the comrade in whose company she bought the first book, "but I was choking with tears / the snow was drifting hard and I could barely be heard."

Coming to terms with the past is dealt with in more oblique fashion of the stories of György Spiró, Ádám Bodor, László Marton, Sándor Tar, and Emese Medgyesi, where the weight of Communism is everywhere felt but rarely mentioned, as if it were atmospheric pressure. These writers witness rather than prophesy. Pomogáts calls for the great novel about the 1956 Revolution; Éva Tóth says that Tamás Benedicty (formerly Horváth) may have produced it in his *Souvenir*, which has not been translated. Meanwhile, Anglophones will have to make do with the marvelous historical novel *Under the Frog*. Written by a man born in England of parents who emigrated from Hungary in 1956, the book recreates the atmosphere of Budapest before and during the Revolution.

Hungarians need to come to terms with the Communist era, and it will probably be a dominant theme for some time. But in *Dust* and in *The Fishing Man*, Ferenc Temesi and Imre Oravecz have, in prose and poetry respectively, gone back to an earlier Hungary, before World War II, before the turn of the century, to use the perspective of history to place and judge recent events. Two writers are not necessarily a trend, but their strategies offer new possibilities. And both books were bestsellers.

These writers offer new and exciting possibilities. And there is other good news. Despite the financial, factional, and artistic struggles, Hungarian writers continue to produce good work. Márton Mesterházi points to the heirs of István Örkény's ironic stance in plays like those of György Spiró (though Spiró has said that he will write no more plays). Ákos Németh and Géza Bereményi are also doing interesting work in drama. (See *Three Contemporary Hungarian Plays*.) Eszterházy, Nádas, and Imre Kertész are, Mesterházi thinks, the novelists best known, and deservedly so, in the West. Miklós Vajda and others have high praise for Ádám Bodor, a Transylvanian who escaped years of persecution in Romania, who links short stories in the manner of Sherwood Anderson's *Winesburg, Ohio*. And though Vajda as a member of the older generation thinks that the post-modernists sound alike, he singles out for praise Lajos Parti-Nagy's absurdist stories satirizing the Kádár-era petit bourgeoisie living on intellectual morsels dropped from above. Unfortunately, Vajda thinks, the stories are untranslatable not merely because of English doesn't lend itself to Hungarian linguistic play but also because the English audience doesn't share the experience. Still, Parti-Nagy has been published in German — not notably more flexible than English.

Lajos Grendel speaks highly of the Slovak Hungarian poets Árpád Tőzsér, the experimental László Cselényi, and, in the younger generation, István Bettes. Among prose writers, the punk writer Attila Győry is a cult figure among young readers. And almost everyone I spoke to speaks of Grendel as one of the finest novelists writing today. Irén Kiss chided me about my ignorance of Hungarian putting me in a (very large) linguistic ghetto and singled out for special praise Endre Szkárosi and Anna Kiss, who have not been translated into English and who don't speak it. Anikó Fázsy mentions poets Magda Székely, Zsuzsa Takács, Péter Dobai, and Zsófia Balla (the last two represented in *Swimming in the Ground*) and fiction writers Nádas and Sándor Tar. (Nádas, Tar, Grendel, and eighteen other contemporary writers of fiction are translated in the two short story collections mentioned above.)

Ferenc Temesi says that there is a new generation of writers who are very exciting. Miklós György Száraz is in his forties; Norbert Haklik is twenty-two and, Temesi hopes and in fact insists, will be a great writer.

If so, he will have to learn, like Márton Mesterházi, that persistence may pay off better than blazing prophecy. After being laughed out of publishers' offices several years ago, Mesterházi was asked to edit a collection of Yeats's plays, perhaps because 1999 was the sixtieth anniversary of Yeats's death. This would, he says, have been unthinkable three years ago. The rows of books at the Balassi office were heartening evidence that scholarly and historical writing are very much alive. And older writers continue to produce and young ones to knock at the door.

The best kind of persistence is finding new readers, and thanks to Adam Makkai and his many collaborators, the two massive volumes of *In Quest of the Miracle Stag: The Poetry of Hungary* give an unprecedented view of the sweep of Hungarian poetry. Besides anonymous folk poems from the early middle ages and equally anonymous kuruc (freedom fighter) poems from the eighteenth century, the two volumes present work by just under two hundred poets from Janus Pannonius (d. 1472) to János Dénes Orbán (b. 1973). Unlike many national anthologies, Makkai and his collaborators include work by poets living outside current Hungarian borders, and not only those from territory lost in the Treaty of Trianon but those who have carried Hungarian literature to places where it had never before existed.

Readers coming fresh to Hungarian poetry, and even those who have some acquaintance with Magyar literature, language, and history, will be in part enlightened, in part overwhelmed, by the apparatus provided. The "Note on the Hungarian Language: Provenance, Spelling, and Pronunciation" assumes a confidence in the ease of the last that someone with more than twenty years' casual acquaintance with the language might regard as misplaced. The "Short History of Hungarian Verse" is quite technical, perhaps more useful to linguists and translators than to mere lovers of poetry. Each poet is accorded a one-page bio/bibliographical introduction and in many cases a pencil sketch.

But László Cs. Szabó's hundred-page "A Nation and Its Poetry" is essential reading for those who wish to see the poets not only arranged chronologically but put into historical context — a context perhaps even more essential for understanding Hungarian writing than for some of its neighbors, given successive invasions, suppressions, and exiles. Besides duly honoring the major names, Szabó notes major national characteristics — linking a concern with Fate to nomadism — and tendencies to identify with countries like Scotland (Edinburgh is to London as Budapest is to Vienna) and to draw upon other literatures. (From the Romantic period on, one could construct a thesis, or at least an essay, on the various uses of Shakespeare.) He notes that Hungarians long ago developed the habit of "emigrating into poetry" for lack of a real homeland, and regards "the passionate defense of the survival of the nation" as crucial for the real Hungarian poet.

Makkai and to some extent Cs. Szabó regard the Miracle Stag of the title as a key theme in Hungarian poetry from the anonymous shamans to Károly Bari (b. 1952). In its earliest version, it is the founding myth of Magyar migration from Asia to the Carpathian Basin, celebrating at first the strength and resolution of the hunters, later grafting Christian symbolism onto the horns, then celebrating the choice of wild freedom over domestic comfort, and finally — at least in this anthology — recognizing that the stag is dying. Makkai sees in some uses of the legend "not only a symbolic rejection of the big city and return to the country where folk traditions are alive," but allusions "to the Hungarians' Asiatic origins...."

Most of the names known to Anglophone readers (from street, square, and monument names in Budapest if not from their poems) are in the first volume: Bálint Balassi, Sándor Petőfi, Imre Madách, Endre Ady, Dezső Kosztolányi, Attila József, Miklós Radnóti. Gyula Illyés, Sándor Weöres, and some others who died too recently to have been monumentalized. Clearly, even in translation, they and many of their successors have written poems that are almost always memorable and often major.

Volume II was designed to include contemporary poets. In the seven-year gap between the volumes, several died, including Ottó Orbán, but most are, at this writing, and happily, still active. Makkai chose only poets who have published at least three volumes and can be defined as contemporary because they "treat universals in a way that is peculiar to the modern context, poets who draw on the eternal themes that are the stock of literary tradition but present them in a way that resonates in the modern day," a passage that describes Éva Tóth's "Memorial Poem" (available for the first time to American readers), Sándor Kányádi's "All Souls' Day in Vienna," and, though it is not obviously about Hungary, Ágnes Gergely's "Shipwreck," and dozens, even hundreds of other poems awaiting new readers, a smorgasbord to be dipped into at leisure rather than a banquet to be consumed from soup to nuts.

There are some obvious omissions. Makkai has no interest in really contemporary avant garde work. (For some of that, see *Swimming in the Ground.*) Perhaps this school will be included in a third volume, proposed for 2006.

Although the brief introductory sketches place each poet in literary, ideological, and religious contexts, Makkai does not attempt to force them into particular schools, perhaps mindful of the reproach implied in Ernő Hárs's "Literary Life": "We stuff one another / into colorful match boxes / according to generation and ideology. / We let an occasional phosphorous sign flare up / then we throw the used up match stick / into the garbage."

I have no way of judging the many translators' linguistic precision and imaginative fidelity. Makkai and his collaborators follow the "Gara Method of Translation"—preparing "a word-for-word, indeed morpheme-for-morpheme ... 'Pidgin-English' translation to help the native poet-translators appreciate the grammatical structure of the text at hand." There is also "a free prose translation in idiomatic Target Language diction," ignoring prosodic elements; then "mock stanzas" that ignore meaning; and finally, at least ideally, taped readings of the original texts.

To an Anglophone, the results seem better than satisfactory. A rather captious Hungarian intellectual (note the redundancy) complains that Makkai did not always choose the best translations. I cannot disprove that charge, but I can adapt Dr. Samuel Johnson's remark about a dog walking on his hind legs: "The wonder is, not that he does it badly, but that he does it at all." "Monumental" is too modest a term to apply to the achievement of Makkai and his many co-workers.

Speaking of captious, on a trip to Budapest earlier in 1999, I sat in a restaurant near two would-be filmmakers pitching ideas to each other. The American had a story about a wonder drug that cured ingrained Hungarian pessimism. Perhaps a drop or two has fallen into the Budapest water supply. Júlia Lázár brightened near the end of our interview. Good work is being published, she admitted. And her own work had been going not that badly. György Orbán was even more hopeful, saying, "It can be done!"

Mártn Mesterházi has something better than a wonder drug. The biggest mistake writers can make, he says, is to die too soon. It's important to outlive the fools. Many good writers were silenced, by death or exile, under communism, a loss that no one in the East can forget and no one in the West should be allowed to forget. Those young and old who managed to outlive communism now have to find ways to outlive the capitalists.

One of the ways of doing so is to remember what communism was like, and three writers from the Hungarian diaspora have kept those memories alive in their fiction by drawing material for their fiction from the world of their parents and even their grandparents. Tibor Fischer, born in England in 1959, has worked in Budapest and recovered some Hungarian, but he regards himself as thoroughly British. Zsuzsa Bánk, born in Germany in1965, writes in German, and Tamás Dobozy, born in Canada in 1969, sees himself and all other North Americans as products of diaspora. Yet all have been compelled to recount events that, as a Fischer character thinks, "grandchildren would be hearing about whether they felt like it or not," and they deal, respectively, with events leading up to the 1956 Revolution, the plight of those left behind, and the psychological wounds suffered by exiles.

Fischer is the best established of the three writers, though at the beginning of his career the manuscript of *Under the Frog* was rejected a dramatic number of times that seems to get larger with every re-telling. His novel draws upon stories from his parents and their friends as well as interviews conducted in Budapest between 1988 and 1990, and though only those who lived during the period covered by the novel, 1944 through October 1956, can judge the accuracy of his portrayal, the sardonic humor about Russians, watch-stealing, the police, and the stupidity of Western leftists closely resembles jokes I heard in the early 1980s. Even at the end of the 1980s, Fischer has said, "you could still see or feel reverberations from the fifties. There were still sort of ideological residual ways of behaving you could easily imagine taking place thirty years earlier." And although Fischer said that he would probably have written the book as it stands even without regime change, the humor would have had a very different tone (Bayer).

In form, the novel is a variation on the picaresque, for Gyuri Fischer, the focal character, drifts from one event to another, from Budapest to Szeged to small towns and even smaller villages where the only attraction is plentiful food to the Chinese Embassy, a factory, and an AVO cell. Flashbacks and character sketches enable Fischer to provide a broader social picture. This is useful because Gyuri is confined, socially and geographically. His only goal is to leave Hungary and become a street sweeper somewhere in the West, partly because his bad "moral credentials" as a member of the X-class bar him from advancement or even from his basketball team's trip to Romania. He and most of his teammates depend on patronage thus earned to avoid the worst of fates, starving and digging ditches in the Army or actually working for the money they aren't paid. As the novel begins, they travel to a game in a provincial town in a carriage made for the SS. They always travel naked, as if this minor act of rebellion, like Gyuri's insistence on passing his Russian exams with the lowest possible mark, will absolve them of complicity in the regime they despise but cannot change despite the refrain, voiced by a number of characters, that "This can't go on much longer."

A footnote to a graffito version of the motif adds, "It already has," and everyone in the novel survives as best he can. Gyuri's father, a former bookie, "looks unbelievably good for a man completely ruined." Tamás, an all-purpose killer in World War II, lives to fuck and fight and survives because he is useful to his factory as an enforcer. One schoolmate is an accomplished shoplifter. A teammate lives purely for sex. A Jesuit teacher and scout leader is not only the most intelligent and by far the coolest character in the novel but, as an accomplished gourmand, defeats in an eating contest the grotesque opportunist who attempts to steal a vineyard in his home village before disappearing, probably to China after predicting, in 1949, that the communists will be around for another forty years.

Gyuri's oldest friend, Pataki, adapts most successfully to life under communism. A trickster figure, he stars in basketball without training, wins at all games of chance, acquires fake secret police credentials, and has many sexual conquests. When he is forced to spy on his scout troop, the Jesuit advises him to copy out its newsletter and to overwhelm his masters with detail. Later he serves as the informer planted in the basketball team, though no harm comes to the squad because of his activities.

Pataki escapes from Hungary in September, 1956, but finds that his magical abilities have not transferred to Germany. Gyuri has declined to accompany him because he has fallen in love with a Polish student and "had something to lose." He has a tangential role in the Revolution, firing a few shots but mostly he observes the initial successes, the groundless optimism of the British at their embassy, and the return of the Russians. When his lover is killed, he leaves for the Austrian border and, having crossed it, looks back and weeps.

There the novel ends, since, as Fischer said later, Gyuri's desire to leave is "one of the engines of the book." Like Fischer's parents, he does leave, but nothing about his later life is even implied. In subsequent fiction, Fischer has moved to other settings and themes, for he felt that he had exhausted Hungary as a subject and in any case did not want to be identified with Eastern European subjects.

Zsuzsa Bánk's *The Swimmer* resembles *Under the Frog* only in being set in Hungary in the 1950s. The simplest way of beginning to explain the differences is to consider the ways in which they treat Stalin's death. Fischer flashes back from Gyuri's English lesson to the memory of his accounting teacher kneeling and weeping in front of Stalin's bust, his wondering whether he could "count on the downfall of Communism or was he actually going to have to read some Marx" for next week's examination and his memory, on seeing newsreel footage of mourning ceremonies in Budapest, that "the only part of him that was standing to attention ... was readily interred and disinterred in an old girlfriend...."

Bánk deals with Stalin's death so indirectly, in a retrospective account presented so obliquely in summary years after the event that Stalin's name is not even mentioned. They and the whole country have to stand silent because "Something had come to an end, a man's life was over, and with it a time, an era, and Zsófi and our father felt something that was almost like mourning." Much later, understanding what Stalin had done, they were ashamed of mourning.

From these differences can be inferred others basic to the two novels. Fischer called his novel a documentary, and the omniscient narrator firmly establishes the time line — each chapter is headed by a date — and the geography of Budapest and of the country through which Gyuri travels. Real landmarks, Communist officials, poets occupy the story's fringes. Some episodes depart from chronological sequence, but they are firmly embedded in the main narrative line. Even when Gyuri flees to Austria and is somewhat disoriented, he is acutely aware of the cold and of the defective land mine, "Soviet rubbish," that he steps on.

Specific dates, places, and historical events come so rarely in *The Swimmer* that they seem surprising when they do. The reader gradually learns that the novel covers the period from the Revolution in 1956 through Russian suppression of the Prague Spring in 1968, but time and space matter little to Kata, the first-person narrator, who wanders about the country from northwest Hungary to Budapest to Szerencs to Lake Balaton and to the northeast of Miskolc and many unspecified stops with her father Kálmán and younger brother Isti as if time had stopped when her mother leaves the family for the West.

Kata struggles to understand her motive, but for more than a hundred pages, the reader and perhaps the narrator do not realize that it may have something to do with news, given in the maternal grandmother's retrospective narrative about her visit to her daughter, that "Something had happened in Budapest." This and echoed phrases about shattered stone heads in the street are the only references to the Revolution. Even then, it may be the occasion rather than the cause of the mother's flight, for some hundred pages later still we learn, in the paternal grandmother's account, that "Kálmán's wife wasn't suited to enduring."

Kata does not seem to understand and certainly does not accept these explanations of her mother's desertion of the family. Most of the novel deals with the truncated family's emotional paralysis at her loss. The father stares as a photograph of his wife, stares at the ceiling, and looks at his children as if he doesn't recognize them. The children call this state "diving." When Isti cannot remain in a similar state, he works at forgetting how to cry, how to make his mother stop being. He takes refuge in swimming — the only thing that the father shares with the children — but, in a simile that reveals his emotional state, moves "like a dog who'd been thrown into the water with a rock tied to one foot," though, Kata admits, perhaps it only seems that way because of his dazed expression. He hears, or pretends to, inanimate objects talk, and near the end of the novel, envisioning his mother on the other bank of a stream, attempts to reach her, falls through the ice and dies of exposure.

Kata, less dazed than her father and brother, is at least able to tell the story of emotional paralysis, but she cannot always remember times and places, and at several points remarks that it makes no difference "whether everything was connected the way I remember it, whether we really were the way I think we were, and the others too." She has lost track of time, but that makes no difference, nor does delay in official permission to leave the country. She does not mention her mother, living in one of never specified locations in Germany, because she has fallen so far behind the events in her mother's life "that now we would never catch up."

Like Pataki in *Under the Frog*, Kata's mother lives wholly disconnected from her home and friends, unable to return, unable to communicate directly with the people closest to her, stuck, like Pataki, in dead-end jobs. Fischer does not trace Gyuri's life after he crosses the Austrian border, but it seems likely that he might get no more than his dearest wish to become a street-sweeper somewhere in the West. Freedom, to adapt Kris Kristofferson's line, may be only a little more than nothing left to lose.

Tamás Dobozy's Hungarian emigrants to Canada would agree. Of the three writers, Dobozy seems most aware of being part of the diaspora, though he also argues that all North American writing is to some degree the result of diaspora. But he also realizes that, "as I grew older and started to write, I suddenly realized what a gift my background was, how it provided almost an inexhaustible source of material — characters and plots and situations and politics" ("An Interview").

In *doggone*, a novel published before Dobozy was thirty, the central character reflects "on the condition of daughters and sons of immigrants. Here it comes: I belong to no country; I belong to two; I belong to one and then the other." However, although the narrator places several scenes in Hungary, in

Canada he seems no more conflicted or disconnected from normal life than characters from long-time Canadian families.

In *Last Notes and Other Stories*, however, Dobozy confronts the issue in far more direct, more thorough, and more satisfying fashion in three stories from that collection. He is able to do so, perhaps, because in moving from novels that weren't publishable to the shorter form, he discovered that "the real appeal of the short story is its complete lack of flab, which is to say that the sentences might be loose and relaxed, but the structure needs to be absolutely tight, without a single incident that doesn't contribute to the peculiar logic of the narrative. Something that streamlined and precise is so beautiful to work with — once you figure out how to work with it properly, that is — so aesthetically satisfying" ("An Interview").

As ordered in the collection, the stories take on an increasing degree of density, and all illustrate Dobozy's attempt to be "cautious about how I represent history, and hope the reader will reflect on the realities behind the story." Given the difficulty of getting at any historical or personal truth, he tries "to include, in one way or another, voices of dissent in the story — by which I mean voices that question what the author has put down, how he has interpreted events, or that point out the holes through which we can glimpse other possibilities. This is what writing is really about for me: sensitivity to alternatives, a doubt as to what was, and the refusal to think that we've obtained the sum total of a person, place, or time" ("An Interview").

This willingness to confront alternatives and not finally to condemn pervades the collection's stories with Hungarian themes. In "Tales of Hungarian Resistance," which Dobozy says "was written as a response to how well I would bear up under torture" ("An Interview"), is set in Budapest during the Communist regime. He uses the experience of the narrator's grandfather, questioned for months by agents of the Arrow Cross about the Secret Hungarian Union, which he probably invented; then imprisoned and later left impoverished as an informant under the Communists. The narrator grandson listens first to the grandfather's tales of marathon confessions that contain, at best one percent truth to ninety-nine percent disinformation calculated to paralyze the authorities. The narrator even attempts to replicate the barrage of names and places presented in various genres and even meters like iambic pentameter, difficult to manage in Hungarian, but he cannot put himself in his grandfather's place.

Later the grandson begins to listen more carefully to his grandmother's often dismissive and derisive commentary on her husband's tale: that he was simply in the wrong place at the wrong time, that he came out of prison fat from the food given in return for information, even, perhaps, that leading to the death's of the narrator's mother and father. But the narrator realizes "that she had no story — only a commentary. Without my grandfather and his tales she could say nothing." Finally, or almost finally, he comes to see that his grandmother's willingness "to offer no excuses ... is what I've come to understand as history," which means "a willingness to say you've done wrong, that maybe there is no way to make amends; or, being so afraid of what's back there, waiting behind you in the dark, that you cut yourself free from all history to see how long you can survive in the thin air...."

Mostly, however, the narrator identifies with his grandfather's interrogator, since neither is able to distinguish fact from fiction in the old man's narrative, but at least the interrogator would know how well he was treated in captivity. But the man, though rehabilitated and given a job under the Communists, cannot be found. The narrator imagines him still worrying over whether the Hungarian Resistance actually existed, "Though probably he was just lost, unable to figure out how he'd gotten so turned around in history in so short a time."

"Four Uncles" deals not with life under Communism but with escape to Canada. The narrator's three uncles are hardly admirable characters. One laments having escaped from one form of socialism to another, unable to distinguish Communists from Canadian Liberals and tyrannizes his daughters and himself, for "by turning [them] into reminders of the country he'd left he'd also turned them into reminders of the consequences of leaving, so that every time he looked at them, they rubbed his nose into a soil he'd risked life and limb for them to walk upon."

A second, anti–Semitic and Roman Catholic, writes reams of hate literature that, when uncovered, would have caused him great trouble had he not been dead. A niece observes that "history ended for him the moment he left Hungary. I don't know what kind of truths [he and his brothers] had then, but it seemed like he held on to them long after they'd become the worst kind of lies."

The third and eldest, outwardly successful in business, a patron of the arts, something of a dandy, curses his brothers in a final delirium for complaining because he remembers trapping crows to make soup during World War II. However, his last words are "how many times, in all the thirty years since, would we have murdered for that taste, killed for it — betrayed everything for just one more bite?"

The narrator cannot bring himself to condemn his uncles — he seems to be the fourth by association — partly because in his year of hiding after the Revolution and in his escape, his memories of them kept him going. But if he had known what they were really like, he would have had no guides. He knows that they were "afraid all their lives" and that "Their principal mistake was thinking themselves in exile when they had always been home." But he realizes that he was an accessory to their crimes because, once he became aware of their sins, he continued to help them, and that in leaving Hungary, like them, he had run "not to save your life but to lose it."

"The Inert Landscapes of György Ferenc" was written, Dobozy says, "as a reflection upon how it is possible for immigrants to be in Canada without being in Canada" ("An Interview"). Here the eponymous painter believes "that for landscape painting to be possible one must have the sense that the geography and people of a country weren't *relative to one another* but *were one another*— that landscape and citizen, like ghosts were mixing their atoms in order to occupy the same spot at the same time." Canadian names, interchangeable, have no resonance, just as, he believes, the country is "art-resistant."

Nevertheless, he continues to paint — once, as a joke, a layered pure white canvas titled "Landscape with Immigrant" that strikes Canadian critics as deeply ironic. Later he gives Hungarian names to Canadian scenes, and again the public buys and the critics praise him as being deeply ironic in highlighting "the disparity ... between the physical geography of a place and the consciousness we impose on it through the act of naming." He discovers by accident that his youngest son has arranged the exhibition and publicly disowns him. He continues to go out to paint but returns with empty canvases which he carefully stores.

The two older sons, including the narrator, seem to have made their peace with exile and with their father's failure as painter and husband, though they accompany him on his futile *plein air* expeditions into the countryside. But the youngest is obsessed with restoring his father's reputation and, still more important, his confidence. He is even worse off than his father because he had lost "his only magnetic north." The equation of father and Fatherland is obvious. And his most severe charge against his mother and brothers for their supposed betrayal is that they are "Canadians."

The youngest returns from exile to steal his father's ashes and wanders through Canada until the Hungarian arrest warrant against the family has been rescinded. He gives the urn to the narrator to take home — but it is empty. Finally the narrator, in Hungary, realizes "what it was to lose a country" and being "unable to shake the sense of infinite distance between the soles of my shoes and the ground they stood upon." He realizes that both he and Hungary have changed and are continuing to change, so that only chance can connect them again. Finally, he realizes, the father attains "the essence of landscape ... by not being able to paint it," and the nothingness common to Hungary and Canada is like the emptiness that stares out of the funeral urn, recognizable "whenever we want a limit to who and what we are. Whenever we want a limit to the places we live."

Dobozy states the theme of limits more overtly than Fischer and Bánk, but structure and detail in their novels clearly imply it. Although Dobozy's characters have escaped physically, they are psychologically imprisoned in their conceptions of what it means to be Hungarian, going round in circles despite the assertion "I have escaped!" Gyuri is physically imprisoned in Hungary, moving aimlessly from place to place, situation to situation, until the end of *Under the Frog*. Kata may or not get official permission to leave — not likely in 1968 — but she cannot escape the paralysis of losing her mother. As all three writers reveal, those who escape physically seem no better off than those who remain. "It can't go on like this," which echoes throughout Fischer's novel, might be used ironically by Bánk and Dobozy, for clearly it can — another thirty-three years in Fischer, as long as the memory of loss of country and loved ones endures from generation to generation in the others. Like the painter's son in Dobozy's story, they can no longer stand on familiar ground.

Fischer is the only one of these writers to use characteristic Hungarian recourse to irony. Perhaps writers native to Hungary can in the future, as their predecessors have, fall back on irony — and on the spirit evidenced in the joke about Austrian and Hungarian commanders leading Hapsburg troops in battle. The Austrian wires headquarters, "Situation serious but not desperate." The Hungarian wires, "Situation desperate but not serious." His descendants may complain, but this spirit seems to enable them to go on writing and publishing.

Works Cited

Bánk, Zsuzsa. *The Swimmer*. New York, Harcourt, 2004.
Bayer, Gerd. "I'm very keen on tea and Shakespeare: An Interview with Tibor Fischer." webdrc.gwdg.de/edoc/ia/eese/artic97/bayer9_97.html.
The Change: Dutch business experience in supporting Central and Eastern Europe. Ed. Julia Djarova and Wim Jansen. The Hague: Delwel, 1996.
Contemporary Jewish Writing in Hungary: An Anthology. Edited by Susan Rubin Suleiman and Éva Forgács. Lincoln, NE, and London: University of Nebraska Press, 2003.
Dobozy, Tamás. *doggone*. Toronto: Gutter Press, 1998.
_____. "An Interview with Tamás Dobozy." http://www.harpercollins.ca/dobozy/index.asp.
_____. *Last Notes and Other Stories*. Toronto: HarperCollins, 2005.
Fischer, Tibor. *Under the Frog: A Black Comedy*. New York: The New Press, 1992.
In Quest of the Miracle Stag: The Poetry of Hungary. Eds. Adam Makkai, et al. Vol. 1: *From the 13th Century to the Present in English Translation*. Illus. George Buday. Chicago: Atlantis-Centaur (University of Illinois Press, distributor), 1996. Vol. 2: *From the Start of the 20th Century to the Present in English Translation*. Illus. Endre Szász and

Márton Barabás. Budapest: The International Association of Hungarian Language and Culture (University of Illinois Press, distributor), 2003.

Kertész, Imre. *Kaddish for a Child Not Born*. Trans. Christopher C. Wilson and Katharina M. Wilson. Evanston, IL: Northwestern University Press, 1999.

The Kiss: 20th Century Hungarian Short Stories. Budapest: Corvina, 1995.

Orbán, Ottó. *The Journey of Barbarus*. Trans. Bruce Berlind. Pueblo, CO: Passeggiata Press, 1997.

_____. *Our Bearings at Sea: A Novel in Poems*. Trans. Jascha Kessler. Xlibris Books, 2001.

Phillips, Arthur. *Prague*. New York: Random House, 2002.

Pomogáts, Béla. "Literature and the New Democracy." *Hungarian Quarterly*, 39 (Autumn 1998), 47.

Suleiman, Susan Rubin. *Budapest Diary: In Search of the Motherbook*. Lincoln: University of Nebraska Press, 1996.

Swimming in the Ground: Contemporary Hungarian Poetry. Translated by Michael Castro and Gábor Gyukics. Saint Louis, MO: Neshui Publishing, 2001.

Szirtes, George. *The Budapest File*. Budapest: Corvina; Newcastle upon Tyne, UK: Bloodaxe Books; Chester Springs, PA: Dufour Editions, 2000, 2001.

Three Contemporary Hungarian Plays. Boston: Forest and Budapest: Corvina, 1992.

Török, András. *Budapest Review of Books*, 8:1 (Spring 1998), 45.

Turner, Frederick. "There Still Stands a City." *Hungarian Quarterly*, 40 (Spring 1999).

4

Slovak Writing in Transition

Slovaks have more modesty than they have things to be modest about. The landscape is varied and beautiful, from the sharp peaks of the High Tatras and the surrounding ranges of lesser mountains, where Germans and Czechs are buying up cottages as weekend retreats, to the fertile plains along the Danube. It has more castles, better preserved, more beautiful, and more picturesquely situated, than Hungary. The capitol is Bratislava — Pressburg to the Austrians, Pozsony to the Hungarians, Prešporok for a long time to the Slovaks — symptomatic of the political and linguistic archeology of Central Europe. It has charming areas, especially Old Town, still partly enclosed by the medieval wall, full of lovely buildings dating from the eighteenth century and later. The castle looks more like a fortress than an elegant residence for a visiting monarch, like the one in Budapest. The opera house is suitably Hapsburg, the art museum suitably modern, the president's residence just dignified enough to suit both its current inhabitant and the former ecclesiastical occupant. Physically, the city stretches from the esplanade along the Danube past the Slavin monument to fallen Soviets that overlooks the town to the crest of the end of the Carpathian range, interspersed with large and lovely parks and row on row of vines.

The curve of twentieth century Slovak history is less lovely. It has five significant dates: 1918, when Czechoslovakia was carved out of the Austro-Hungarian Empire; 1948, when the Communists took power in Czechoslovakia and imposed alien economic and cultural systems; 1968, when the Prague Spring was suppressed and a federal system, with a separate Slovak government, was established; 1989, when the Velvet Revolution restored the opportunity to recreate the climate as well as the institutions of capitalist democracy;

and 1993, when the Czech and Slovak Republics arranged a more or less amicable divorce — opposed by some family members — and for the first time in close to a millennium Slovaks were free at least to attempt to define themselves and to determine their national identity.

The transition was difficult, in part because independence was linked to the nationalist politics of former communist, and boxer, Vladimir Mečiar, whose pugilistic and political past characterized his rule. Understandably, the speakers at the 2002 conference at the University of Ottawa by nine members of the Slovak government then in power can find them ably stated in Stolarik's introduction. Of course, all of the speakers were looking forward to possible membership in NATO and the European Union, and everyone was anxious to emphasize the fact that the bad old days of Vladimir Mečiar's authoritarian and very nearly lawless rule were over and that Slovakia was marching forward in harmony with the values of their neighbors to the west. Most of the respondents, academics and Canadian officials alike, sound like Slim Pickens in "Blazing Saddles": "Ditto!" Only practical men, like Anton Jura, of U.S. Steel Košiče, speaking on economic conditions, and physician George Fodor, speaking on health, seem at all critical.

In 2004, the situation changed again. Eduard Kukan, the final speaker and, until the recent elections, the favorite to succeed Rudolf Schuster as president, ran his campaign so poorly that he finished a poor third, out of the runoff which Mečiar lost to Ivan Gašparovič, a former ally whom *The Slovak Spectator* described as "Mečiar lite."

Still, if one wants to know where Slovakia has been rather than where it is going, this is a useful book. There are many charts and figures. Some are startling. There are 218 Jews left in Slovakia. Faculty-student ratios have risen from 6.74 in 1990 to 9.58 in 1998, largely because there are 60.3 percent more students, including far more Ph.D., part-time, and external students, and budgets have not increased by anything like that percentage.

The reasonable conclusions, drawn both from this book and from a recent visit to Slovakia, is that the country has fared much better under independence than many critics had any right to expect. Problems from the Communist and Mečiar past remain, especially those connected to questionable deals in privatization, corruption in general, and the condition of the Roma. But foreign investment has increased, the currency seems stable, and Mečiar, who seems as resilient as Richard Nixon, was once again been rejected by almost 60 percent of the voters in the 2004 elections.

More important in considering modern Slovak history is the fact that for more than a thousand years it had been subject politically and culturally to other governments and languages — first to the Hungarians and then to

Austria-Hungary, when Slovakia was called Upper Hungary and Slovak could not be taught in the schools, then, after 1981, at least culturally, to Czechoslovakia, where the very name indicates second billing. Dominik Tatarka (1913–1989) maintained that the Czechs were "the most democratic" nation in the world, while the Slovaks "are a nation forever being liberated" ("God's Community — A Community of Humankind," *Slovak Literary Review*, February 1997; originally published 1968). Or, as Pavel Vilikovský's cynical monologist puts it in the title story of *Ever Green Is...*," "the Slovaks, an unlucky nation, for a millennium they bemoaned their bondage ... they have never had an opportunity to get out of practice...."

More than a decade after separation from the Czechs, some Slovaks talk about them rather in the way that Midwestern American farmers talk about New Yorkers: very clever but not always reliable and perhaps, as the following joke suggests, not really manly.

The difference between Czechs and Slovaks? When a Czech gets drunk, he sings, "My girl has left me. I think I'll kill myself." When a Slovak gets drunk, he sings, "Someone has taken my girl. I think I'll kill him." Sounds a lot like the American rural South.

But the Czechs are rather like extended family. The remaining Hungarians within Slovakia, about 600,000, are seen as a standing temptation to irredentist movements in Hungary, disturbingly close just across the border. In fact, a bridge over the Danube between Hungarian Esztergom and Slovak Šturovo, destroyed by retreating Germans in World War II, was only repaired almost sixty years later using funds from the European Union.

Centuries of subordination created in Slovaks a diffidence that can be charming, and they have a sense of relief in finding that they are not, after all, at the bottom of whatever heap there is. For example, James Sutherland-Smith, an Englishman responsible for many of the translations quoted below, asked why Slovak writing was less well known than Czech, and got replies that "varied from 'We're not as good as the Czechs' to the less disarming 'Foreigners never get further than Prague'" (*One Hundred*). A Slovak writer complained that the rest of Europe thinks that Slovaks are poor, dirty, and ignorant.

"That sounds like Oklahoma," I said.

What did I mean by that?

"That's the popular American view of Oklahomans, or Okies. I even heard a local radio announcer use that word. The only thing that saves us is Arkansas."

How so?

"Well, according to popular belief, people in Arkansas are even poorer, dirtier, and more ignorant than Oklahomans — and incestuous besides."

Look of enlightenment. "Ah, like the Ukraine!"

Slovaks are less charming when defensive-aggressive, like the woman in a provincial town who asked, sharply, "Why do you not speak Slovak?" The answer, that there was no one within a thousand miles from my home to teach me, didn't please her, and she wasn't any happier with the information that even the Czechs in Prague, Oklahoma, pronounced it "Prayg" and have forgotten the language of their forebears. Another Slovak trotted out clichés like "All Americans are fat" (was I? Any fatter than he?) and "America is a violent nation." I'd heard that, I said, and almost believed it until my first trip to Europe, when, in southeastern Hungary, I was taken to a large, beautiful synagogue. But there weren't any Jews. These experiences were akin to an encounter at an Oklahoma banquet when a woman asked where I was from. Norman — right in the middle of Oklahoma but also the chief university town. "Oh," she said, "you're not a real Oklahoman."

One of my Slovak friends complains of similar exclusionary attitudes among his countrymen. He owns a cottage in the village where his father was born and recalls commenting to a local storekeeper that the quality of some apples was not good. "Yes," he was told, "but they are *our* apples." The view that the customer is probably wrong may be due as much to the legacy of socialism as to local chauvinism, and he regards it as pervasive. But he was appalled when I told him that a restaurant in Bratislava had altered a credit card receipt to something like five times the original charge, implying that this would never have happened under socialism.

It may be a stretch to see these two incidents as indicative of Slovakia under the Mečiar government, which ruled until September, 1998, by appealing to Slovak fear of Hungarians, Gypsies, and anyone who wasn't a "real Slovak" and by making sweetheart sales of privatized assets. But he was voted out of power, though his legacy and continued presence on the political scene continue to be troubling, and Slovakia has since joined NATO and the EU, which those organizations would not even consider as long as he governed.

But even then the public face of Slovakia, especially Bratislava, was pleasant. The newest public art in and near the main square in Bratislava, all in burnished metal and all by Viktor Hulik, is charming. The figure of a Napoleonic soldier leans over a park bench underneath a heroic statue of Roland, patron of Bratislave, raised high on a column above the real life of the town. Another statue portrays a man raising his hat, a memorial to "Polite Johnny," a local character. Fifty feet or so away, Viktor Hulik's bust of a man in a hard hat peeks out of a fake manhole.

He may be regarded as a typical Slovak, cautiously peering into the post–Communist, post–Mečiar, post-transitional twenty-first century. This is especially true of the writers I have read and interviewed since 1998. The Slovak literary community is fond of the line, "Writing is not an occupation; it is a destiny." Writers throughout the world would probably agree, though some would emphasize the economic disadvantages implied by the first clause and others—especially when the work goes or is received badly—the more Sophoclean aspects of the second.

Slovak writers in chorus are very un–Sophoclean in their eagerness to discuss circumstance rather than fate. And to an even greater degree than is usual in central Europe, the circumstances are partly economic, in larger part political, and in the largest sense historical.

Slovak writers historically have had not only a place in the country, in a sense difficult for American to understand, but they were instrumental, indeed essential, in creating the idea of a country. As one Slovak writer said, for a hundred and fifty years writers represented the only means by which a people—not officially a nation—could define as well as express itself. In the Renaissance, writing in the vernacular was for Dante and other literary nationalists an act of assertion. Writing in Slovak—rather than in German or Hungarian under the Hapsburgs or later in Czech—was an act of defiance.

So was opposition to Russian domination. Now the Russians are gone, and with them, as the Bulgarian writer Ivailo Dichev points out in "Desires: The Erotics of Communism," a source of energy, at least for Mr. N., a dissident whose "happiness was his battle" and whose life has lost all color with the disappearance of communism. (*Description of a Struggle*). Under Communism, some writers found energy in indirection. Milan Richter, the Slovak poet, says that when his work was suppressed, he was forced to develop a sub-text. In "The White Dog," Rudolf Sloboda's character describes one way of doing this: composing his autobiography by using the point of view of a white dog. Of course, the dog can't laugh or talk, and the writer has to omit all sorts of things as inappropriate to a dog's point of view. But, the speaker concludes,

> ... no one can blame me for making a dog think.... It's important for the future reader to know how this could have been seen in our own time. And this way I don't even have to worry about someone who can't understand any of my memoirs calling me an idiot; he'll simply blame it all on the white dog [*Description*].

Gustáv Murín points out that "white dog" was, under Communist censorship, a term used to describe anything that was put into the text to seem like nonsense, to deflect the censor's attention from more problematic elements, and to wear him down in general.

Some writers had more difficulty. A significant number were blacklisted after 1968 and could publish only in *samizdat*. At worst, Dominik Tatarka, after asserting that he "was trying to prevent my own division into a private and public man, for I knew that with that division madness began" ("The Demon of Conformism," *Slovak Literary Review*, December 2001; first published 1956) could not find work, had to live "on an invalid's pension on the edge of starvation under constant supervision by the state police." He wrote in the form of "a diary with neither an ending nor a beginning" (*One Hundred Years of Slovak Literature*), and a friend taped conversations with him which were later published. In *Letters to Eternity*, published in Toronto in 1984, he or his persona writes to a lover who is also involved with the Party about a writer who has bowed to the Regime which

> has enslaved a small nation into self-forgetfulness. The greatest representative cries of feeling (in this amnesia) are for the wealth we have won. He writes an emotional article for a world-wide publication, Thirty Years of Free Life. In his speech there isn't the slightest mention that in these thirty years he was humiliated in prison for eight of them. Every day he appears on television in the role of a naïve although male sexual organ, raped at least 1000 times on postage stamps, streets, TV screens, celebrations, anniversary days of an ever-present man, known intimately [*One Hundred*, trans. Viera and James Sutherland-Smith].

In "A Horrorscope of One's Own," Ivan Kadlečík's narrator talks to friends, one of whom is later arrested because of a magazine, about "criminal matters ... literature, the Czech edition Petlice (the Clasp), culture, ethics of civil cowardice and courage; historical ethos that — according to the moral and intellectual personality of Dr. Šimečka [the writer and journalist Martin Šimečka's father] — has for some of us become so stale and bureaucratic it can't be moved or removed, that ethos; it makes us feel helpless and vanquished; we were talking about the apostle Dominik who has just passed away ... we were more lonely without him." Later he is approached by police while boarding a bus, and "I felt like a criminal, a looter, a disguised punk or, at least, a Slovak writer — a mass murderer of his own children (may they have mercy on me)." He returns home safely, but he and his fellow writers "were under stress permanently and alone like targets of anonymous remote-controlled destruction: such was the price for being agents of truth."

> As his house doors open, behind them appeared the contorted face of Franz Kafka, the Gemini, who said in English: My house is my castle. To which I replied, also in fluent English but with a soft Central Slovakian touch: Fucking bastards.
> (If published in the Elementary School Reader, the last expression can be

replaced by "sweet little pigs." Or, better yet: it can be replaced according to one's own individual experience. And so, on the authority of my profession as a writer, I am granting an absolute free expression to each and every citizen including the censor, the office-holder, the policeman, and the bureaucrat.) [*One Hundred*, trans. L'uben Urbánek].

Kadlečík and several of the other writers whose careers were affected by "normalization" present characters whose lives and bodies are constricted, sometimes in an apartment, feeling threatened by an unknown presence, once in a grave. Several younger writers reverse the image to present characters penetrated or possessed by alien forces. As Martin Šimečka (1957) shows in *The Year of the Frog*, a rare example of Slovak fiction to be published in the United States, he was barred from education and jobs, and his character looks longingly toward the West from his confinement in Slovakia. In one passage, however, the character witnesses a surgical operation and "felt how that cold needle entered my brain" (*The Year of the Frog*). In "The Virgin in the Underground," Viliam Klimáček's (1958) narrator claims that "My body is a cage. Ribs are its frontiers. There is a funny creature living inside, he climbs the bones, keeps nagging and sometimes asks questions. I do not know whether he wants to help me or to trouble me" (*One Hundred*, trans. Vladislav Gális). Balla (1967) — the only name he uses as a writer — has a more extreme image of a boy "with a rat instead of a brain" with "A pair of glaring eyes [looking] through a pair of pale extinguished eyes, a pair of eyes through another pair of eyes" and "a scaled mobile tail protruding out of his right ear." Balla is more obviously postmodern than Kadlečík, for instead of allowing any reader to revise his work, he offers alternative scenarios and, at the end of the excerpt, which describes genital self-mutilation and "bites of the brain-hungry rat," he mutilates his own story with "The previous sentences were later deleted by the author" (*One Hundred*, trans. L'uben Urbánek). However, it could be argued that the differing metaphors in the two generations both describe the effect of an oppressive regime. For the first, it was imposed; for the second, it occupied them from the beginning of consciousness.

Of course, much of the writing published during those years was quite orthodox, and it is important to realize that not all writing not banned by or even encouraged by the Communists was necessarily bad, though much of it will probably remain untranslated. For example, Miroslav Válek (1927–1991) was Minister of Culture for the Czechoslovak government during the post–1968 repression, and some of his poems hold to the party line. But he was an important figure in the 1950s and 1960s, and, as his poem "Aesthetics" (1959) shows, ideology does not always play a part; in fact, the poem might have been written by any European disciple of Baudelaire:

> In us the night lies down.
> We're assailed by a drumming fusillade of melancholy,
> a tearful spleen forces us down upon the earth.
> And from the not-so-distant past a sad, small
> multiplication table of courage tangles in us:
> We write
> > we erase,
> > we erase,
> > we erase [*One Hundred*].

And his "Killing Rabbits" combines the routine with a kind of guilty excitement at the blow:

> Once more sense in your palm the reflex
> of a futile leap,
> a heaviness in your hand,
> sweet on your palate,
> listen how rabbit heaven opens
> and full handfuls of fur fall from it [*One Hundred*,
> > trans. Viera and James Sutherland-Smith].

Hana Zelinová (1914) apparently had no official position, but "The Order of Wolves" (1970, *In Search of Homo Sapiens*) should have met with wide approval. Set in 1450, it compares the aristocracy with marauding wolves. But the writing is eloquent, the relationship between an elderly woman and her dying husband convincing, and the recurring image of the dying fire extremely powerful.

But in 1989 dissidence and conformity both became pointless and writing in Slovak routine, and routine is less heartening than resistance. On the other hand, Martin Šimečka regards the new conditions as encouraging because they help to dispel "the perception that any intellectual effort, including writing, is only useful for rousing the nation from thick-headedness. This enlightening role of literature ruined the taste of writers until the second half of the century" ("Learning to Write"). The new conditions also mitigated, if they did not entirely destroy, the connection between writers and the government.

The separation has been painful. Like other former Soviet bloc countries, Slovakia is making the difficult transition from socialist to capitalist ideas and institutions — with the added complication of developing institutions independent of the former Czechoslovakia. In 1948, the government nationalized publishing houses and split editorial, distribution, and printing functions into three separate divisions, putting the first two under the Ministry of Culture and the third under the Ministry of Economics. Only six publishers were licensed, and each was confined to a narrowly defined niche. All bookstores were owned by the government.

Under this system, those who belonged to the official Union of Slovak Writers could do fairly well. Typical press runs for best sellers were twenty to thirty thousand copies, and government subsidies kept prices so low that, as translator Peter Kerlik says, people could decide whether to buy a book or a bottle of wine—lover and bread optional and extra, presumably.

In 1989, four hundred publishing houses emerged, most very small. But printing and distribution were and to some extent still are separate, so that publishers have no control over costs. And some have not figured out the connection between demand and supply. One novelist complained to his publisher that copies were not being distributed. Well, the publisher replied, we should keep some for people to buy in a year or so. The novelist, though hardly a trained economist, tried to explain that it might be possible to print more copies and thus increase sales. Apparently he was not successful, for in 1998 we were unable to find a copy of his new book in any of five bookstores in a large provincial town—or in Bratislava bookstores outside a five-block radius from the Writers' Club.

But even if books were distributed rationally, prices are now so high that even the most popular books sell about three thousand copies, and press runs are more typically one thousand for prose and six hundred for poetry. Gustáv Murín reports that in the 1990s, prices of books increased ten-fold, but sales dropped fifteen percent a year. Of every 100 crowns spent on books, only one was for new Slovak fiction. And while the average number of titles published between 1991 and 1997 increased from 2,700 to 3,300 per year, circulation of those printed decreased from 31 million to 4.5 million copies, and the average circulation per book dropped from 11,300 to 1,350. In 2003 more than a third of Slovaks surveyed claimed that fiction was not essential to their lives (private communication). As a result, no one can make a living solely from writing.

Therefore, most writers rely increasingly on external support. A major source is the Slovak Literary Fund, which receives two percent of royalties paid for all creative work. A board independent of the government and composed of members chosen by the various writers' associations administers the fund. Writers who have contracts and can show that they have completed sixty percent of a manuscript can apply for fellowships which free them to write for three or six months, although by 2006 it had become a symbol of approval and was spread to more writers so that it represented about one-seventh of a normal month's salary.

In addition, members of the various writers' organizations can apply once a year for thirty day residencies, housing and food paid, in one of several houses for writers, including the very plush late nineteenth-century Budmerice Castle. (In the words of Gustáv Murín, self-described as the oldest young Slovak writer, not all Communist ideas were bad.) That is still available, but the writers' residence in Bratislava has been sold, so that writers outside the capitol have no convenient and inexpensive place to stay when doing research or dealing with publishers.

Writers can also apply for research grants and for publishing subsidies. But on a day-to-day basis, the most important job of the Literary Fund is to subsidize the Writers' Club in Bratislava, for that not only provides a gathering place for writers but features reduced prices for meals prepared by a leading Slovak chef.

The Ministry of Culture is another source of funds. By law, one percent of the annual budget of Slovakia must be devoted to culture. The Ministry has never received anything even close to that, but it still has enough money to subsidize publication of some books and to support the National Center for Slovak Literature (now the Literary Information Center, *http://www.litcentrum.sk*), described "as an institution contributing conceptually to the revitalization of the literary process in the new economic conditions." It is subdivided into sections for literary criticism, literary translation, international promotion, distribution, and publishing, including a number of literary magazines and, in English and German, *Slovak Literary Review*.

This is an bi-annual tabloid devoted to translations, biographical sketches, news of conferences and recent publications, and stories about Slovak publishing houses. For non–Slovaks, this is the most accessible and perhaps the most reliable source of information about Slovak literary life. It seems to represent writers of all genres, schools of opinion, and ages — the youngest in the first three issues born in 1967. Recently the Center has published a monograph, *Slovakia and Its Literature* with an appendix on Slovak history, and a twenty-page pamphlet, *Contemporary Slovak Literature*, both by Vladimír Petrík. Discussions of individual writers are necessarily brief, especially in the pamphlet, but they do give English-speaking readers information about schools, themes, and methods to which they did not have access. The problem, as with many translations into English, is that these books are extremely difficult to get in America.

As recipients of official support, writers have found it useful to organize. Under the Communists, of course, there was only one organization, the Union of Slovak Writers. (Slovaks insisted on their identity even when they were officially joined to the Czechs.) In December, 1989, a group calling itself the "Community of Writers of Slovakia" split from the Union, in order, as its president said, "to protest against the inability or unwillingness of the Congress' participants to clear the communist-totalitarian past of the Union."

The Slovak PEN Center was established the same year, and four other groups subsequently emerged. The Ministry of Culture persuaded them to form the Association of Slovak Writers (AOSS) in order to be able to deal with one group. But in 1992, partly because of the strains over impending separation from the Czechs and the accompanying political controversies, a group calling itself the Slovak Writers' Society withdrew. Not all of these writers were former Communists, but most emphasized Slovak nationalist issues and advocated separation from the Czechs, and in varying degrees supported and were supported by the Mečiar regime.

Until May 1998, the Society seemed homogenous, but at the annual meeting late in that month there were reports that questions were for the first time raised about the distribution of money to members and about the use of funds gained from privatization to pay ministerial salaries rather than to fund cultural activities.

The other writers' organizations, sometimes described as democratic or cosmopolitan, were generally less enthusiastic about Slovak independence and about the Mečiar regime. The Community of Writers, for example, is "dedicated to keeping the sensibility against attempts to build new versions of totality and dictatorship, attempts to liquidate democracy." Currently six groups make up the AOSS: the Community, the Club of Independent Writers, the Club of Nonfiction Writers, the Slovak Center of PEN International, the Union of Hungarian Writers in Slovakia, and the Union of Ukrainian Writers in Slovakia. They describe themselves as "a voluntary and democratic organization of equal and independent writers' organizations [that] pursues the overall interests of Slovak literature and literatures of the nationalities living in Slovakia."

The Society and the various other organizations in the Association have over three hundred members each. To be admitted to membership in any of these groups, a writer should usually have published two books and be recommended by two current members. Only members can use the Writers' Club, but all writers whose royalties are paid into the literary fund are eligible for residencies at the houses for writers. But young writers seem to be less interested than their elders in membership or in the divisions that the two large organizations represent.

Among the older writers, it is generally accepted that people in the two groups are hostile toward each other or at least communicate very little. Ostensibly the divisions are ideological, but in practice the conflict seems to have more to do with limited resources and perhaps even more with the attempt of older writers to see that their work gets into print. One cosmopolitan says that the Society's members are like a man driving a car without brakes down a steep hill. He can steer a little left or right, but basically he is out of control.

Another writer agrees that the conflicts have little to do with literature. Debates would be healthy or at least potentially productive if they focused on the role of literature or methods of representation. But there is no real debate or even discussion. The current climate is stultifying and leads, he says, to "thinking along stupid lines." Recently, though, another writer described the situation as chronic rather than serious.

Writers in the Association resented the higher level of funding given to those who supported the Mečiar government, which in turn was suspicious of those who sought funds and contacts abroad and criticized the regime at home. And, as I said, younger writers apparently ignore both the writers nostalgic for tighter control and the accompanying support of pre–1989 days and those who seek to canonize the dissidents or to put themselves into that group retroactively.

Mečiar's coalition did not survive the 1998 election, but the situation of Slovak writers as a whole has not improved markedly. The Association may get more funding, the Society less. But the pot will not get larger. Most books are distributed primarily in Bratislava, where only ten percent of Slovaks live. Writers are therefore isolated from most of the population—so much so that they are not even aware of their isolation. And even if the books got beyond the city limits of Bratislava, book prices are too high for wide distribution. And even if they were distributed, according to one intellectual who befriends writers but is not himself a writer, ninety-five percent of Slovaks don't read books at all and the remaining five percent read books only in translation. That leaves the writers to read each other—if they are on the same side politically.

That may be unduly cynical. However, another intellectual is no more hopeful because, he says, readership and everything else in Slovakia is divided along geographical lines, plains (with a large Hungarian population) in the south and three mountain chains with numerous sharply separated valleys in the north. As a result, he says, Slovaks are prone to what Italians call "campanilesmo," a devotion to the area from which they can see the bell tower of their parish church and an inclination to distrust anyone or anything—including apples—from anywhere else.

This tendency to stake out territory can be seen in the Junec family in Peter Pišt'anek and Dušan Taragel's "On the Influence of Drinking Coffee in Solving Questions of Accommodation" (*Transitions*). Of course, the story is partly a satire on the effects of urbanization, but the authors also seem to be pointing to something engrained in Slovak village life. As the family grows, each member tries to carve separate quarters from the family home, but since individual entrances are expensive, one door is cut out of the bedroom wall, another out of the bathroom ceiling, and so on. When the parents die, each brother receives his inheritance: Sanyo the kitchen, Juraj the toilet, Matej the bathroom. No brother will let the others use his room. Finally all are dispossessed by the encroaching town, move to a new development, and are reunited by their "common destiny" and by a hatred of what the town has done to their village.

According to Martin Šimečka, this tendency toward walling oneself off was true of many Slovak intellectuals, who "traditionally were shut off from the world" ("Learning to Write in Freedom"). The National Center for Slovak Literature has attempted to overcome the division between writers inside and outside Slovakia by holding, in 1996, a meeting of expatriate writers from Romania, Yugoslavia, Hungary, and Poland (*Slovak Literary Review*, February 1997).

Ondrej Štefanko, a Slovak writer, editor, and translator living in Romania who attended that meeting, nevertheless believes that Slovak writing from the "Low Lands" (Romania, Hungary, the former Yugoslavia) has little readership in Slovakia because of "the lack of interest on the part of the cultural community in Slovakia in what is happening in neighboring or geographically close countries. I have the impression that in Slovakia nobody cares what is happening next door. A certain isolationism has set in, as if the Slovak cultural community was self-sufficient" ("Slovak Literature from Dolná Zem [Low Lands]," *Slovak Literary Review*, December 1999). This attitude limits another kind of market accessible to some small countries and linguistic groups: the expatriates. Hungary is a good example. But Slovak intellectuals maintain that Slovaks abroad are not a viable market because they carry with them regional rivalries and resentments.

Perhaps more hopeful is the attempt to bring Slovak literature to a wider audience through translation. SLOLIA, or Slovak Literature Abroad, a branch of the Literary Information Center, was established in 1995 to fund translations of Slovak literature and to subsidize publication in books or in special sections of foreign magazines. And it is prepared to invite foreign publishers to Slovakia and to conduct seminars and symposia to encourage wider dissemination of Slovak work.

All of this has to do with structural rather than textual matters — that is, with the general situation of the writer rather than the actual writing. That is more difficult for the outsider to comprehend. Still, it is clear that writers are dealing with various legacies from the past: Milan Richter and Ján Johanides write about the Holocaust; Martin Šimečka deals with life under Communism in *The Year of the Frog*.

The novel has for the most part been read as a document of life under Communism, and rightly so. Milan, the narrator, barred from secondary school and university because of his father's dissident writing, drifts from one menial job to another, taking breaks until required by the authorities to get another job. The novel, originally three novellas published in samizdat in the 1980s, covers episodes in his life from the time he is twenty-two, in 1980, to twenty-seven. Often the time scheme is difficult for the reader to establish, perhaps because of the circumstances of original publication, perhaps because, as the texture of the novel makes very clear, not much changes in society or the life of the protagonist.

Šimečka does not attempt to present a broad view of Slovak life under Communism. Milan is occasionally hassled by the police and once jailed for two days; his father is jailed for a longer period in the second section and, between the lines, released at some point during or before the third; as a clerk in a hardware store, his chief task is to tell customers that the store doesn't have what they want, though Milan introduces an innovation by telling them not "We don't have it" but that the articles will never appear. Flats are cold; roofs leak; money is short; Austria is tauntingly close across the Danube; he listens to news from Vienna because "it did not come from this world, and the female broadcaster's voice smelled of Colgate toothpaste and hot Nescafé Gold." But Milan rejects advice to leave because "It's my only free choice, and I will not give it up so easily."

However, reading the novel from the perspective of 2003, one could argue that the Communist regime constitutes the conditions rather than the causes of Milan's problems. As a top-notch distance runner, he could have been admitted to university had he won a big race. But, he admits, he didn't "because I was afraid." In fact, Milan is afraid of many things, especially of the life ahead of him, but he wants to live nonetheless.

Yet he fears that he is not living, and that others see him differently from the way he sees himself, that in his circle "No one has anything really interesting to say anymore." To escape, he runs long distances into the hills above Bratislava, exhausting his body and turning off his mind. His main link to life is his lover, later his wife, and descriptions of her beauty and goodness and his alternate exaltation and despair about their relationship fill rather too much of the novel.

His other passion is Nature, which at times he identifies with Tania, especially on trips into the forests and mountains. At other times, especially working as an orderly first in the neurosurgery ward and later in the maternity (and abortion) ward, he sees nature as both nurturing and destructive. In his personal life, fertility is always thwarted. Tania suffers an ectopic pregnancy and at the end of the novel a premature birth which the child does not survive. Married friends lose two children. He witnesses many abortions in a kind of cold horror, and near the end of the novel attends the birth of a hideously malformed child which does not survive. The novel's title comes from passages near the beginning and end of the eponymous section: first he runs over thousands of frogs, "swirling and scattering in a deranged ecstasy. They were popping under my shoes like tiny balloons." And he is "angry at the meaninglessness of life and the cruelty of Nature." At the end of the section, he comes across large toads, "double-headed monsters with goggle eyes, because they had made on that day the decision to mate." A car runs over them, and he runs through "this horrible zone of sex."

This and the medical procedures described even more graphically, as well as many of Milan's self-doubts and recriminations, would occur whatever political regime was in control, though political oppression certainly reinforces physical and metaphysical oppression. Nor is Milan's solution, "Goodness is the antidote against nothingness," peculiar to young men in dictatorships. I do not mean to discount the political situation but rather to suggest that the novel's lasting power, if it is to have any, will depend not on politics but on what humanist critics once called "felt life." Memories of life before the Velvet Revolution in 1989 should not be forgotten, but they will not have the same power that they once had.

At least one writer has attempted to deal with the paradoxes and ironies of political life before and after 1989. Gustáv Murín agreed with my quotation from Marx (which he did not recognize) that history repeats itself: the first time as tragedy, the second as farce, in characterizing the contrast between the generations of 1968 and 1989 in *Ako Sa Mas* (How Are You?), published in 1998 and not yet translated.

Murín's experience with that novel may not be typical, but it indicates some of the problems faced by writers, even those not officially debarred, as Šimečka was, from education and good jobs, over the past twenty years or so. He completed a first draft of a novel in 1984 and sent it to two Slovak publishers. Both rejected it as too sensitive politically, so it was distributed privately. Murín says he didn't think of it as samizdat, though that is what it was. Three years later, he entered the manuscript in a Czechoslovak federal contest — and won. The prize guaranteed publication, and the manuscript was submitted to Smena, a publisher that had rejected it in 1984. They recognized the story, and it still made them nervous. Since they couldn't reject it officially, they temporized until a Prague publisher, Mlade Fronta, issued it in Czech. This was in June, 1989, four or five months before the Velvet Revolution.

Then Murín wanted the novel published in Slovakia, and he offered it to Archa, a publishing house founded in 1990 by former dissidents. Like their predecessors, they didn't refuse it, but they didn't accept it. Thinking that revision might help and encouraged by the possibility of a film version, Murín kept working on it. Finally he realized that Archa was not going to publish it. Meanwhile, he had become involved with Slovak P.E.N., and this gave him new insight into issues that previously he had seen as black Communists and white dissidents. But, he realized, some of the dissidents had been communists, and in the final revision, he deals with the compromises the dissidents made before 1989 and their subsequent attempts to whitewash themselves — themes that, he maintains, are new in Slovak literature. Finally, with financial help from a friend, it was published in 1998.

The strongest attacks on the book have apparently come from Šimečka's anti–Mečiar paper, *Domino Forum*. One contributor to a feature called "What I'm Reading" claimed that she wasn't reading Murín's book, and a week later another contributor and ex–Party member wrote that it would be better if Murín were silent. Even Jan Budaj, a leader of the 1989 revolution later discredited by revelation of his association with the KGB, was said to regard the book as an attack on the current leaders.

Clearly the controversy over the book was more political than literary. The dissidents wanted to defeat Mečiar. So did Murín — but he felt that dissidents need to admit their pasts in order to establish credibility with the people — with whom, like most intellectuals, they have less contact than right-wingers and pragmatists like Mečiar.

Regardless of the quality — or fate — of Murín's book, he was attempting to write about contemporary issues. Of course, not every work of literature is overtly political, though this is hard to judge because relatively little has appeared in translation — amazon.com lists only a few titles still in print, and some of those are about Czechoslovak literature. Charles Sabatos notes that "Not a single work of contemporary Slovak fiction appeared in English between the Soviet-led occupation in 1968 and the end of Communism in 1989 ... (*Ever Green Is...*)." Martin Šimečka maintained in 1998 that "No more than a few dozen Slovak books [including *The Year of the Frog*] have been translated into a world language and, aside from a few exceptions, were published with small print runs and were virtually overlooked by European critics" ("Learning to Write"). The "Bibliography 1990–2000" of translations of Slovak writers (*Slovak Literary Review*, December 2000) bears this out. It lists ten books in English — only one published by a very small press in the U.S. and one in England. All the others seem to have been published in Slovakia and are almost inaccessible to Anglophones.

As a result, it is hard for an outsider to get a sense not only of trends in writing but of the shape of individual careers. But there is enough to get some sense of themes and trends. Much of the fiction available is rather mordant. Although Central European writers probably weary of being compared to Kafka, many stories exhibit striking similarities to his work. Most obvious is the flat, almost matter-of-fact tone, even when the subject matter might seem to invite high emotion. This may be related to the tendency of some writers to adopt the attitude of folk-tale and fable. Some, like Václav Šuplata (1956) and Ján Uličansky (1955), write overt fables for children. Some, like Vincent Šikula (1936–2001), move from children's stories to a child's point of view in "Grannie" (*In Search of Homo Sapiens*) using very simple language and seemingly unrelated episodes in which he resents and tries to escape from his grandmother and then mourns her death. "Mandul'a" (1964, translated in *Transitions*) begins as if the audience were already familiar with the story, which is told in the present tense by a first-person narrator who gives terse descriptions and interjects lines like "So it was!" and the refrain "Cuckoo" into a story about a woman who is impregnated and then deserted, first by her lover and then by her son. The fragment from Šikula's *Not Every Cloud Has a Silver Lining* (1966) mixes the tone of the folk tale — "There was a forest, in the forest there was a small hill, on the hill there stood a church" — with that of oral narrative, as in "Frankly, all of this was maybe not even half-true. Wanderers like to spread all sorts of nonsense around the world, and other people only add up to their nonsense. But enough of explanations" (*One Hundred*, trans. Viera and James Sutherland-Smith).

Stanislav Rakús has been linked with Šikula and others as a member of "the School of Lyrical Prose" (*Transitions*). His "Jasanica" and "Mother Dorothy" (both 1979) reflect, thought they do not imitate, oral tradition. The first story, folkish rather than folk, deals with a woman thought by the villagers to be a witch, befriended only by an itinerant tinker. In the second, the omniscient narrator addresses a corpse. Like Kafka's, Rakus's and Šikula's stories verge on allegory, though the events cannot quite be made to fit an abstract pattern, instead circling back on themselves to deny correspondences and closure.

But the most Kafkaesque quality of the stories of all schools is their sense of enclosure, almost claustrophobia, both spatial and emotional. Readers will be more aware of the constriction than the characters, who are made uneasy by too much space, too many choices. Martin Bútora's statistician Kmetik wakes in a sweat, prowls his apartment in search of intruders, carrying a flashlight and a ladle, worrying about a mysterious man outside and about who might have entered his flat. Part of his anxiety is political, for two idealistic students have asked to publish his research which shows that "the obligatory courses on dialectical and historical materialism were utter nonsense," and if he complies, he may not get the fellowship to America that he may or may not want. These and other, personal issues from the previous day give him unsettling dreams. Still, "He was comfortable with his opinions of the previous day, he agreed with them. On the other hand, whether he liked it or not, something made him continue thinking. He wonders, "Who was he arguing with for God's sake? There was no one contradicting him." The story's title — "You'll Pick It Up, It'll Be Bad. You Won't Pick it Up, It'll Be Worse" — sounds like the punch line of a mordant Central European joke but, according to Bútora, comes from "a Slovak fairy tale" in which "Janko asked his magical steed if he should pick up a golden feather from the ground, or a golden hair, or a golden horse-shoe," and the horse replies with the title of the story. And Kmetik concludes that "It would never be good: it would just go on, not making mistakes in tiny nuances, distinguishing between the bad and the even worse" (*Transitions*).

This is certainly true of "A Parting Gift" by Ladislav Ťažký (1924). Touring Slovakia with a script editor in search of story lines which "were to have their roots in the most topical, most burning questions that gave rise to conflicts in lives lived to the full, but they were not to omit the poetry to be found in people's lives, in nature and in the post-revolutionary upsurge of energy and the prospects offered by our easily-won freedom" (*In Search of Homo Sapiens*). Although the narrator is weary of travel not only in search of film material but of discussions with readers and writers, he continues "because my conscience tells me that just now, in our turbulent times, our Slovak people need the living word...." The first two episodes of the story take place before the Russian troops have departed. In one, a half-drunk beggar not only refuses to pick up a cigarette dropped by a Russian officer but grinds it under his shoe, even though he is clearly longing for a smoke. In the second, the narrator sees a Russian enlisted man trailing longingly after a gorgeous gypsy girl — who demands money. The soldier has no money, and the narrator, remembering his own days as a soldier, lets fellow-feeling overcome political resentment and gives the soldier the price. Only later, in the third episode, does he learn that the girl has contracted a virulent sexual disease, previously unknown in the area, from the now-departed soldier. So, it seems, the legacy of Russian occupation is not that easy to get rid of.

"A Parting Gift" is unusual in dealing with the transition period. More often, writers included in *In Search of Homo Sapiens* identify themselves with particular regions of Slovakia, though non–Slovaks may be puzzled as to where the action takes place, and few of the stories are set in Bratislava. The earliest story was published in 1963, the latest in 1999. With a few exceptions, the stories are set in the present, and most of them follow neither lyrical nor postmodern practice. Alexander Halvoník's "Fear" is a kind of parody of a private eye story; Peter Holka's "Love as a Crime" is a comic tale of sexual fantasizing, Ján Tužinsky's "A Murmur" peoples a deserted railway station with Dostoevsky characters, Ján Lenčo's "On the Way to P." posits an alternate and possibly backward universe, Andrej Ferko's "Intra Muros Populis" traces in a single, monstrous paragraph the attempt of his character Gregor (can any Central European writer ignore the obvious allusion?) to find an ideal way of life. But even some of these exceptions to straight-ahead realist narrative draw upon folk and oral traditions.

Things are grimmer and more constricted in the work of Rudolf Sloboda (1938–1995). Like Kmetik in Bútora's story, Sloboda's ex-priest turned road-mender in "The Ring" wanders his flat, with a machete or a pistol, alone and fearful in the dark: "As soon as the sun sets misery overwhelms me. This misery lasts until it is dark. When at last it is dark I am afraid." Like an Ingmar Bergmann priest, he has lost his faith but believes that "somewhere we must rely on God, for instance, in the granting of consolation." Although "I stopped loving the last person on this earth," he "did not wish to repent" and hopes that "isolation from living people could only bring gain to me, that I would not know the bitterness of real isolation" (*Transitions*).

Sloboda's "The Brains" (1982) [in Slovak connoting reason or sanity rather than the physical organ] is much less tightly wound and more realistic than "The Ring." The translated excerpt is framed by the narrator's frustration with his daughter, but for the most part deals with his acting in a film, a conversation with a colleague, seeing an American film, issues of mixed-race dating, and an argument with his daughter and then his wife. The excerpt ends with the narrator's feelings of worthlessness and the reflection that "Maybe poverty would solve everything," so that his daughter could not ask him for money, but then decides that "without money I would be completely finished. There was at least one thing that put me ahead of my wife and daughter — they are unable to make money" (*One Hundred*, trans. Pavol Lukáč).

This story illustrates Jelena Paštéková's view that "Sloboda created a stylistic figure of the 'writing I' having life data corresponding to those of the author.... In this way, the author diagnosed the socially imposed schizophrenia of the 'real socialism' as well as his own life" (*One Hundred*) and, she says, enabled him to avoid the restrictions of "normalization." The novel ends, "I'm a killed man," a painful irony in view of Sloboda's suicide.

However, this method, or at least this excerpt, is less successful than

"The Ring" or "The White Dog," in which author and character are distanced from each other. In "The White Dog," the narrator is a traffic supervisor for the transit system who writes about writing his autobiography when he is not wandering off onto the history of dog ownership and other topics. But when he is on the topic, he centers on issues familiar to modernists, though anathema to post-structuralists: the question of the value of words (he believes in it), the purpose of recording the events of his life ("Who is going to remember this, if it is not written down?") and the question of truth v. fact ("Every fact may look like a lie, but years later it becomes a truth. That's why it's necessary to write a lot and unceasingly"). He writes for the future, because the future is all there is, and there is no point in deceiving the future. But he is concerned that his wife will find and read his manuscript, so in order to avoid blame, contradiction — censorship? — he writes from the point of view of the white dog and concludes with the passage quoted earlier.

At his best, Sloboda's fiction has an energy and sense of movement that works fruitfully against the trivial and obsessive concerns of his protagonists, and they show that a little distance and artifice can be an advantage for a writer. So, of course, can close attention to the texture of everyday life. This is shown not only in Sloboda's fiction but in "The Sources of the Sea Attract the Diver" (1963; *Transitions*) by Ján Johanides (1934). The story's narrator is a cook put on disability leave to be treated for a cancer which does not seem on the surface to alarm or depress him, though at moments he is aware of everything slipping away. But for the most part, unlike characters in the stories discussed earlier, he is relatively tranquil, in his apartment "surveying it quickly and noting what we had. I nodded and thus continued in peace and forgetfulness. I went to sleep immediately, as usual." On another occasion, he does not want to go home too early, because his wife, whom he likes, "but in the way I liked other people," often entertains other men. A colleague reproaches him for his complaisance "as if he'd tried hard to teach me to hate or as if at least he'd attempted to awaken my interest in hatred." Later he learns that his friend's wife is also having an affair, and though he does not try to console him, he stays with him. He also convinces a woman colleague not to have an abortion, and after meeting his wife's lover, whom he finds intelligent and sympathetic, he looks out into the night, where "The stars were trembling too far away to be in sympathy. I was the only one who was sympathetic and I didn't wish to learn to hate. I was thinking about humility when I closed my eyes."

While in the hospital for treatment, he is called to the hospital to view the body of his wife, killed in a car accident while driving with the lover, who displays far more emotion than the husband, who tries to convince the lover that "life had meaning and importance." The letter she had written to the narrator in explanation has been lost. At the end, "I was considering everything that life had given me," he realizes that he grew to love Marta because of "her desire to be happy," and that she was insolent "because she made me into a bridgehead ... to the goals she thought might make her happy." Realizing her sense of isolation, he does not resent being used because "The trivialities I gave her during her life were only to show that they wouldn't make her especially happy. I don't know if she understood."

For Johanides's narrator, the fabric of everyday life serves to distract, even to console. He could be a secular saint, truly humble in the face of adversity, or a man who has numbed himself to all genuine feeling. Marlowe Miller thinks that the narrator is genuinely peaceful and that the story "reveals [Johanides'] existential belief in determinism, or Fate. It is the fate of the character with the greatest reason to disintegrate to become the magnet, the physical cipher, for all the emotional pain around him" (*Transitions*). Zora Puršková notes that the story was made into a film, "322," and that "The presentation of a diagnosis of a catastrophic illness in both the writer's and director's interpretation has an unambiguous value — showing the relative and always ambivalent character of an undeniable and fatal evil" (*One Hundred*). Whatever conclusion one reaches, it cannot be easily arrived at, and the story deserves wider and deeper reading. The story is not at all political; it is not even specifically Slovak. But like all literature worth reading for more than documentary value, it is very human, though without the connotations of "heartwarming" that often burden that word.

Johanides' character endures because he does. Pavel Vilikovský's character in "Alive and Well in Bystrica," an alcoholic official investigating a suicide in the face of indifferent witnesses, thinks, "Perhaps we will endure. But why?" (*Transitions*). Characters in "Shall We Use 'Thou' with Each Other? (Escalation of Feeling III)" (*Transitions*) and "Escalation of Feeling" (*Description*) endure the loss of possible love after the couple acts in a pornographic film in the first case and rape in the second without questioning fate or anything else in prose that is cool and objective. The stories were written in the 1970s but not published until the 1980s because Vilikovský (1941) neither cooperated with nor resisted censorship during "normalization" but withheld his work from publication between 1968 and 1989.

While these stories might not have been written by any other writer, they have a family resemblance to the work of Johanides and others. But the stories in *Ever Green Is...* are very different from any Slovak fiction available in English translation, for in this volume Vilikovský is revealed to American readers as a major postmodern technician with a firm Central European sensibility. (Perhaps there is no real distinction between the two.)

In "Ever Green Is..." (taken from Goethe's "Grey is theory and ever green is the tree of life"), one man says to another, "I'm a follower of Marx." The other says, "Me too." "Karl?" the first one says. "No, Groucho." This joke has been dead for decades, but Vilikovský brings it back to life. While the narrator, trained professionally and sexually under Col. Alfredl, clearly modeled on the Austro-Hungarian super-spy, never breaks into a chorus of "Hurrah for Captain Spalding," he clearly could if Vilkovský wanted him to. Among many Groucho moments is this passage from a long paragraph in the monologue that covers more than a hundred pages:

> All in all, the theory of relativity is just a harmless joke, a rebus, but let's take, for example, the five principles of extinguishing forest fires! Let's take Ludolf's number, also known as pi, or Madame Bovary — who was, incidentally, a Hungarian Jewish woman by origin. You can object, and essentially I agree with you, that it's a decadent book, but remember the right-hand rule in the Highway Code, or, if you like, the Marconi-Popov wireless transmitter. Now come up with something yourself.

Framed as a monologue delivered to a recruit who turns out, as the result of a prolonged bout of vaginismus in Slovakia (ended by the narrator's calculated impregnation of the woman to force out his penis), to be the narrator's son, whom he leaves tied up as a lesson to him, the story reads like a vaudeville version of a James Bond film. Employed by Lloyd's of London to overthrow the King of Romania, the narrator gets instructions from Harold Lloyd. There is a literal cliffhanging episode in which the narrator kills a rival spy, and a metaphorical one in which a crucial encounter with a Romanian chambermaid who is not a chambermaid is broken off by an ellipsis. Every cliff-hanging chapter ending is followed by a general disquisition on a totally different topic, and except for the narrator's treatment of the listener (a surrogate for the reader?), no episode is resolved. Every situation is interrupted by general observations and remarks (here, in spite of Gertrude Stein's injunction to Hemingway, remarks are literature). There are rules for interrogation, as for almost every other topic, though the narrator prefers the well-tried method "kicking the shit out of someone" (69), and recipes for fondue and tabbouleh. There are dozens of Slovak jokes, including one in which "in Slovak literature all works are prominent," and insults directed at almost every other country. There is a bibliography of works cited or alluded to which could be regarded as Nabokovian if my search of the World Catalogue hadn't turned up a sexologist named Josef Hynie — though not the title cited.

However, as Dr. Samuel Johnson said of *Clarissa*, if you read it for the plot, you would hang yourself. Puns, parodies, and allusion carry the reader along, but finally one must ask if the story has a point. Perhaps it tries to portray a mind, an attitude towards humans as disposable, toward history as manipulable, and toward atrocities as governed by rules which come to be ends in themselves. All this, presumably, was created in the Hapsburg empire and maintained itself, almost for esthetic purposes, through the shambles that followed and then into the Soviet era, very much not a dead father, for at the end, the colonel caps the title with "...the horse of life," climbs from (Houdini's?) cabinet, and neighs. If Slovak did not have the concept of a horse laugh before, it does now.

Although "A Horse Upstairs, A Blind Man in Vráble" uses some of the same post-modern techniques as "Ever Green Is...," it is easier to describe — but only after one reaches the end. It too is given continuity by a frame: a bus ride to the town in the title by the unnamed narrator, who, it is finally clear, is trying to answer the question, "Do you love your mother?" Before it is answered, obliquely, the narrator avoids the issue by beginning the story several times, gives superfluous statistics and historical data about the towns he passes through, wanders through observations about cats, the ideal Bratislava behind the real one, and personifications of abstractions like "last year." He tells a sad story about a boy who doesn't exist or had another name. At one point, describing other vehicles on the road, he confesses that they are invented and besides, "This has never happened, not to me anyway; it is happening if at all, at this very moment, and to you" and says that the purpose of literature is "to convince humanity, that frustrated yet still rather vain woman, that despite everything, she has a beautiful little pussy." Or, put theologically, "We desire a God in order to have our own narrator." Later he says, "I don't deserve my own narrator."

As the story progresses, it becomes clear that the narrator's obsession with precision is a means of evading the real subject: his mother's last illness, her descent into a near-vegetable state, and his smothering her to end her, and his, suffering. It is, he insists, a happy ending, "and so what if none of the characters are happy?" But the story ends with the memory of his mother, youthful, in a meadow with goslings, and "everything, including the horse and the blind man," is truly in its place. While the story has fewer pyrotechnics than "Ever Green Is...," it produces a much stronger emotional effect because it combines post-modern technique with strong, if obliquely expressed, emotion.

The work of Lajos Grendel (1948), who collaborated with Vilikovský on *Slovak Casanova*, a collection of stories, is difficult to place because he can either be regarded as Slovak writer writing in Hungarian or as a Hungarian writer who lives in Slovakia. This confusion represents to some degree the position of all ethnic Hungarians in Slovakia, for attempts to preserve their language and culture — aided in various degrees by the Hungarian government — are regarded with suspicion by the more nationalist Slovaks. Still, Grendel has held prominent positions in Slovak writers' organizations, and though he goes to Budapest to launch his books, he writes them in Bratislava.

Grendel may not identify completely with the narrator, although he clearly understands his feelings, in "The Vagaries of Oneirism — I" (*Slovak Literary Review*, December 1999) who

> felt no more at ease in Budapest than anywhere else, though not any worse either, And even if it was nice to hear everybody around me speak my mother tongue, I had long since given up the solemn illusion which in my eyes used to transform even a bandit should he happen to speak Hungarian. I thought it natural that I was, am, and can never be anything else but Hungarian. I had got used to being an itinerant traveler everywhere and never felt, beyond nostalgia for long outgrown intimacy, greater emotion in my hometown than on any of the open balconies running in tiers round the walls above the courtyard in some old, rundown tenement house in Budapest.

In this fragment from *Esmeralda's Rainbow* (1999), the narrator visits the studio of a painter who urges him to have the strength to dream, but the narrator flees, deciding to "expunge from my life even the recollection of the man I was but a reflection of, who stayed on in the house to remind me, as the better and freer half of my self, of freedom in his absence, and to torture me." Years later, looking back on the experience, he is content to have learned conventional roles, so that "The outer zone of my existence is encircled by that frightening milieu guarded and watched over by good manners, the laws of the land, and a night squad of policemen."

No such contentment is possible for the narrator of "The Contents of Suitcases" (1987; *Description*), a story dedicated to Jorge Luis Borges. The narrator, like Grendel both writer and editor, is followed by a mysterious man who flees when the narrator turns to confront him. The narrator begins to write a story, this story, about the experience, and realizes that events will not correspond with his completed text but consoles himself with the idea that "Lies, when they are self-oblivious and to the point, can bring us closer to the truth than pure naturalism." Later he realizes that although his goal in writing has been to understand himself and reality," in fact, holding the mirror up to nature reveals "not life, but literature itself. If we smash the mirror to pieces, we discover there is nothing behind."

He does so because the man has turned up again with a suitcase — one of as many as fifty, it turns out — filled with a manuscript that he wants to submit for publication. The manuscript has no beginning and no end, and the sequence does not matter, but the narrator is struck by the variety and vividness of the situations, characters, and settings portrayed and at the same time convinced that the manuscript "was an outrageous travesty of literature," a blow to everything that had motivated him to write, and — worst of all — destroying the illusion that creation is possible. He realizes that somewhere the endless manuscript contains his own story and thus renders it meaningless, unconnected.

Still, the narrator has finished and published his story, a paradox rather like that of Romantic poets who wrote poems about being unable to write poems. The mirror is an illusion, but the writer still polishes it. Perhaps self-reflexiveness at least supports the idea, or illusion, of a self.

Unlike their colleagues in Slovenia and other countries, Slovak women prose writers have thus far not been widely translated into English. Many of them seem to have spent at least part of their careers writing for children — but so have many of the male writers mentioned earlier. Etela Farkašova, introducing the December 2002 *Slovak Literary Review* devoted to women's writing, values it because "it articulates women's experience in its variety 'from inside,' describes the world of other women's emotions and thoughts" and "reveals the depths of the female imagination" and in the process "can expose layers and dimensions of human reality which male writers dismiss as irrelevant, uninteresting, or trivial...."

Two women writers born in the 1930s certainly reflect these concerns. Both Jaroslava Blažková (1933) and Alta Vášová (1939) present first-person accounts of a mother concerned about the future of a son, and the fact that the former has lived in Canada for years matters only in the details of the setting. This son has come back from India, where he has been unsuccessfully seeking God, and rejects his mother's overtures to comfort or even to communicate ("The Garden of Earthly Delights," 1998; *Slovak Literary Review*, December 2000). In Vášová's "Hands on a Beer-Stained Table" (1995; *One Hundred*), the mother sees her son's coat on an emaciated young man and worries that the two have exchanged more than coats. Then she finds her son in bed with a young woman and cannot decide which is worse.

In "Zombi" (1996; *One Hundred*, trans. Viera and James Sutherland-Smith), Jana Juráňová (1957) takes a much harsher view of a youngish man, balding, who has "lost the appetite to be in an American film" in his imagination, who knows that he is not as famous as his father, who relies on a succession of women to feed his self-esteem and to save him from drinking. "He doesn't have the energy to be wicked," but on the other hand "He hasn't the energy to be good or honest or open or truthful." Lacking any goal or discipline, he merges with whatever crowd he can join.

Uršul'a Kovalyk writes, under a pseudonym, of a character who suffers horrendous abuse by a drunken father and neglect by a harsh grandmother in fragment from "Betrix and I" (*Slovak Literary Review*, December 2002) and falls in love with her cousin because he is "the first man who would not beat the hell out of me." Judging from the title of her first collection of stories, *Cheating Women Hate Eggs*, she is no easier on women.

FEMINA, the Club of Slovak Women Writers, is attempting "to promote and support the work of Slovak women writers" (*Slovak Literary Review*, December 2002), and Etela Farkašová (1943), one of its founders, is also a strong fictional voice. Her "Day After Day" deals with the "depressing, endless circle" of dealing with a handicapped child whom she cannot but love but for whom she cannot have hope (*Slovak Literary Review*, March 1999). "A Sky Full of Migrating Birds" (1988) is almost as static, reminiscent of Virginia Woolf in a story structured by a woman's following flocks of geese across a winter sky which remind her of a Chinese poem about desolation and emptiness, leading her to feel that "language is like forming a chain, passing on and receiving, because existing in language is like taking part in a never-ending relay" (*In Search of Homo Sapiens*, 34). Reflecting on her life, she realizes that "I am, only so long as I desire" and that in seeing the birds,

> she has found something half-forgotten, she has touched those distant places of her own within her, something she had considered long suppressed, not existing, that she had ceased to call to mind ... she delights in this newly discovered feeling, she relishes it to the full, with her gaze still lifted upwards [37, 38].

Only two of her stories seem to have been translated, but she deserves a wider and not only a feminist audience. But until FEMINA succeeds in having the work of some of its anthologies translated into English, American readers will not be able to get a better sense of her accomplishment and that of other Slovak women writers of fiction.

Still, there is some progress. Although only six women writers out of twenty-three (unless you count the nonfiction introduction and conclusion) are included in *In Search of Homo Sapiens*, that is a major advance on *Transitions*, which had none, and even *One Hundred Years of Slovak Literature*, which included seven women out of sixty-two poets and prose writers. Mária Bátorová's (1950) "Tells" (1999) excerpted from a longer work, moves from pathos about an elderly dog to political argument between a young woman beggar and a hypersensitive musician, and the fragment, at least, ends inconclusively. Marína Čeretková's (1931) character in "The Actress" (1983) models her role as an old woman on someone abandoned in a nursing home and discovers that the neglectful son is now her lover, a government minister. All are very well done, but none is technically as interesting as "A Sky Full of Migrating Birds."

The playing field for women and men poets is somewhat more level, but only because no full volumes of work by Slovak poets seem to have been translated into English, or at least to be available in the U.S. Still, brief selections of poems in the *Slovak Literary Review* can give some sense of techniques and themes. At present, the chief sources for Anglophones are three anthologies, only one, *In Search of Beauty*, available in the United States.

Unfortunately, either because many of the poets chosen are not very good in the original Slovak or because the translators have on too many occasions no ear for rhythm, little command of vocabulary, and little knowledge of English syntax, *In Search of Beauty* is not likely to advance the reputation of these poets or of Slovak poetry in general. The thirty-eight chosen, only eleven under sixty, are members of the Slovak Writers' Society.

A good many of the poems read like hymns, some addressed directly to God, even more to Saints Cyril and Methodius as bringers of the Word, both spiritual and Slovak. Many, like Milan Kraus's "Sleepwalker," are lofty and vague at the same time. And there is a fatal attraction toward generalization, as in Viliam Turčany's "Sonnet on Relationships" — and, for that matter, in the separate editors' prefaces. Too many rainbows; too many invocations of the word; too many simplistic definitions of poetry and the poet, as in Svetloslav Veigl's view of the bard whose "eyes are dreamy and it suits him, / he rolls drops of joy like children's marbles, / although he has never joy completely in his soul."

There are some gems to be found: Kraus exhibits some wit in addressing his mistress as a jug; Vojtech Mihálik achieves genuine emotion in "Orphans of Parents Still Alive" and "Cactus," in which he contrasts his juicy and abundant youth with his current dry age, resolving "to roll my leaves into points / and surround myself completely with thorns." And Eva Kováčová's "Powder Puff" is at least about something concrete, while drinking songs and ballads have life and some narrative drive.

The other two anthologies have been published only in Europe. One is *Not Waiting for Miracles: Seventeen Contemporary Slovak Poets* (three of them women). All were born after 1940, the youngest in 1967; each is represented by at least five and as many as eight poems; each is introduced by a brief biographical sketch.

Wider ranging in genre as well as time is *One Hundred Years of Slovak Literature: An Anthology*, published in both English and Slovenian editions for the 2000 Vilenica literary event. The apparatus, especially the biographical and critical introductions to individual writers, is much more thorough than the poetry anthology. Many of the recent prose writers in the anthology have been discussed earlier.

Nine of the poets from *Not Waiting for Miracles* are included in *One Hundred*, and some of these have had additional poems published in *Slovak Literary Review*. The last two sources take care to identify poets by school and period, but readers new to Slovak poetry will probably be more attracted by individual achievement than by labels. Again, I must point out that brief selections from a body of work make it impossible to get a sense of a poet's achievement. Moreover, it is difficult to give, in brief discussions and quotations, a sense of the quality either of intensely lyrical or of philosophical poems. The fact that I discuss poets whose work deals with the nature and mission of poetry does not mean that it is better but that it is more readily accessible.

One of the oldest poets to survive "normalization" was Ivan Kupec (1922–1997). Silenced during the Seventies and Eighties, he worked on *The Book of Shadows*, which he published in 1990. "The Heretic's Creed: Mother" ends with what seems inescapably to be a triumph of his survival as a poet:

> Naturally, death changes
> Life after the third bend in the road it trims shadows
> and in the fear of poetry, which once piled earth over me,
> it sees just the budding shoot
> with which a child enters a burnt city.

"A Second Shortest Poem for the Year 2000," written in 1988, looks prophetically, if uncertainly, toward the Velvet Revolution:

> And we still remain, feet in the sand
> on a yet more unconsoling bank. We haven't forded the river,
> the dawn of a fortunate star flickers for us
> from a distance further than the half century.
> The myth is vanishing; perhaps we wanted
> much too much, one heave of our shoulders
> and we swim to the other bank, prisoners of yesterdays,
> also with descendants dead before birth.

Štefan Strážay (1940) has a similarly gloomy look at the future in "The City" (1992):

> In the city statues have been veiled,
> a long time.
> It is like an ominous sign.
> Theme: despair.
> The past does not exist,
> the future is covered
> And time keeps working on
> what is under the impregnated
> Rubber-coated sheet
> without us knowing how,
> as we can't see.

Ľubomír Feldek (1936) was apparently not affected by normalization, but in the 1990s he published far more work than in previous decades. "Jaroslav," for the 1894 Nobel Prize winner Jaroslav Siefert, takes a wry look at the poet's profession. Siefert, told while in hospital that he had won the Nobel Prize, responded with "I don't feel well, but joyful," and Feldek ends the poem with:

> he managed to conduct
> a fast course in poetry.
>
> In six words
> he explained to millions
> where that dog was buried,
> the one with the odd name
> *Beingapoet.*

Two women poets, Lýdia Vadkerti-Gavorníková (1932–1999) and Mila Haugová (1942) take a more sensual attitude toward the nature of poetry. In "Desire" (1977), Vadkerti-Gavorníková enjoins the reader "To sweat in [the poem] / as in your own skin" and notes that "the poet is / naked," clothed only by "Words Words Words." In "Ecrive" (11.11.1992) Haugová begins with an ellipsis, as if what follows were part of a continuing conversation:

> ... leave everything noc- [*sic*; "con-"?]
> cealed in a word; arrogant light of
> darkness; music of sonorous vowels;
> incest of sounds; palpably im-
> palpable words; smell of tongue's
> sex; gestures of hands touching;
> warmth (mine only?)
> I step towards to you like an Egyptian woman;
> one hand inside you, the other round
> you, here, now (in a sentence which God
> commanded us), we make love without a single word.

Taťjana Lehenová (1961) writes poetry about sex without linking sex to poetry. "A Tap like a Water Main" and "A Little Nightmare Music" respectively resent or envy and celebrate the phallus. After the scandalous success of these poems, more philosophical work like "I Call Her the Sybil" seems overblown, and more colloquial work like "The Chosen Few" seems flat. There seems to be little record of her publishing after the early 1990s, and she is now living in Prague unconnected with literary circles.

Viliam Klimáček (1958; see above) has a somewhat more industrial view of the force of love in "A Moment of Geology" (*Not Waiting*):

> ... a chestnut-haired girl
> with an unpitying smile

> a welding torch braises a piece of me
> with the acetylene of her sharp
> tongue she melts and rounds me out...

His other poems are more emotional, even playful, rather than primarily erotic, as in "Fireafresh" (*Not Waiting*):

> especially to consume the fireafresh
> to lay down growing
> make love
> and the fireafresh in your fair hair
> — soft it is —
> to throw
> and in the little-by-little night blazing
> to play knucklebones
> — the hopscotch which awaits...

Jozef Urban (1964–1999) was one of the most popular and prolific poets throughout the 1990s. Obviously influenced by the Beats in poems like "I Blow My Nose Inartistically" (*Not Waiting*), he thumbs it at a polite society composed of cannibals. And he begins "Inspire" (*One Hundred*, trans. Marián Andričik and James Sutherland-Smith) with

> I stopped listening to music while writing.
> I'll deny myself references to masters. Hardly anyone knows them.
> No strategies. And I've grown out of shouting
> at a woman critic with a soul of bakelite, who in her way hates me
> clean and tenderly:
> GESTAPO!
>
> Awareness of futility is beautiful. As when it rains and dries up.
> And that fragrant and singularly soft air between it...
> I don't know what it smells of but I would say
> fig tree [1996].

In other words, although he seems to reject "culture," like many of his predecessors in Slovak poetry, he turns to the natural world for inspiration and solace.

Peter Macovszky (1966), who writes in Hungarian as well as Slovak, looks less to previous poets than to literary theory. "This Is the Real Thing" (1994) begins "This is a structured speech of poetic expression. / It denotes a level of textual bondage, / structuring text in the guise of form." And so on, as if Ezra Pound had compressed his manifesto on Imagism into a few lines. This theoretical, abstracting tendency is even clearer in "The Bridge" (1995):

> the words of this poem
> need the other words
> of this poem
> to create a chain:

> a chain bridge
> over which they could
> stroll and shed
> obsolete sounds
> and withered
> disabled meanings
>
> with which they've never
> coincided
> and never fashioned
> any bonds [*One Hundred*, trans. Martin Solotruk].

These terse, almost abstract poems have more energy and vitality than the longer and more superficially vivid philosophizing of some of his contemporaries, and it will be interesting to see how Macsovsky develops into middle age, now that he is an editor at a major commercial publishing house.

Some of the poetry of Peter Šulej (1967) could be used to support Dušan Mikolaj's view that "when it comes to communicating in an interesting way, it is above all pure, genuine, spontaneous and humanizing humor. We have begun to neglect it shamefully, partly because we take ourselves in particular far too seriously..." (*In Search of Homo Sapiens*, 154). Šulej's "Toys" begins "Every poem is just a toy," and the purpose of poems is

> to delight distract entertain us
> they have been waiting simply for the call
> for just the right signal
> sentences pedal-cars dolls' words
> without a manual without instructions without plan
> a little laughter a few tears
> when the toy is broken — scattered
> a newly-assembled world like Legoland
> the fabled library of Babylon — geometry
> words stuck together from circles and spirals
> an unending so unending game [*Slovak Literary Review*, March 1999].

Of course, soberer, simpler and more direct poetry still has a place, as in the work of Viera Prokešová (1957), whose poems grow out of a particular place, situation, or emotion, as in "After a Week" (*Not Waiting*):

> 1.
> After a week only, you won't exactly
> recollect him, maybe his smile
> over the round table,
> the movement of a hand, everything is isolated
> detail and unconnected —
> more down-to-earth are one's morning
> fellow travelers.

2.
But if you miss him everywhere you needn't
be sad, on the contrary
you can think that perhaps he is
well and you are glad
as if somehow it could depend
on you.

Many of the poems in *Not Waiting for Miracles* have themes which can be described as both local to a situation and universal — love, loss, longing, a rueful recognition that a teenage son will never again outgrow his shoes or have a haircut. For the most part, poems in *Slovak Literary Review* and *One Hundred Years of Slovak Literature* are less domestic. Obviously, the range and themes of these poets vary widely, and it is regrettable that they have been available to American readers only in scattered selections in literary magazines.

However, that is the fate of most writers, including American writers, and the situation of the Slovak writer is like that of writers everywhere: it is difficult to get work done at all. For Slovaks, publishing that work is easier politically than it was before 1989, but financially things are much more difficult. And emotionally the situation is tense.

Before I left the U.S. for Bratislava in 1998, Gustáv Murín e-mailed that he would be glad to see me because Slovak writers are so divided by ideology that he had no one to talk to. This is clearly compared to what, for on our first walk through central Bratislava toward the Writers' Club, we halted every fifty feet or so to greet a friend of his, sometimes a cluster of friends. Many of them are writers. Therefore, if all writers were on speaking terms, they not only wouldn't get any work done, they would be in Zeno's paradoxical universe and never reach any destination. The outsider is forced to conclude that while Slovaks may not relish disaster with quite the gusto of their Hungarian neighbors, they are not ready to tempt fate by seeming too happy or fortunate.

Still, if there are nearly seven hundred members of writers' organizations who have published at least two books each, not to speak of unnumbered members of hungry new generations, literature in Slovakia can hardly be regarded as moribund. Alexander Halvoník (1945) writes and edits because "I think that the most important thing is that new books should be written and that together they should form a source of inspiration on which I can draw in my cultural life and to which I can also make my modest contribution. Culture must be created and its foundation built bit by bit" (*In Search of Homo Sapiens*, 57). Perhaps even more encouraging is the remark of a Slovak boy attending Atlantic College with 350 students from eighteen countries. Asked the difference between Slovaks and Americans, he replied, "none at all, we just have to know more" (*In Search of Homo Sapiens*, 172).

Works Cited

Description of a Struggle. Ed. Michael March. London: Picador, 1994.
In Search of Homo Sapiens: Twenty-Five Contemporary Slovak Short Stories. Ed. Pavol Hudík. Wauconda, IL: Bolchazy-Carducci; Bratislava: Slovak Writers Society, 2002.
Not Waiting for Miracles: Seventeen Contemporary Slovak Poets. Ed. Braňo Hochel. Levoča, Slovakia: Modrý Peter, 1993. As of June 2003, available from amazon.com.
One Hundred Years of Slovak Literature: An Anthology. Ed. James Sutherland-Smith. Bratislava, Slovenia: The Union of Slovenian Writers, The Association of Organisatons of Slovak Writers, 2000.
Petrík, Vladimír. *Contemporary Slovak Literature*. Trans. Sharon Milošová. Bratislava: Center for Information on Literature, 2003.
———. *Slovakia and Its Literature*. Trans. Sharon Milošová. Bratislava: Center for Information on Literature, 2001.
Šimečka, Martin. "Learning to Write in Freedom." www.tol.cz/transitions/letown1.html.
———. *The Year of the Frog*. Trans Peter Petro. New York: Simon & Schuster, 1996.
Slovak Literary Review. Bratislava: National Center for Slovak Literature. http://www.litcentrum.sk.
The Slovak Republic: A Decade of Independence (1993–2002). Ed. M. Mark Stolarik. Wauconda, IL. Bolchazy-Carducci, 2004.
Transitions: Slovak Stories. (*Slavic and East European Arts*), vol. 9, nos. 1–2 [Winter 1999]). Ed. Nicholas Rzhevsky. Stony Brook, NY. Slavic Cultural Center Press.
Vilikovský, Pavel. *Ever Green Is....* Trans. Charles Sabatos. Evanston, IL: Northwestern University Press, 2002.

5
Romanian Writing Redivivus

At the beginning of the twenty-first century Romanians are still trying to fill the gaps and resolve the contradictions created during four decades of repression and of isolation from the West during Communist rule. The most obvious contradictions, as in every post-communist country, are evident on the drive into Bucharest from the airport. Glitzy signs for Western consumer products only partly mask Communist gray.

Much of the gray is literal. What seems on landing to be a golden ground haze turns out to be smog that rises higher and grows thicker towards the center of the city. By day, the grime visibly coats the buildings and dusts the cars (mostly Dacias assembled locally) that crowd streets and clutter sidewalks. By night, the haze, not quite as thick as that in "Blade Runner," softens signs and street lights, making the vendors' stalls and the cobbled side streets of the Old Court district look like the Left Bank in Paris.

Bucharest was, by older accounts, a lot more like Paris before various disasters: earthquakes in 1940 and 1977, the bombing of World War II, and the megalomania of Nicolae Ceauşescu, who wanted, like Nero, to demolish large sections of his capital in order to build a monument to himself.

From what is left — nineteenth century neoclassical government and commercial buildings, domed at the corners and chastely ornamented; Romanian Orthodox churches, the older ones aged into individuality and distinction; the mansions of the nobility and higher bourgeoisie turned by the Communists into museums, writers' clubs, and other cultural sites — one can see what early twentieth century Bucharest must have been like.

Now there are literal gaps in the city, especially in the south center, where the market was cleared and remains empty and boarded up. Hundreds, perhaps thousands, of other buildings fell to the wrecking ball, their sites like open wounds. Bucharesters especially mourn the lost churches, and the more superstitious felt that their destruction released forces even more malign than Stalinism and what they called Ceauşism.

Given Romanian attitudes toward what Ceauşescu managed to build before his fall, they should be more tolerant of the ruins. They shrug at the Exposition Center to the north and sneer at the National Theater at the center, but they seem compelled to take visitors first to see the enormous House of the People, second largest building in the world after the Pentagon, with a perverse form of pride.

By American standards, the buildings aren't that bad — or at any rate are no worse than most of our municipal architecture. People in former Communist countries tend to blame party ideology for what is merely official bad taste. For the Exposition Center, the builders dug a large circular hole and put a dome over it, and the symmetry is much more pleasing than the Stalinist block nearby. The National Theater, a cube slightly rounded at the edges, would grace, or anyway not disgrace, a good-sized American city. It may not harmonize with the classical buildings to the north of University Square, but compared to the dark glass rectangle of the Intercontinental Hotel just to the southwest, it looks restrained and even elegant.

Even the House of the People could be worse. Like the Pentagon, it doesn't look that big because it's a lot broader than it is tall and because from the front its full dimensions aren't observable. True — and again like the Pentagon — it has no features which would tempt one to take a closer look. But the Romanians will insist that any visitor see it, so prepare to be appalled.

Gaps and attempts to fill them are not confined to Bucharest. In Transylvania, churches built in the fifteenth and sixteenth centuries by Saxon settlers are largely deserted or turned into monuments because Ceauşescu allowed the parishioners, still largely German-speaking after more than eight centuries in the region, to emigrate after the German government paid large exit fees. Those that remain are regarded with less suspicion by ethnic Romanians than the much larger Hungarian minority. In Cluj, (Klausenberg under the Austrians, Kolozsvár under the Hungarians, to give an indication of the complexities involved), the mayor removed the part of the plaque identifying King Matthias Corvinus as a Hungarian king and has dug large holes in front of the statue, apparently to demonstrate what no one disputes: Cluj was a Roman settlement. Now the mayor has been removed and, with little or nothing discovered, the hole has been filled in.

And this leaves out of account the Jews, who suffered under the Iron Guard in the 1930s and even worse under the Nazis during the war. Or mention of the Rom, or gypsies, whom sooner or later everyone does. Ethnocentric racism is a real problem: the second largest vote-getter in the November 2000 elections was the head of the Greater Romania Party, opposed to Saxons, Hungarians, Rom, and apparently anyone else not pure Romanian — this in a region where ethnic purity is often an impolite fiction.

Romanians have had to try to bridge cultural and social as well as ethnic gaps. Communist attempts to industrialize a predominantly agricultural people brought to the cities a number of those who found difficult the transition to urban life. Even the casual visitor to Bucharest will see far more evidence of peasant ways than in Central European capitals: wagons drawn by horses, women in rural dress (not colorful peasant costume) sweeping sidewalks with brooms made from twigs, two-wheeled trash carts rumbling on iron wheels down sidewalks past store windows displaying luxury goods from the West. Off the main streets, one can see women teetering on spike heels across cobblestones, symbol or symptom of Romania's struggle to accommodate new and old.

The new seems to have an edge. During the 1980s, Romanians were quarantined from toxic Western influence, and they were and are hungry for cultural fare more substantial than Big Macs — though they clearly want those too. Theaters and cabarets mount avant-garde works that, for example, combine lyrical reading with intricate choreography involving shopping carts that would have delighted Busby Berkeley.

Romanians I spoke to have not had enough time to become disenchanted with the west. At a symposium on postmodernism, held in a seventeenth century building in a district established by Vlad Tepeş (model for Dracula), a central European participant observed that discussion always seemed to come back to America as a reference point. The only (mildly) anti–American sentiments were expressed by a performance artist from San Diego.

Romanians are even more enthusiastic about the American political system, though they expressed wonder and dismay at the confusion about our 2000 presidential election. As I left Bucharest, the passport control officer sympathized with our confusion. To him, "America means democracy." I replied that, in fact, most Americans weren't worried, and in any case, it was better to wait three weeks go get the results than to know them in advance. He did a quick take and agreed. (Several years later, I am less sure.) At that point I didn't know that Romanians would soon face their own disputed election. Happily, they had to wait only three days for the final result.

These are conditions in which Romanian writers work and have worked. During the years of Communist domination, and since, Romania has in part reflected the political and cultural situation in the rest of the Warsaw Pact and in part served as augury of what was to come. As in Hungary and Czechoslovakia, for example, the state controlled cultural publication if not production. Those who fell in line were rewarded; those who did not were punished in periods of repression and subjected to various kinds of inconvenience in more liberal periods. After 1989, writers and other artists gained political freedom but lost a significant part of the economic support and cultural importance that many of them had come to count on when, under modified free market conditions, government subsidies began to disappear and audiences dwindle as a result of competition from other media.

The difference between Romania and other nations in the Communist bloc was its relative independence of Russian domination after the early 1960s, accompanied and strengthened by Nicolae Ceauşescu's cult of personality as "Helmsman, Hero, Savior" and the fostering of Romanian nationalism and what Eugene Negrici calls a siege mentality in order to strengthen his regime (Negrici). Romanians were insulated from contact not only with the west but even with citizens of other Soviet bloc countries, a political and cultural constriction that helps to account for the explosion of interest in the West and America in the 1990s. These moves, particularly the emphasis on national identity and the need to defend it, anticipated the policies of Vladimir Mečiar in Slovakia, Franjo Tuđman in Croatia, and, most notoriously and destructively, Slobodan Milošević in Yugoslavia, and various presidents and premiers in the Eurasian former Soviet Republics.

Except for the darkest days of what Negrici calls the "Fundamentalist stage" of Communism, from 1948 to the death of Gheorghe-Gheorgiu Dej in 1964, party control of literature was never total, and there was considerable easing of restrictions between 1964 and 1971 in what was called the Lyrical Revival. And even under Ceauşescu, though writers were encouraged to write in praise of him, poet and translator Ioana Ieronim says that no individual writer was obliged to do so, whatever some who did praise him say now. Magazines and editors were under more obvious pressure to be sure that Ceauşescu was praised. (Obviously Romanian television had to feature the Leader, and the programs in praise of Ceauşescu were beyond parody.) Still, as Negrici says, even when the government could "pretend to be careless and allow harmless criticism, harmless refreshing innuendoes," even "a little dissidence," writers could never be sure when the censors would impose rules, at first written and then vaguer, because it needed enemies to justify its existence. Adam Sorkin notes that work published in magazines might not pass the censor for book publication, and work published in the Seventies or early Eighties might not be republished in the late Eighties. There were seemingly more trivial instances of censorial meddling. Ieronim was not allowed to use her real name, Moroiu ("spirit" or "ghost" in Romanian) because it had religious connotations. There were obvious forbidden words like freedom, liberty, religion. Other restrictions were more subtle. Ieronim was forced to change the color of a setting sun from red to orange because the censor thought it referred to the Communist Party. Another poem, in which God views the world through a drop of dew, was thought, because of a complicated process of allusion, to refer to Ceaușescu. But writers who used the approved vocabulary—Negrici has a hilarious list—in a kind of duck speak were assured of a hearing. Even suspect writers, as the rueful joke went, could be sure that at least some people would read their work, even if they were paid to do so.

But as Sorkin told me, "It's amazing what could be gotten away with. For instance, you could write about concentration camp Romania and address the poems to a 'then and there,' such as to Anne Frank. (Mariana Marin did this to get a book approved, as I understand the story.) And you might not refer to Ceaușescu, but you could refer to the Pope, as did Mircea Dinescu [see Sorkin and Sergiu Celac's translation of "Cats in the Vatican"], and since Communism was anti-religious, how could it be censored?" Sorkin added that even supposedly pro-regime figures published coded critiques of the regime. And in his essay "Hard Lines," Sorkin gives further details about the difficulties under which poets labored in the last years of the Eighties, while Norman Manea testifies to the absurdity of life under the clown as dictator in "On Clowns." And Ilie Rad takes a more scholarly approach in "The 'Stylistics' of Censorship."

Oddly enough, according to Oana Cristea Grigorescu, even before 1989 theater was somewhat freer to discuss sensitive issues, even to talk directly about politics, even to produce *Coriolanus*, in the forty years up through 1989, and it remains vital in various regional theaters as well as in Bucharest, where in November, 2000, the National Theater, built under Ceaușescu, was playing Ionesco's *Macbett*. Two months earlier, the Central and East European Festival for Alternative Performances in Unconventional Spaces was held in Bistrița. Romanians are apparently used to that kind of venue: a production of Vladimir Holan's *Toscana*, featuring choreographed interweavings of shopping carts, was mounted at the Toaca Cultural Foundation, in a mid-nineteenth-century villa in central Bucharest. But, Sorkin notes, not all plays that were produced could be published.

Visual art (like fiction) was apparently more susceptible to being pressed into state service, first as Socialist Realism, then in the 1980s to praise Ceaușescu. Some artists left the country voluntarily and have stayed abroad. Unlike the writers of the diaspora, they were apparently not regarded as exiles. (Some writers, notably Magda Cârneci and Saviana Stănescu, are in varying degrees involved in the art scene, arranging exhibits, writing art criticism and theory, and supporting visual artists in other ways.)

Writers who emigrated had their own problems, like Nina Cassian, who writes in "*Invitation au voyage*" that her difficulty in learning to write in English was more than Herculean and questions whether she can shed Romanian as a snake does its skin.

Writers who stayed in Romania and who were not well-regarded by the regime could publish work not clearly offensive to it, though it might be delayed, some times almost intolerably, for reasons like lack of paper, a clerk's dislike of the poet's face, Elena Ceaușescu's disapproval, or no reason at all. Dan Verona outlines the more than Orwellian process of attempting to publish in a system that was absurd but not funny (Vianu). Some of the most deeply felt work was either published in samizdat or kept "in the drawer." Or, in the case of Daniela Crăsnaru, "in her aunt's cellar, in a box under some onions, because her own flat was liable to be searched." After the fall of Ceaușescu, she was "free to send you my real poems" (Adcock in Crăsnaru).

Crăsnaru managed to survive under the Ceaușescu regime as writer and also as an editor until the pressure of censorship became so heavy that she resigned. All of the twelve stories in *The Grand Prize and Other Stories* were written before 1989. Four were originally published in 1983; five others were published in 1990 after Crăsnaru discovered them in the drawer of the Communist former editor who had told her they were lost. (Adam J. Sorkin, personal communication. See also Sorkin's, "The paradox of the fortunate fall: censorship and poetry in communist Romania," *Literary Review*, Summer 2002; available through www.24hourscholar.com).

Even those casually aware of recent Romanian history can guess that at least three of them, including the title story, could not have been published before the overthrow of the Communist regime — although as Adam Sorkin, the co-translator, said on another occasion, it was surprising what writers could occasionally get away with. In "The European Mechanism," a "fully contemporary" restaurant has "a miasma of cheap cigarettes and the fumes of rum, beer, and sweat." And the director of personnel at a factory is unable to admit not only the failure of urbanization programs but of the attempts to rehabilitate every youth dislocated by the system.

"The Grand Prize," set at a twenty-year class reunion, is the most complex in showing the effects of totalitarian conformity. The professor who campaigned against the use of "good morning" as superstitious and counterrevolutionary has outlived his error because "people have become used to forgetting stupidities easily" because of even greater stupidities, in a kind of dialectical progression. Christian, an editor who has quietly and almost unconsciously played the Party's game, is a brilliant success in Bucharest. He endures the satiric gibes of a classmate and the tedious conversation of a man who has an idea for a book, and he hears without fully understanding it and certainly without applying it to himself the story of another classmate unable to believe in his fortunate life who retreats to a hospital. But he is unable to escape guilt for his unwitting betrayal, at official urging, of a friend who wanted to be a film director but is forced to remain in a different, dead-end program. The friend, "totally become what he was doomed to be," shows Christian the script and documentation for a pageant — and it is dreadful, Party-line conformism written in doggerel. Unable to confront what he has done, and become, Christian sleeps with the wife of a classmate and returns to Bucharest humming "For she's a jolly good fellow...."

Even stories which were probably published in the 1983 volume — none is dated — deal with people whose lives go awry, sometimes by accident, sometimes by pressure from demanding relatives, as in "Everything's OK," sometimes by mistaken identity, as in "Local News," sometimes by a glimpse at life's other possibilities, as in "About Happiness" and even more dramatically in "The Fallen Oak Tree."

Except for this last and the title story, in which characters and setting are more fully realized (though both could easily be turned into novellas) the point of view is detached, analytical, proceeding by a series of vignettes. But all convey a sense of loneliness and disaffection not confined to the borders of Romania, even though physical and social details place them firmly in a time and place.

Ieronim's *The Triumph of the Water Witch*, written in the dark months before Ceauşescu's overthrow, and Marin Sorescu's *Poems Selected by Censorship* are two examples of "drawer poetry," though they are very different in approach.

Ieronim is aware that "the century was breaking in half" and "a never-resting star drew the earth out of its orbit." And she reaches into the past in an attempt to put the world back together. Most noticeably in the comma-less series of nouns jammed together, and from the temporal and cosmic patterns implied in the quotations just given, Ieronim re-creates the physical and mythical world of the Bârsa region of Transylvania. This tightly linked sequence of prose poems begins in the spirit and language of saga and fairy tale — the world of childish wonder, when her mother, boiling soap and handling the poisonous sodas, seems like a witch whose spells the child shrinks from learning; the bitter neighbor woman Ida lurking like the witch in Hansel and Gretel; "MARXENGELS-LENINSTALIN," bearded and apparently mouthless, mythical-looking, so that the child wonders aloud, "how do they eat?" and is quickly silenced.

Then, without quite losing that frame of reference, the poems blend in oral history from her elders, the "once upon a time" of legend becoming the broader, more opulent, more generous world of gowns, chocolates, festivals, Paris, Vienna. Her Uncle Fritz repastes the calendar's "days into next year using the days from years gone by."

But though the child finds continuity and consolation in the sights and scents of the changing seasons, she begins to see the erosive effects of time — clocks and circles are major motifs in the book — and the years of oppression that wear away feast days, memories, even the words once used to describe them. The child learns the clipped and cautious language necessary for survival: "I know how to speak without moving my lips / my face motionless...." The water witch of Romanian folklore has been supplanted by the witch of the slang term connoting ruthless bad taste, a fearsome Russian woman, "the demon's hair permed into wire, her snout smeared with chemical rouge, a pistol in her boot, a train station clock on her wrist."

Yet the spirit of fairy tale does not quite die. A woman marred by imprisonment in Russia returns, and though she cannot by magic return to what she was and she and her husband live without hope and meaning, their beautiful, red-haired daughter "revealed ancient folk memories from the Rhine." And the witch-like Ida is transformed by the kiss of a little boy.

Nevertheless, the land and water are poisoned, literally and figuratively, and at the end the speaker prepares to leave the arc of the Carpathians, the circle of the Lord's protective arm withdrawn so that she and her family are "Totally naked suspended in the moment."

After the constricted and oppressive atmosphere of *The Triumph of the Water Witch*), Ioana Ieronim's new volume available in English, *Omnivorous Syllables*, displays an expansiveness reaching "from Paradise to Inferno"; Manhattan skyscrapers feed on neutrinos; emotions swing between "deepest historical fear" and "highest historical ecstasy"; "signs will migrate / to the infinite."

As if to signal release from the Ceauşescu regime, physical settings range from Romania to the Pyrenees to Manhattan, and the first twenty-three poems in the collection were written in English. (Despite the title, eighteen are in a section headed "Lyrics before 1989.")

Poems are dedicated to poets from many countries. One has "a special exemption from the force of gravity"; another becomes the keeper of "the echoes of her people's songs"; another, on his cell phone, is "Transfigured by love"; others call their fellows from all over the world.

The power of the word may be, as the title insists, omnivorous, but these poems often find it difficult to express the plenitude of the universe, so that to write a poem one must "shut every window / except, perhaps, for one" and to learn from the example of the Spartan boy "how to write a poem / that you will e-mail in an instant / and still /have it written durable /sacred /like an ancient prayer carved in a rock."

Less problematic is the poet's belief in "a woman in full power / invulnerable" who may, like Romanian woman of the past whose powerful songs rang from mountain to mountain, "wail over the fate of my country / wash away its dirt with my tears / burn its vicious tatters." Or, in a poem written before 1989, a woman coming home from an ordinary shopping trip protects the pages of her manuscript from "celery's wet tentacles." At times it seems that nothing changes: "you just keep polishing / the teeth of the omnivorous syllables."

As in this case, flux, uncertainty, recurrence in history, the cosmos, and the relations of lovers recur. "Out of nothing things happen to be born," and "escalators clatter upward / mount for a thousandth time." Lovers are aware that "our bodies have burned several lives" and that, rather than unmarred and unmoved stones resting beside each other in a mountain stream, they may be like "apples rolling apart in the tall never harvested grass." Love is "Uncharted Territory" in which an embrace may be intensified by being delayed. And at its best, the lovers are "bigger than life / crossing toward one another" to "reenact the world's beginning."

Poems written before 1989 tend to be less expansive and personal than those written later. In the ironic "Pastoral," Ieronim asserts that evil is invisible when it doesn't exist — and when it does. "Certainty" is a decoy, created by a mad and savage god, and silence can be seen as victory. Of course, themes persist over the dividing line of 1989, and I have interwoven quotations from both periods. And even in the later poems Ieronim recognizes that the human brain is hard-wired to see in terms of black and white, ignoring "undecipherable facts."

Still, there is a qualitative change in tone. And much as one could wish to ignore recent history and to concentrate on aesthetic qualities, it will be a long time before we are able to do so.

Most of Marin Sorescu's *Censored Poems* were written in Romania before 1989 at a time when, as Sorescu writes, "The prison for ironists / was bursting at the seams." Nothing else was full. A butcher is denounced for saying that he has no meat. In frigid hospitals, there is ice in the bedpans and the brain surgeon has to bring his own candle to have light to operate. Death is an economic boon to the state, saving on pensions and food.

When Sorescu moves out of the Ceaușescu period, the world is no less grim. Vlad the Impaler speaks of a victim "Transpierced, in agony ... like manure on a fork." Martyrs, their bodies "Fed to bestial mud," produce no miracle. The Crucifixion does not result in Resurrection, for "through all the endless sleep of death, / an ingrown toenail jabs."

As the brief quotations show, Sorescu's language is blunt, largely monosyllabic — "no wrapping paper, no baroque ornament" — as if there were no time for circumlocution or evasion of harsh facts or even complex grammatical structures. There is undeniable power in "With minds in manacles, shaven-headed, / we move cautiously, always on tiptoe, / not to offend some thug."

Elsewhere, the directness can seem more flat than forceful. The brain surgeon opens the skull to find a question, "What the bloodsucking hell?" This may be a justifiable emotional response, but it is a very weak last line. And some poems, like "Landscape," are not exactly bad, but the imagery of skulls and fear ridden like a horse are not terribly compelling.

The larger question, not only about Sorescu's poems but about all of the literature resurrected after the fall of Communist regimes in 1989, is not merely how many variations on even this once compelling theme readers can stand. More important, as the horror and black comedy of this period recede — to be replaced, of course, by different horrors — is the question of how many of these works will have enough energy and originality to speak to readers ignorant of the circumstances which occasioned them. Every reader forms a jury, and most of the juries are as yet unimpanelled.

There may not be much more recovered poetry. Writers with bad filing systems cannot recover their work. And Adam Sorkin notes that "there was surprisingly little drawer poetry, because much eventually could be gotten into print, perhaps a bit injured but not terribly eviscerated" (See also Mircea Martin in Vianu). And some supposedly "drawer poetry" may have been written afterward to establish the secret dissident bona fides of establishment writers. But the situation had an effect even on work that could be published before 1989. Grete Tartler was born in 1948 and knew only communism. In her "Sahel," words wither into skulls that, however desiccated, somehow live and confront the poet as the poet confronts them in a stand-off that is not at all sterile. While these lines could be read in the modernist tradition of distrust of the decay of language (cf. T. S. Eliot's *Four Quartets*), the political connotations for Romanian poets are inescapable

Mircea Dinescu, born two years later, is angrier and more direct. "Manuscript Found in a Bottle Lamp" ends with the abbreviated conditional syllogism to the effect that if it were permissible to eat idiots, intellectuals would be less popular at butcher shops.

In the Nineties, when intellectuals were less often on the plat du jour, some writers in Romania, as in other former communist countries, felt obliged to devote time that might have gone to writing to party politics, the diplomatic corps, and other kinds of public service in order to help create a democratic society.

Now writers are free to publish what they like, when and if they can. Of course, as Petre Ghelmez points out, although political censorship is dead, "we have economic, commercial censorship now ... and the censorship of bad taste" (Vianu). And now poets are free to divide themselves not so much into conformists and dissidents (though some of those divisions are perpetuated by the latter group) as into schools and periods, most conveniently by decades. The Sixties group was described as "the old elephants" by one young poet. During the difficult years of Communist rule, Magda Cârneci says, they attempted to link with modernist writers before World War II as a way of escaping from socialist realism. Carmen Mușat thinks that the project of modernism was never fulfilled in Romania and that in her country World War II ended only in 1989.

The Seventies poets, according to Adam Sorkin, the major American translator of Romanian writing, "tended to be less spontaneous in their lyrical revelation and less experimental, more culturally centered, more self-disciplined and critical, more guarded and restrained, yet more self-confident" (Sorkin, "'We Do Not Know Anything Else,' p. 6). Major women poets who emerged in this decade were Daniela Crăsnaru, Denisa Comănescu, Ioana Ieronim, and Liliana Ursu (Sorkin, "Too Much"). Others include Adrian Popescu, Ion Mircea, Dinu Flamand, Grete Tartler, Mircea Dinescu, Nicolae Prelipceanu, Angela Marinescu, and Doina Uricariu.

The generation of the Eighties, called the "blue jeans generation" group, was dominated by writers who embrace varieties of postmodernism, also termed "young wolves." Their ranks include Gheorghe Crăciun and his friends Mircea Nedelciu, Gheorghe Iova, Ioan Flora, and Ion Bogdan Lefter, and the poets Magda Cârneci, Traian T. Coșovei, Nichita Danilov, Mariana Marin, Marta Petreu, Elena Štefoi, Mircea Cărtărescu, and Liviu Ioan Stoiciu. And many others.

Given the political climate of the Eighties, issuing manifestoes would have been unwise if not impossible, but Magda Cârneci finds that the group had, and have, in common "the refusal of the 'high,' pure, abstract modernist forms; a new opening towards the surrounding reality, towards the 'authenticity' of the real human person; the striv[ing] to regain and express all the levels (biological, biographical, sexual, social, cultural, spiritual etc.) of human existence; a new 'realistic' style affirming the democratization of the artistic language...." (Cârneci, Art) Looking outward, she argues that "postmodernism encourages a state of mind offering a chance to a faster and normal integration of this cultural area into the international context." (Marcel Cornis-Pope offers a broad historical context as well as a detailed examination of the work of individual writers in *The Unfinished Battles*.)

As Adam Sorkin says, the work of the "Eightyists" "was always implicitly political, rather obviously so when foregrounding and deconstructing the slogans and phrases of official collective life, less apparently so when alluding to the Western pop music, movies, or TV that the government tried to keep out of this progressively closed society" (Sorkin, "Too Much"). However, they escaped censorship, for the most part, because their work was too oblique and apparently parodic to seem threatening. As Lefter said in a November 2000 conference on postmodernism, much of that writing had a subversive role, but it undercut the pretensions of art and was not politically dissident. Now some critics ask whether they take a position at all, and at a Café Europa conference on postmodernism, a majority of the speakers dismissed the term as dated or meaningless or called for an emphasis on ethics to counterbalance that on aesthetics. Lefter argued that we have to relativize something and called for a position of "limited relativity." But they were — and seem still to be — a cohesive group, and their work is reportedly much anthologized and therefore canonized. For example, Lefter is director of *Observator cultural*, an important weekly, and author and editor of several books published by Editura Paralela 45; Crăciun is associate editor of *Observator cultural* and one of the major editors at Editura Paralela; and these two men and Monica Spiridon have edited that publishing house's *Experiment in Post-War Romanian Literature*.

In addition to serving as president of the board of the International Center for Contemporary Art (CIAC) in Bucharest, Magda Cârneci is co-director of the art magazine *Atelier* and is associated with *Observator cultural* and Editura Paralela as editor, as critic (*Art of the '80s in Eastern Europe: Texts on Postmodernism*), as deputy director of the Romanian Cultural Institute in Paris, and as poet. If her *Poeme/Poems* in the Editura Paralela 45 Gemini bilingual edition are at all representative of her work and beyond that of the Eighties generation, then it is clear that postmodernism means something very different to Romanians than it does to Americans.

The book draws from three sources: *O Tacere Asurzitoare/A Deafening Silence*, published in 1985; *Haosmos/Chaosmos*, published in 1992; and *Poeme Politice/Political Poems*, written between 1985 and 1997 and published in magazines over the past ten years. (Some are now more readily available to American readers in her *Chaosmos* [White Pine, 2006]). The poems of 1985 could be used to illustrate the situation of writers before 1989. Even the lines are more constricted than the poems of 1992, although both periods share a vocabulary — "swirling," "swarms," "absorbed" and dozens of participles of intense action — and images like blood, absorption into cosmic or oceanic vastness, a sense that "disorder reaches perfection," that in "the cosmic dream ... Vision and Extinction are one and the same" and "disintegration ... is reintegration ... fusion ... is confusion." The later poems may remind an American reader of Whitman, though of a post–Einsteinian celebrator of the body hydrodynamic rather than electric.

The political poems, though recognizably in the same voice, are reminiscent less of Whitman or postmodernism than of the nineteenth century Central European poets of burgeoning national and linguistic consciousness. "Requiem in a Classical Style," dedicated to "those who died in Bucharest, December 1989," could, with obvious changes in vocabulary and attitude, have been written in the aftermath of 1848. The poet gives up, in a violent blazon of body parts, everything so that the country

> may awaken, rise up, redeem yourself,
>
> o homeland, that you may bear us again,
> but now born unsullied, purer —
> o bear us for one last time.

The generation of the Nineties contains, according to Ieronim, a number of very talented writers (See also Braga.) For the most part, they are less violently energetic and certainly less cosmic than Cârneci. Some of these whom I was able to read in translation are Iustin Panţa (1964–2001), Ruxandra Cesereanu (b. 1963), Saviana Stănescu (b. 1967), and Ion Manolescu (b. 1968). In the work I have seen Panţa writes short, highly compressed prose pieces, alternating between indented dramatic scenes and longer-line presentations of the setting and milieu — often the privations imposed by the former regime — and ruminations on the significance of the event or relationship from a perspective later in time. The ending of "A Confession" encapsulates this method: "I went away then, and here I am now, near you, telling you this tale." The content or meaning of the tale is rarely conclusive. The relationship existed; it was exciting, though not always transforming; it is past. In "Prologue" (like "Confession," seen in manuscript and apparently not published in English), the reality of the woman observed is like

> an earthen pitcher left outside overnight...
> in the morning you may find in it part of last night,
> as a liquid forgotten there; (exactly as much as could enter in that
>   pitcher — one litre, two...
> as if the pitcher would have been left mouth downwards,

and darkness was caught inside as in a snare) -
for the rest, the landscape is, as you well know it from always.

As poems like "Hysteria," "Ugly, Alone, and Violet," "Desolate Horizon (Antipoetry)," and "Dissection" promise, Cesereanu's imagery and vision are far more violent and disturbing than Panţa's. Mud, blood, decay, and, in Sorkin's term, "neurotic fantasy" characterize these poems which reach not into memory but into fantasy, almost hallucination. "Father," which may or may not echo Sylvia Plath, ends

> Father, your dreams plunge
> in the mouth of a sewer,
> where the animals wait for me.
> My love will keep on decaying for ages and ages
> until I've fallen among the roots.
> My life is running in the pipe [*Transylvanian*].

Cesereanu's *Lunacies*, her first full-length collection to be published in America, is almost self-consciously labeled. Although the title sequence of fifty-nine relatively short poems is separated from the half-dozen longer poems which follow, all clearly come from the same vintage. But rather than Keats's blushful Hippocrene, this is a brew, like Frost's of death and blight, compounded of blood, darkness, screams, mutilated and mutilating birds, ravening dogs, moons that threaten and are threatened, nuns twinned with insects, and angels more like furies that would disturb Salvador Dalí.

The Dalí allusion might seem fanciful, but just over halfway through the sequence a "knife slashes night's armor across the eyeball," a clear reference to the Dalí-Buñuel film, and "The stubs of the trees' fingers wear ruby rings," an image worthy of Dalí at his best.

It is difficult but not impossible to describe what Cesereanu is doing; it is much more difficult to discuss why she is doing it. One clue may come from the recurrent Christian symbols, especially those that invert the attributes of the Virgin Mary. In the first poem of the sequence, the speaker finds "here in my womb, the angel-homunculus," and throughout the volume's remaining poems the generative power becomes, for the male, threatening snakes, and for the female dark, deathly, a "coffin" from which "babies rush pell-mell to the slaughterhouse."

In the middle of the sequence, it begins to look as though the speaker is on a pilgrimage or quest that may lead to something, but by the last poem, more or less in the form of a cross, the idea of redemption seems only another means of torture.

Yet the final effect of the volume does not seem quite despairing because of the furious energy that comes in large part from the involuted and repeated images, so that in "The Fool of Delights," which seems to be addressed to an inverted savior, a "phosphorescent heart sizzles" and "the soul with its little milk teeth / nibbles death, crunches death, / beheading the angels who flutter drunkenly, / come to herald your coming." That much energy cannot seem entirely futile.

Stănescu's poems and plays, which I have seen only in manuscript translations, are less violent but no less fanciful. In "Haunting Deep Within You," for example, the speaker inhabits and ultimately infects the blood of her lover. And the sequence about the "Mindog" concludes with "Angel and Demon" linked in the "Poe Try flat" with a whole imagined menagerie and, incidentally, linking to angelic references in work by a number of Romanian women poets. In her plays *The Inflatable Apocalypse* and *Outcast (a text to be performed)*, characters with generic names circle around each other.

Manolescu is the youngest writer included in *The Phantom Church and Other Stories from Romania*; his "Paraphernalia" is set in what seems to be an American town, with WASP names like Robinson, Tittleton, Grant, and so on, though according to the editors there are many references to Ceaușescu's last years in power. They go on to characterize his stories as "based on a technique he calls 'phantasmatic,' which connects literature to pop art forms, such as advertisements, comic strips, and video clips."

These writers may not be representative of the generation in its thirties, but their distinct visions may indicate some of the boundaries.

The distinctions between generations are to some degree complicated by regional divisions. Ernest Latham, an expert on Romanian history and politics, points out that Romanian cultural life is much less centered on the capital than that of most European countries because only Bucharest was part of nineteenth century Romania. Transylvanian cities like Sibiu, Cluj, and Timișoara were heavily influenced by German and Hungarian culture and politically dominated by Austria-Hungary; Iași was influenced by Ukrainian and Jewish cultures and Constanța by Greek culture. Each region is very much aware of its cultural heritage and its differences from the rest of the country. Two recent anthologies base their principles of selection not on literary schools or on generations but on region. In fact, *Transylvanian Voices*, though it concentrates primarily on writers from Cluj, translates poems from what were once the dominant languages in the region: Romanian, Hungarian, and German. *City of Dreams and Whispers* presents poets from Iași and Moldavia. Iași was home of the national poet Mihai Eminescu; it is now the home of the iconoclastic writers of Club 8, including, Sorkin notes, Radu Andriescu, Mariana Codruț, and Ovidiu Nimigean. Each of these three has poems in *City of Dreams and Whispers* calling attention to or questioning language. Nimigean wonders

> wherefrom comes that feast of metaphors
> in a country so poor wherefrom
> such perverse refinement of enjambment
> rhythm and alliteration
> wherefrom the virgin-bride freshness of comparison
>   ("The Rhetorical Drug").
> Codruţ warns
> don't let yourselves be taken in
> by the folkloristic props
>
> words are a land
> full of too many pledges ["Untitled"].

And Andriescu's "The Sour Cherry Pie"—like some of his other poems, using as epigraph a reference to American blues—picks up at the end a motif that runs throughout the poem in

> those migratory lines
> commonly known as
> self-referential.

While images and motifs may cross old boundaries, each region has its own publishing houses and magazines, and some of the most significant journals, those most open to new work, are published outside Bucharest. Cluj, for example, has several journals. The newest is *Apostrof*, which began in 1990, publishes poetry, prose, critical essays and, as Cesereanu puts it, "'files' of literary history, presenting unknown or censored documents from the life of the writers." *Echinox*, edited by Stefan Borbely and Corin Braga of Babes-Bolyai University, is multi-cultural, publishing studies in Romanian, Hungarian, German, French, English, and Italian. In 2001, *Echinox* continued in its traditional form, but it has added *Echinox Journal*, in which current books are reviewed, and an on-line forum for cultural debates.

Steaua (star) a review of "Romanian Literature, Culture, and Spirituality," has just undergone editorial re-structuring. It began 1949 as *Literary Almanac*, becoming *Steaua* in 1965 after the censors rejected *Hyperion* because it sounded too cosmopolitan. From the beginning, its editors tried to foster an aesthetic rather than a political viewpoint and concentrated on world literature. After censorship was relaxed in the 1960s, they published Romanian writers like Lucian Blaga and Ion Barbu, who earlier had been silenced. However, it remained anti-dogmatic, and until 1989 it was an outlet for leading writers and for a cosmopolitan viewpoint.

After 1989, it faced competition from other magazines with similar editorial outlooks and forward-looking staff. *Steaua* was not in tune with postmodernism, and it became, in Ruxandra Cesereanu's term, "dusty." Under the editorship of Adrian Popescu, beginning in November, 2000, the journal will become more flexible, encouraging debates on such controversial subjects as the direction of Romanian culture, the relationship between the center and the provinces, and the battle between literary generations. It will also present new work by leading writers, portraits of writers from the diaspora, and books from other countries as well as Romania. And in each issue the editor will confront an important current topic. Some of these will be the rejection or acceptance of postmodernism, the process of surviving by culture during the Communist regime (Cesereanu and Popescu disagree on this issue), and the battle for the literary canon. And there will be poetry and fiction — but no poetry for six months in order to make a sharp break with the old version of the journal and to discourage amateurs, for, Cesereanu said, "Every Romanian is a poet, especially in Cluj."

Journals published in Iaşi include *Literary Conversations, Time,* and *The Poem*. Many of the writers included in Adam Sorkin's *City of Dreams and Whispers*, which gives a brief account of the city's literary tradition, are or have been associated with one or more of these journals and, as students, professors, or both at the University of Iaşi.

Euphorion: Review of Literature and Art, based in Sibiu and supported by the Writers' Union, was founded in 1989. A handsomely produced tabloid, it publishes original work in Romanian and reprints and translations of work in other languages, especially English, French, and German. *Transilvania* is a more traditional journal, and *Saeculum* is an academic journal. Hermann issues bilingual editions of poetry and fiction and translations of American works; Anglophone Academic Society of Romania publishes books on teaching English, the history of ideas, philosophy, doctoral dissertations, and other scholarly works.

Still another region is represented in *Sorescu's Choice*, which feature ten young, or youngish, poets (no birth date is given for half; the youngest pair were forty when the volume was published) associated with Marin Sorescu's home province of Oltenia and its capital Craiova, described in rather suspiciously glowing, almost chauvinistic, terms in Claudia Cochina's "Craiova Seen from the Wagon." The translators are ten poets from Northern Ireland, which Sorescu visited in 1991.

John Fairleigh notes in his introduction that "many of the poems" (none dated) were written before the fall of Ceauşescu in 1989, and that therefore "little sense of time and place is betrayed." Instead, the poets tend to focus on the inner life with a view that is "somber, passively resigned to the inhospitable natural world and the other beings within it."

Most of the poems are somber enough — Grigore Balanescu's poems are full of stone and ice; death, both word and concept, echoes throughout those of Carmen Firan; Ion Hirghidus's of blood, bones, stars falling "rotten to earth," and a "black city" being gnawed by rats. Patrel Berceanu writes of "stars rotting" and, even more depressingly, of the fact that Romanians are "a melancholy people. / We hear poetry at the party congress." Cold, scarcity, privation testify not too obliquely to conditions under the Ceauşescu regime in many of the poems, especially in Hirghidus's "Tomorrow Is Piously Blooming" and Berceanu's "Food Chain."

Very few of the poets give much sense of other beings except individual lovers or ex-lovers. The focus is very tight — on a door, a frozen windowpane, creases in clothes, though in contrast there are many appeals to the stars, silent, remote or near, rotten or whole.

Ion Munteanu's poems have a kind of wit and edge absent from most of the other poets. In "The Poet in His Field" and "Open Letter," he writes of the poet as elusive, perhaps dangerous, "A forceless force / To be reckoned with — so long, that is, as such a thing / Is not against your own interests." In "No Fears of Dying Young," Constantin Preda writes that even "if these words are only poetry.... My goblet, throbbing with a mystery wine, brings back / The first time breasts were ever bared / In my oil-lamp's rosy glow" — in one of the few positive views of love in this collection.

Even Hirghidus finds some consolation in poetry, but Florea Miu presents the most positive view: the poem is "a rest in the clarity / of vowels, the victor's satisfaction, / weary after the wars with himself." And in "Song with Closed Eyes," he closes them in order to be able "to say / that everything — but absolutely everything —/ is possible." Ironically, then, the strongest hope for poetry arises in the bleakest circumstances.

Still, Bucharest is the largest center of literary activity for obvious political, economic, and demographic reasons. It is less influenced by Hungarian, Saxon, and other cultures. It is large enough to support the privately owned and self-sustaining *Observator cultural*, a thirty-two page tabloid-sized weekly, national in scope, founded in February 2000. Editor Carmen Muşat says that "our main purpose is to establish a vivid dialogue between Romanian and European culture, between Romanian and American culture as well," and especially with intellectuals in other countries dominated by totalitarian communism. To do so, the journal reviews foreign books and does frequent reviews of cultural issues in the world press as well as devoting sections to debates on cultural topics, to philosophy, to theater and film, and to interviews. Perhaps more important is the commitment to fostering young writers and intellectuals, whatever their literary allegiances. In fact, Muşat says, *Observator cultural* is less interested in generations or schools than in work of good quality. Moreover, the editors want "to provoke an attitude towards artistic and political events, to make people think about their place within society and about their reaction towards culture (as an artistic, historical, and political phenomenon)." That, she says, "distinguishes us from the other literary reviews on the Romanian market at the moment. We refuse to think about culture only in its aesthetic dimensions, which include literature, music, visual arts, theater, and movies."

Mușat and Ioana Ieronim seem bullish about the prospects for Romanian culture, but other views of Romanian literature and culture, though expressed with equal vigor, tend to be cautious, even captious. Aside from having too many poets, Cesereanu thinks that Romanian culture, or perhaps the administration of culture and the logistics of delivering it, has three major problems. First, it is implosive, not explosive—there is no spine, no general cultural vision. Second, it is inoperant, backward-looking, full of peasants and folklore rather than considering the current condition. Third, it is too choleric, full of fury to no avail, controlled by schools and vogues that subordinate real values to generation politics and are too imitative of literature in other countries. The penchant for imitation may be connected to Gheorghe Crăciun's view that "Modern Romania has always been a country of the forms without a background." He goes on to say that "Romanians get bored so very quickly with the new forms. We always want something else and always something exclusive. I think that experimental liability of Romanian literature is a fundamental component, with a serious tradition" (Crăciun).

Western Europeans seem to feel, Cesereanu thinks, that Central and Eastern Europeans will produce a whole new kind of novel, but there is little publicity for the good work that is being published. One of the problems is getting work translated. One experienced translator of other literatures into Romanian thinks that quality has declined since 1989 because the formerly rigorous certification process has been abolished, so that anyone can claim to be a translator. There seems to be less of a problem, because there is less of a profit motive, with translations from Romanian. The University of Iași has a translation program, and dedicated translators like Fleur Adcock and Brenda Walker in England and Adam Sorkin in America have worked with Romanian writers, especially the poets, to bring their work to Anglophone readers.

Of course, translators and publishers are still trying to catch up with the youngest writers and the most recent work of their elders. Most of the books available in the library of the University of Oklahoma, however recent the copyright date, represent work done in the 1980s. The most recent volume to appear in the West is Ieronim's *The Triumph of the Water Witch*, and it was written more than ten years ago, and until the appearance of *Omnivorous Syllables* translations of her work I have seen in manuscript are of work 1979–

1987. The companion anthologies *Romanian Poets of the '80s and '90s* and *Romanian Fiction in the '80s and '90s*, are published by Editura Paralela 45 (www.stormloader.com/paralela45. See especially the collections Gemini and Mediana), are not listed by the major online bookstores or even in the World Catalogue and therefore are almost inaccessible, at least to American readers. Fortunately, the Center for Romanian Studies (www.romanianstudies.ro) has offices in the U.K. and the U.S., and its anthologies of Transylvanian and of Iași poets are more easily acquired, as is *The Phantom Church and Other Stories from Romania*.

As might be expected, views of the current situation in Romania range from Cesereanu's view of implosion to Gheorghe Crăciun's view that "the audience that should have been watching the show were missing, being too busy with the literary gossip and making plans for the first date of the Romanian literature to the world," while for the past decade "Romanian literature seems to have fallen into skepticism" because of the lingering corruptions due to communism (Crăciun). Sorkin notes that "the contemporary poetry sections get smaller every year." Still, he says, "the impression of high quality lingers, and many of the writers of the communist years have produced major new collections [during the Nineties], while new voices speak new ways" ("Too Much"). Others, like Ioana Ieronim, are even more hopeful, pointing to new writers who are doing excellent work.

This generation may be less burdened by the past, but they and their elders have to work in a context. The political and economic situation in Romania may be uncertain, but the cultural infrastructure — book and magazine publishing, performance and exhibit space, and foundations like the International Center for Contemporary Art to sustain activity in all the arts — seems to be sound. Writers may not be able to afford to eat in the dining room of the Writers Club, housed in a mansion built more than a century ago for the aristocracy, but the people I spoke to seemed, without forgetting the past, to look to the future with considerable confidence.

Works Cited

An Anthology of Romanian Woman Poets. Edited by Adam J. Sorkin and Kurt W. Treptow. East European Monographs, No. 197, and New York: Romanian Cultural Foundation Publishing House, 1994.

Braga, Corin. *Ten Studies in Archetypology*. Cluj: Dacia Publishing House, 1999.

Cârneci, Magda. *Art of the 1980s in Eastern Europe: Texts on Postmodernism*. Pitești: Editura Paralela 45, 1999.

_____. *Poeme/Poems*. Translated by Adam J. Sorkin with the poet. Pitești: Editura Paralela 45, 1999.

Cassian, Nina. *Take My Word for It.* New York: W. W. Norton, 1998.
Cesereanu, Ruxandra. "Feature Interview" and selected poems. *The Bitter Oleander*, vol. 7, no. 1 (2001), 45–74.
_____. *Lunacies.* Trans. Adam J. Sorkin and Ruxandra Cesereanu, with Claudia Litvinchievici. New York: Spuytin Duyvil/Meeting Eyes Bindery, 2004.
Cornis-Pope, Marcel. *The Unfinished Battles: Romanian Postmodernism Before and After 1989.* Iaşi: Polirom, 1996.
Crăciun, Gheorghe. "Postmodern Tale With an Uncertain Ghost." Paper delivered at Café Europa, Bucharest, 25 November 2000.
Crăsnaru, Daniela. *The Grand Prize and Other Stories.* Trans. Adam J. Sorkin with the author. Evanston, IL: Northwestern University Press, 2004.
_____. *Letters from Darkness.* Translated by Fleur Adcock. Oxford: Oxford University Press, 1991.
Dinescu, Mircea. *Exile on a Peppercorn.* Translated by Andrea Deletant and Brenda Walker. London: Forest Books, 1985.
Ieronim, Ioana. *Omnivorous Syllables: Lyrics 1990–2006.* Illustrated by Tom Brândus and Adrian Tăbăcaru. Bucharest: Liternet, 2006. No price given. ISBN 973-7893-49-2. Available as free .pdf file, http://editura.liternet.ro.
_____. *The Triumph of the Water Witch.* Translated by Adam J. Sorkin with Ioana Ieronim. London: Bloodaxe Books, 2000.
Manea, Norman. "On Clowns: The Dictator and the Artist." *Literary Review*, 35:1 (1991), 5–25.
Negrici, Eugen. *Literature and Propaganda in Communist Romania.* Translated by Mihai Codreanu. Bucharest: The Romanian Cultural Foundation Publishing House, 1999. Negrici includes short and pointed biographies of the major literary and political figures of the era.
The Phantom Church and Other Stories from Romania. Edited and translated by Georgiana Farnoaga and Sharon King. Pittsburgh: University of Pittsburgh Press, 1996.
Rad, Ilie. "The 'Stylistics' of Censorship." polito.ubbduj.ro/EAST/East_3/rad.html.
Sorescu, Marin. *Censored Poems.* Trans. John Hartley Williams and Hilde Ottschovki. Higreen, Tarset, Northumberland, and Chester Springs, PA: Bloodaxe Books and Dufour Editions, 2001 and 2002.
_____. *Sorescu's Choice.* Edited by John Fairleigh. Highgreen, Tarset, Northumberland and Chester Springs, PA: Bloodaxe Books and Dufour Editions, 2001 and 2002.
Sorkin, Adam J. *City of Dreams and Whispers: an Anthology of Contemporary Poets of Iaşi.* Portland, OR: Center for Romanian Studies, 1998.
_____. "Hard Lines: Romanian Poetry, Truth, and Heroic Irony Under the Ceauşescu Dictatorship." *Literary Review*, 35:1 (1991), 26–33.
_____. Personal communication, 16 February 2001. Quotes not otherwise attributed are taken from this message.
_____. "Too Much," unpublished essay.
_____. "'We Do Not Know Anything Else': A Translator's Reflections on Contemporary Romanian Poetry." *Pennsylvania English*, 16:2 (Spring/Summer 1992), 1–11.
Tartler, Grete. *Orient Express.* Translated by Fleur Adcock. Oxford: Oxford University Press, 1989.
Transylvanian Poets: An Anthology of Contemporary Poets of Cluj-Napoca. Edited and Translated by Adam J. Sorkin and Liviu Bleoca, assisted by Emese Egyed. Iaşi: Center For Romanian Studies, 1997.
Vianu, Lidia. *Censorship in Romania.* Budapest: Central European University Press, 1998. Interviews, comments, and poems by Romanian writers confronted by censors during the Communist regime.

6

Transition — And After? And Beyond?
Geopolitics, Marketing and Literary Anxieties in the New Central Europe

After the fireworks and the heady speeches delivered in the spring of 2004 when the European Union expanded to the borders of Russia and Romania, from the Baltic to the Balkans, both the fifteen older members of the European Union and the ten new ones will have to face the uncertainties expansion will bring. And so will the countries outside the fences that are supposed to make good neighbors.

On a recent trip through Central Europe a few weeks before the new members were officially welcomed into the fold, I talked with people from both new and older EU states and discovered, along with hope and enthusiasm, some uneasiness about what expansion would bring.

For those previously inside the pale, the chief anxiety had to do with migration. The most obvious problem is the possible immigration of unwashed and unemployable hordes from the East, especially those who want to use the new member states as stepping stones to the more prosperous West.

This fear is not entirely due to paranoia. A former employee of the British Embassy in Bratislava told me several years ago that most of his work day was consumed by Roma (gypsy) applications for asylum. And according to an Open Democracy report, many of those immigrating to Hungary, legally and otherwise, "do not see [it] as their final destination."

The new ten have been scrambling to address this issue by tightening their borders, with help from the EU, and by changing visa regulations. Slovakia, for example, recently denounced a free movement agreement between itself and Cuba and the former Soviet Republics. The older members of the EU, meanwhile, have placed restrictions on migrants from new member states. Under these restrictions, migrants can receive limited benefits for two years, though some countries may extend the limits to as long as nine years.

Migration poses other problems, too. The new ten worry that many of their citizens will leave, though various studies point to low emigration rates, especially among unemployed or low-income workers. A more pressing concern is the possible brain-drain of highly trained young professionals to the older and wealthier states.

Meanwhile, some in "old Europe" worry less about who is coming in — partly because, with declining populations, workers are desperately needed — than in what is going out. One headline wondered whether the new EU members will mean the end of farming in Scotland. Some worry, as Frankfurt entrepreneur Wolfgang Klotz puts it, that faltering economies like East Germany's will get worse "because even those companies still located in Dresden or Leipzig might transfer their production lines to the Czech Republic or Slovakia." In fact, the day before the ten joined the EU, German Economics Minister Wolfgang Clement confronted this issue, threatening cuts in subsidies if the new states did not increase taxes because, in Deutsche Welle's paraphrase, "Germany cannot finance low tax rate systems outside its borders."

Not everyone in the new member states is altogether happy about the change. Some fear high taxes; some, like Hungarian pig farmers and milk producers, worry that they will be unable to compete with their counterparts in the West. Others worry that their countries will become a source of cheap labor or, as the Slovene writer and political critic Aleš Debeljak puts it, a target for carpetbaggers; some fear that national autonomy, won so recently, will be lost. Some have grown weary of EU demands, warnings, and threats of punishment, since, as even some EU officials admit off the record, "applicants have been scrutinized more closely than existing member states" (Debeljak) like Germany and France, which have not met budget regulations.

And there are more practical fears. Hungarians in Transylvania, the Ukraine, and Serbia will find it more difficult to cross borders unless they are granted Hungarian citizenship. Klotz predicts that descendants of Germans expelled in 1945 from new member countries will, now that Poland and the Czech Republic are under EU laws, sue for restitution of expropriated property.

Then, of course, there are centuries-old ethnic rivalries. In Bratislava, for example, a Hungarian diplomat told me that he wanted to emphasize the thousand-year common history of the Slovak and Hungarian peoples. Privately, I wondered if this was a good idea, since at one time Slovakia was called Upper Hungary and the Slovak language could not be used in any school. These kinds of wounds are not easily healed.

Still, every new member state conducted a successful referendum on entry into the EU, and there seems to be a good deal of hope that membership will bring some measure of prosperity and order. As Debeljak put it, "the interests of Slovenian citizens might be more comprehensively safeguarded if they are protected not only by the Slovenian constitution alone but also by European regulations and laws."

In fact, some of the most forward-looking Central and Eastern Europeans urge that the EU border be moved still farther east. Alexandr Vondra, a Czech diplomat, argues that "the only way is really to seriously contribute to the stabilization of the European periphery, in the South, in the East, because otherwise I think that there is a serious threat that the instability from the East and South could be imported into the core." The alternative route, Debeljak complains, is that "instead of investing its joint efforts in creating a federal Europe with a high quality of life, the European Union is becoming more and more like the 'gated communities' of America, where the inhabitants of wealthy neighborhoods keep their territory ethnically and socioeconomically homogeneous by means of armed security guards, high real-estate prices, and limited access."

Several of the new border states have taken steps to ensure that those outside can at least look through the gates and even, at least culturally, participate in the new Europe. Debeljak has called for Slovenia to establish a University of Southeastern Europe so that "Slovenia could define itself as a European bridge for transferring knowledge, critical observation, information, and skills to the less fortunate parts of the former Yugoslavia and the Balkans, rather than shunning the region as if Slovenia is a kind of cordon sanitaire between the stable and unstable regions..."

A recent conference on "Border Regions in Transition" offered perspectives and precedents, if no solutions. The conference was led by a group of geographers and political scientists and was held in locations in Hungary, Croatia, Serbia, Romania, and the Ukraine. Among the issues discussed were the developing industry in border towns, the effect of EU enlargement on Romania and Moldova, and "The Roots of a New 'North Great Plain' Identity."

That kind of cultural awareness was also evident at the conference of

"Intellectuals for a United Europe" held in Debrecen, Hungary, the weekend before expansion, with participants from Slovakia, the Ukraine, Romania, and Hungary. The organizers concentrated on spiritual and cultural matters. There was an exhibit of books and folk art from the region, a concert of regional music, an ecumenical church service, and a series of papers on science, politics, music, language, and education. The organizers called the meeting a hopeful beginning of "higher educational, economic, cultural, church, and scientific relations" among the four countries.

Ultimately, the hope is that Slovakia, the Ukraine, Romania, and Hungary will enter into some sort of partnership. The idea is, that by banding together, they can achieve an economic, cultural, and political influence that none could achieve alone. Romania and the Ukraine are as eager for membership as the other two countries, now in the EU, but none of them, or any of the other new and prospective members, wants to be completely overshadowed by the older member states.

Literary entrepreneurs had not waited for the politicians to work things out. In the last decade of the twentieth century, the mood of Central and Eastern European writers and publishers may not have been despairing, but it certainly seemed subdued. State subsidies had disappeared, and while writers were free to say anything and publishers to print it, the distribution system was in disarray; dissidents with nothing to dissent from lost much of their attraction for Western publishers and readers; and no one seemed to know how to improve the situation. Now, judging from admittedly incomplete evidence from the 2003 Frankfort Book Fair and subsequent correspondence with publishers, the literary world of that region seems to be not only more hopeful but more proactive in bringing ideas and technologies from the West and in using them to bring their writers to a western audience.

Before publishers and literary organizations could begin to export the work of their writers, however, they had to make it possible for international readers to acquire them, and to do this, they had to correct or, better still, ignore practices inherited from communist times. This requires not just a new frame of mind but new people, and, according to a Serb writer who falls between generations, young writers as well as publishers are much less interested in drinking, smoking, and groping and more interested in getting down to work.

For example, Croatia has not yet joined the EU, for various reasons, but some publishers are determined to enter the Western market. Valerij Jurešić of Faust Vrancic Ltd. may not be quite typical of the younger generation, for he seems to have more ideas and energy than are suitable for three or four people. He edited the first student newspaper in Croatia, ran an international literary festival for eight years, brought the first slam poetry competitions to his country, and sponsored the first contest for the best novel manuscript. Now he is trying to revolutionize Croatian publishing with KIS — books information system, or Croatian Books in Print, later expanded to include a monthly update.

He offers a barrage of arguments to show why this is both necessary and possible. Most important is the rapid growth of consumer spending in Croatia — twenty to twenty-five percent since the end of 2001. This is due in part to the stabilization of the banking system under the influence of Austrian and Italian banks, which have brought new products and services to the market and have forced Croatian banks to adapt to the new competition. This new confidence has benefited the book market which, as in all other former communist countries, had slumped badly. Book sales increased twenty percent, then slumped, but Jurešić expects a rebound by 2008.

Unlike other countries, subsidies from the Croatian government had not been cut under the Tudjman regime, though it was not at all clear who was getting how much and for what reasons. The new government has made the process more transparent, but only large and mid-sized publishers get much of the €3 to 4 million, and only to publish established writers.

Moreover, Jurešić says, the Ministry of Culture has not done enough to create a healthy market. Authors have had difficulty collecting royalties. And distribution is no better than in countries like Slovakia. Instead, the book business is in "the wild stage of capitalism." Publishers who have money act as though they have none, paying commissions to bookstores irregularly and in some cases creating monopolies for their lists through book clubs. He attributes some of the problems to strong government intervention which prevents the establishment of healthy relations based on the realities of the book market.

Jurešić hopes to change the whole process by means of Books in Print, which began as an on-line service (www.knjiga.hr) and is now available in hard copy for €60. It can connect booksellers to all publishers, not just the big ones, so that they can order books on demand, speed delivery time, and avoid the inefficient and borderline corrupt commission system. In 2003, the average bookshop carried from 1,000 to 3,000 titles from 100 to 250 publishers, and it was generally assumed that some 8,000 titles were available in Croatia. By 2003, the KIS catalogue made available 15,000 titles from 1,200 publishers, by 2006 the number of books listed in the database had risen to 22,000, and its website already had more hits than other Croatian web sites combined. KIS now issues a monthly magazine on books and publishing and Op.a (a Croatian abbreviation for "author's note" on a commercial basis, available on newsstands and by subscription. Every working day its website carries three to ten news items, more than 4,500 since its inception in 2002.

Beginning in 2004, KIS has generated weekly, monthly, and yearly bestseller lists of bookshop sales for the leading Croatian daily newspaper. In the same year, it established small on-line bookshops for publishers and booksellers, and at then end of 2006 it started a wholesale business, mostly for export.

Jurešić has faith in all the ramifications of a project that has not thus far worked, at least without state or other subsidies, in other Southeastern and Central European countries. Jurešić realizes that his project will have to survive without government subsidy since, in his view, the large publishers, who have influence at the Ministry, see his Books in Print as a threat to their domination of the market. He wants to rationalize and expand that market within his country, but of course publishers understand that foreign sales can mean larger audiences and therefore larger profits. Croatia has 4.5 million literate readers of the language; other former Yugoslav republics have another 15 million readers; and worldwide more than 3 million people can read Croatian. A Croatian Books in Print helps give Croatian writers a worldwide market presence.

Some writers from smaller languages, like Tomaž Šalamun or György Konrád, have managed to break out more or less independently, but lesser-known writers have had to be promoted by literary societies or publishers, both of which have, as a rule, funding from their governments or from foundations. For example, Beletrina, the student publishing house in Slovenia, issues a series of chapbook translations in various genres, though most of the fiction is excerpted from longer work. The Slovene Writers' Association publishes longer works, mostly by established writers but sometimes anthologies of the work of their juniors. But outside the country, these works are hard to come by.

There are some initiatives to get work translated and published in other languages and countries. For example, the Trubar Foundation, under joint sponsorship of Slovene PEN, the Slovene Writers' Association, and the Center for Slovenian Literature, with funds from the Ministry of Culture, will pay up to half of printing (but not translation) costs for the publication in translation of living and preferably established Slovenian writers.

The Hungarian Book Foundation will pay sixty to a hundred percent of translation costs, but not publication costs. Since its beginning in 1997, the Foundation has spent about $500,000 to support translation of roughly three hundred books — almost $1700 per grant — out of five hundred applications. Languages most popular for translation, twenty or more books in each, are

German, Bulgarian, Polish, Russian, and French, with only five in English. Of the 120 authors translated, the most popular have been Sándor Márai, Péter Esterházy, Péter Nádas, and Imre Kertész, each with more than a dozen translations. So far, 220 books have been published, and only fifteen cases did the publisher not produce the book on time or failed to publish it at all.

More and different material about Hungarian literature is now available from the website of Hungarian Literature Online (hlo.hu) which includes excerpts from newly translated volumes of poetry, interviews with writers like Imre Kertész, and news about prizes, book fairs, and other literary events.

More ambitious is the Romanian Liternet (liternet.ro). Razvan Penescu says that the project began in 1998, on a smaller scale, with Gusztav Demeter's website, in English, created to promote Romanian writing abroad. At the same time, Penescu began a newsletter, still circulated among his colleagues and to a group of 2,000 subscribers, about cultural events — movies, plays, concert, television programs — in the coming week. Later he added links to reviews, written by both volunteers and some of the most preeminent Romanian critics, in a special section of the site called Agenda, and in Atelier, poems and excerpts from prose works, together with music, photos and essays. Next Penescu and his colleagues established the e-publishing house Editura LiterNet which issues poetry, prose, and theater and film scripts (many of which have subsequently been produced) not only by well-known Romanian writers but new voices in Romanian literature — free on the internet in pdf files. So far Editura has issued more than 190 books to half a million readers (at the moment 600,000 downloads, with more than 1,000 downloads per day), and its translation section has issued books in English, French, German, and Hungarian, and translations from these languages into Romanian. The next project, "A Novel for the Nobel," will publish English translations of some excerpts from the Romanian prose, like all other Liternet material, free on the internet. This solves to a certain extent the problem of distribution in the West, especially in the U.S., faced by most publishers in Central and Eastern European countries.

Another innovative publishing venture is the CD, later issued in hard copy, *Inso(mno)lent P(r)ose*, edited by Nenad Velickovic of Sarajevo, and distributed at the Frankfort Book Fair, with full text in English, German, Bosnian, Serbo-Croatian, and Bulgarian, judged the best in a competition for writers born since 1969. Thirty of the best stories from 172 authors who submitted a total of 538 stories from more than sixty towns (the most from Sarajevo and Belgrade) are published in the collection, an English version of which I have seen in hard copy. Sponsored by Omnibus and UNESCO, the contest was established for the purpose of "renewing cultural links in the region and bringing young people from various countries, who share a common history and language, closer together" and "making possible a fuller representation of our recent writing on the European literary scene." I'll discuss the stories later; the important thing here is that the collection gives evidence of vital literary culture in the region.

Equally important is the method of distribution — digital texts (here available in Adobe, Netscape, and Word versions) are cheaper to produce and distribute than older methods. The organizers of the Vilenica International Writers' Gathering are also moving away from printed to digital text to produce their multi-lingual anthology of work by each year's participants from numerous countries, and this should allow them to make copies far more widely available.

By far the most ambitious project, digital or otherwise, I saw at the Book Fair is the Central and Eastern European Online Library (www.ceeol.com), which now has a database of 13,500 articles from journals in humanities, literature, and social sciences from sixteen countries. And counting. Founded in 2000, the Frankfort-based project is directed by Hungarian Bea Klotz and Romanian Cosmina Berta.

The value of the project, Wolfgang Klotz explains, is three-fold: it provides a central source for back issues of journals and makes available content previously inaccessible to Western or for that matter most Central and Eastern European readers; it protects the journal's subscriber base because downloads of single articles cost more than hard copies of the journal; and it gives publishers an additional source of income — seventy percent of the net from each article sold online that may help them to become financially independent or at least less dependent on subsidies. And, not incidentally, CEEOL gives all contributing journals free access to the entire data base, an intellectual advantage that in the long run seems far more important than any financial support.

The database depends upon individual editors' using CEEOL's software to provide zip-files of their journals' contents by email. This material is made available to subscribers the following day. CEEOL hopes to become viable by selling its services to institutional subscribers and by selling downloads of separate articles to individuals.

Browsing is free to everyone, and accessing the site is the only way to begin to understand what a powerful new research tool the database provides. From what I have seen, it is, within its obvious limits, to the MLA International Bibliography what that is to a box full of 3 × 5 note cards. The user can do, among other things, some of the following. Access domains like art, cinema, philosophy, and so on. Search by keyword, author, title, language.

Provide spelling correction for Slavic and other names with non–English characters. Give, in English, abstracts of all 7,000 articles. Provide tables of contents for all issues included in the database. Automatically list all available articles by an author, give biographical details, and allow the author to update information.

The directors have also begun to digitalize old books — seventy-four in ten languages thus far — as .pdf files which maintain line and page breaks of the printed text — a major help in citations. And Klotz and Berta hope to add other services, like a pool in which translators can offer their services, and to establish links with other online services like Cambridge Scientific Abstracts, ProQuest, Ebsco, and Swets.

Recently Wolfgang Klotz has founded Textor Publishing House, which will issue more than sixty titles at the beginning of 2005. The books are re-digitized nonfiction books in German, French, and English written by an Eastern European writer or dealing with one or more of these countries.

Perhaps the most exciting thing about CEEOL is the assumption that Central and Eastern Europe has something that the West needs — that, in other words, the East is not the sick person, or persons, of Europe. Perhaps even more important, as in the case of Croatian Books in Print and the continued efforts to make new writing available to readers in other languages, is the evidence that a new generation of cultural business people has faith in its cultures and in itself.

Writers and critics from Central and Eastern Europe seem to share that faith, but at the same time they more obviously struggle to deal with the legacy of the past in Central Europe and the Balkans and with the influence of critical movements from the West. For example, writers and critics from seven countries who gathered at the International Center for Contemporary Art for the Bucharest meeting of Café Europa in November, 2000, were supposed to discuss the "Flavour of Postmodernism," and as one might expect from a highly diverse and polyglot group, postmodernism seemed to have almost as many flavors as Baskin-Robbins. But the speakers and respondents spent far less time discussing what postmodernism was than when it happened.

In fact, no one seriously disagreed with the notion that postmodernism is a thing of the past. Chris Keulemans, the youngest participant, said that the topic made him nostalgic for the bookstore discussions he remembered from the Amsterdam in the 1980s. (And on my flight back to the U.S., the thirtyish woman seated next to me, director of adult education at the Chicago Art Institute, asked, "Are people still talking about that?") Several Romanians agreed that the term described for them a state of mind and kind of writing that subverted official Communist aesthetic by avoiding politics, overt commitment, and formal closure. Antonje Zalica, a Bosnian émigré novelist and filmmaker, dismissed the term by contrasting "post" with "ex" and remarked that concentrating on the first was like climbing a mountain backward in order to see where you'd been rather than where you were going. People from the Balkans tended to be impatient with too much emphasis on undecidability and detachment, and even Englishmen like Peter Jukes complained about postmodernist emphasis on aesthetics over ethics.

This attitude is reflected, at least indirectly, in two collections of writing from Southern Europe. In *Voices from the Fault Line: A Balkan Anthology* contains work ranging from scholarly abstracts to experimental poetry and drama by twenty-four writers from six countries, most of them from the southern three-fifths of the former Yugoslavia. almost all born after 1950 and most a decade or so later. The least vital work is that influenced by Plath, Borges, and Barthelme.

For purposes of discussing east-west relations as well as for its high quality, Bulgarian Alek Popov's "Shits-Giving Day" is the prize of the collection. Sometimes resembling Kafka, sometimes Swift, the story is based on the premise that Western Europe sends excrement to nourish the East — which experiences a renaissance of art and culture while the West, trapped into providing the material, becomes more and more bloated physically and intellectually. It calls to mind "A Modest Proposal," and does not suffer by the comparison. In a prose piece that may delight minority readers and writers from any nation who deal with paradoxes of bureaucratic liberalism and affirmative action, the Rom Dragoljub Acković asks what a Rom head is worth and posits a fluctuating market in which even inferior merchandise is bought by governments as a sign of enlightenment. These and other short satires have an ironic edge not always visible in some of the laments about the condition of these countries during and after Communism.

Some writers are willing to criticize their fellow Slavs. Macedonian Venko Andonovski offers in a fragment from the play "The Slavic Chest" an analysis of the Slavic character — "showing off your insides, the most intimate parts of your body and soul" — that only an insider could make this scarifying.

A bit more experimental is Bulgarian Vladimir Levchev's fragment from the novel "The Balkan Prince," part told as if by a traditional bard (with some modernist ironic touches), part by a sober historian, in Bakhtinian dialogic fashion. Western and other readers should have a chance to see the structure of the whole, for the part given here is very intriguing.

Inso(mno)lent P(r)ose, whose marketing strategy I discussed earlier, features even younger writers than *Voices*, born between 1970 and 1985, most in Serbia, Croatia, and Bosnia-Herzegovina. They are identified only by name, for instead of the usual biographical data, the volume concludes with answers to a ten-item questionnaire which is quite personal — write a haiku, contribute a recipe, what to take from Earth on a spaceship — but not, in the usual sense, informative.

Like the narrator of Hemingway's "In Another Country," most of the characters do not go to the war, but the war is always there, in memory, in metaphor, in seemingly casual allusion. Some characters escape the war but return, finding that they can no longer live in their homelands. The prize-winning story, Amir Kamber's "Amir Kamber: Organ and Piano Tuner," is in artistic terms not notably superior to many of the other stories, but it does combine nostalgia for the world of the narrator's grandfather, a dislocation of language and identity, the brutal facts of deportation, and the anguish of a writer who has to try to find himself in "a quality search engine. / I type myself. / And enter."

Not all of the stories are this bleak or self-reflexive, but as a whole they give a strong impression of the mood of a generation who survived the recent Balkan war and who are now trying to make psychological and artistic space in which to live. Or not. While one contest judge notes that no one in the stories is arrested or turned into a dung beetle, a significant number have a surreal, indeed Kafkaesque quality. Nisad Hasanović's "The Plateau" is narrated by an executioner who discovers that he is killing his twin and in the process becomes aware of his own imprisonment; Mikica Ilić's "The Perfect Labyrinth" turns from a defense against an unseen enemy into a locus for fratricide and then suicide in what can be taken as an allegory of Serb paranoia in the 1990s. Some stories have an atmosphere of hallucination, as in "Pinocchio's First Sexual Experience" and in "The Bear and Nightingale," in which characters float just above the ground and the narrator finally drifts away above the clouds.

Judging from these two Balkan anthologies as well as from the comments at the Bucharest Café Europa meeting, Aleš Debeljak (who had to cancel his appearance) may be worrying needlessly, or too locally, about the privileging of aesthetics over ethics. But his "The Political Meaning of the Slovene Neo-Avant-Garde" points to the difficulties faced not only by writers but by all kinds of workers in the transition from managed economy to the free market. Industrial workers were first to feel the effects because their equipment and production methods could not compete with those of Western Europe and America. As a result, full employment is only a vague memory, and Budapest, for example, has many homeless people and even hobo jungles or Hoovervilles sheltered by woods along railway lines and in the Buda Hills.

Central European writers face analogous conditions. Before 1989, they could either submit to the dictates of what Debeljak calls "sentimental humanism" (the adjective sounding odd to an American raised during the Cold War) and attain financial security and official status or resist or ignore the official line and amass moral capital at home and some prospect of readership in the West.

Now, Debeljak complains, writers who wish to be engaged face attacks from "the lackeys of the formalist dogma" in a massive popular and scholarly media front that represents a "pathological flight from the bridge connecting a work of art to the life of the community...."

Some of this rhetoric seems to echo that of old and for now discredited critical technologies, though it may be used with some validity. I have been in Central Europe six of the last seven years and have never seen phalanxes of formalists occupying the squares. On the other hand, I have seen signs for a club called "Tito" in Ljubljana and for something I couldn't identify called "KGB" in Bratislava. And even a mint-condition Trabant, the once-despised East German car with a two-cycle engine that now has a certain nostalgic chic, put-putting its way along St. Istvan Korút in Budapest.

I should add that I have learned a great deal from Debeljak's writing in translation and have been moved by his poetry. Nothing in my response invalidates his point that writers have every right, and depending on their talents and inclinations, even the obligation to be engaged with the world. On the other hand, writers also have the right to refuse, as he puts it, "to vibrate on the wavelength of shifting historical, national, and social movements."

This issue can be approached from an historical or at least a temporal perspective. Debeljak is approaching his mid-forties. He was once part of the avant-garde and admits that its usefulness as well as its vogue has passed, and while looking for a new aesthetic he hears the hungry and noisy younger generation treading behind him. Perhaps, though it sounds odd for an American to counsel a European about historical perspective, he needs to see, as I have, several more critical schools come and go in order to attain a degree of serenity.

Debeljak takes a broader view of politics and culture in *The Hidden Handshake: National Identity and Europe in the Post-Communist World*, especially with the cultural and political roles, or their absence, of the newest nations within the European Union.

Debeljak is particularly concerned by the EU's failure to adopt some of the values of the nation-state, in his view a European creation, which at its best transformed nationalism into patriotism, allowed not only the existence but the flourishing of minority cultures, and fostered, through its cosmopolitan atmosphere, fruitful multicultural competence. (He is, of course, aware of the ways in which Germanic culture in particular inhibited Slovene political and cultural life, and he worries about majority languages becoming the exclusive vehicles of political discourse in the EU.)

In fact, Debeljak seems to be a thoroughgoing Euroskeptic, and in view of the recent French and Dutch rejection of the EU Constitution, his analysis seems not only acute but prophetic. He cites four reasons for skepticism: worry about diminished state boundaries; desire to protect ethnic identity (often, I think, used to mask the desire to protect local economic interests); a "democratic deficit" in the management of EU affairs, from Brussels down; and "the failure to form a 'common mental framework.'"

The last concern pervades the book. Debeljak maintains that the impulses behind the EU are primarily technological and economic; that "Europe" is defined as Western Europe, which accounts for the EU's failure to intervene in Bosnia; and that "Old Europe" is acting as if it were an American gated community, constructed to exclude lesser cultural, ethnic, and economic breeds, accepting the implications of divisions which date back not just to the Cold War and the Schengen Treaty but to the Treaty of Trianon.

To counteract this exclusiveness — and to insure a place for Slovenia and other smaller nations — Debeljak proposes the construction of "a common grand narrative," "a substantial imaginative framework of general identification, material for 'common dreams' that can give all the citizens of Europe a certain minimum of existential meaning and emotional density, through which we recognize a commitment to something that transcends us as individuals with particular identities."

Just how this is to come about, and what would result, is not at all clear, and Debeljak admits that "such a construction is idealistic, hinged as it is on a search for balance between ethnic and cultural traditions on the one hand, and loyalty to a supranational, overarching cultural habitus on the other" before lapsing into near-duck speak about "mutual acceptance of a publicly shared sphere within which such reciprocity can take place."

Happily, this kind of language is rare, and much of the book is devoted less to the making of a new European consciousness than to the definition and preservation of the cultural importance of small nations, specifically Slovenia, their languages, and their cultural heritages. In fact, Debeljak begins by discussing issues of national identity, particularly important to Slovenes because, beginning with independence from Yugoslavia, they have been riding "the last car on the last train of nationalism." Like any citizen of a small country, he is, sometimes reluctantly, aware of the necessity for "concentric circles of identity." Once part of the Hapsburg Empire, then of various avatars of Yugoslavia, now of the European Union, Slovene writers must either find a way to export their visions or to retreat within their own borders. On the one hand, "Liberal tolerance [as distinct from cosmopolitanism] camouflages what is essentially something passive" and "cannot be fully divorced from a self-congratulatory and highly patronizing attitude." At its worst, it can reduce a minority culture to the status of folklore, Disneyfication. An example is Peter Handke's desire, discussed in *Transitions OnLine* (Tobias K. Vogel, 20 July 2005) to keep Serbia isolated so as to keep its charm.

Looking up and out rather than down, Slovene writers must neither over-value other traditions nor, like the *népi* in Hungary, who wish to concentrate exclusively on local traditions and ethnicity, ignore them in ultra-nationalist fervor. Debeljak realizes "that the boundaries of my language [are] to a considerable degree, the boundaries of my world"—not just "linguistic skills" but "a whole symbolic, mental, and social experience deposited in the layers of a nation's historical existence and collective mentality" and constitute "the encapsulation of a metaphysical worldview." On a less abstract level, one's language allows one to give names to everything, to understand inside jokes and to follow the implications of subtle cultural references—the kind of thing that can make poetry untranslatable.

As a result, in Debeljak's desire to make literature an important instrument for constructing the "common grand narrative," he rejects purely aesthetic approaches to literature. Postmodernism blurred "the distinction between the pragmatic and artistic dimensions," so that "Postmodern art is no longer the embodiment of an alternative world that derives meaning from its aesthetic and ethical tensions with the existing order; on the contrary, postmodern art by and large supports, maintains, and justifies the existing order." In Debeljak's view, "the artist brings together a variety of existential, social, and national aspects of experience in a search for meaningful balance."

Some critics and literary historians seem rather pleased that the younger generation in Central and Eastern Europe need not become prophets, dissidents, or moralists like their elders; others are clearly nostalgic for times in which writers were the unacknowledged legislators and mentors of their countries. Still, it is one of the costs, as well as one of the signs, of freedom that writers and others can muddle along to find new, or very old, ways of doing things. To confine the discussion to writing, perhaps Kipling was correct in saying "There are nine-and-fifty ways / Of composing tribal lays/And—every single one of them is right." Or, to paraphrase invert Joseph Heller's line in *Catch-22*, outside there is not a war going on, and some funny or at least not desperately serious things are happening. And for all people, not just writers, that can be considered as progress.

Works Cited

Debeljak, Aleš. "The Political Meaning of the Slovene Neo-Avant-Garde." *World Literature Today*, 78:2 (January-April 2004). See www.ou.edu/worldlit.

Inso(mno)lent P(r)ose. Edited by Nenand Veličkovič. Translated by Celia Hawkesworth. Sarajevo: Književna radionica Omnibus, 2003.

Voices from the Faultline: A Balkan Anthology. Ed. A. Johnson and Žakalon Nežič. Hampton, VA: ZayuPress. 2002.

Epilogue

In America, people may be mildly interested if you say that you are a writer, but if you say you're a poet, they might start edging away. In fact, one woman friend said, "Don't tell my family you're a poet!" in much the same tone as someone might insist that you not mention that you are alcoholic or HIV positive. However, poets probably still rank ahead of mimes and performance artists.

Some Americans harbor delusions that poets are special. Years ago, I heard an aggressively ignorant graduate student proclaim that "It is dangerous to be a poet." She may have meant psychologically, referring to what, in *The Loved One*, Evelyn Waugh called "that zone of insecurity in the mind where none but the artist dare trespass." Being myself of more neo-classical than Romantic temperament, I replied that being a poet was no more dangerous than being a shoe salesman.

But before the countries of the former Communist bloc became independent, it could be dangerous to be a poet in a quite different sense — legally and even physically. Now it is not. After the euphoria of 1989 dissipated and writers realized what life without subsidies and persecution could be like, they have been in the position a child who would rather be punished than ignored.

Even now, although writers in Central Europe no longer have the income they had before 1989, they have a lingering prestige that may seem strange to Americans. When in Europe, I tell people that I am a writer, not a professor, because that gives me a higher status.

There is a corollary effect, however, for often, at least in groups, they want to know my standing as a poet and also who is the leading poet, novelist, and so on. My response to the first question is that I am below the radar and to the second that America does not have those jobs any more, at least since Allen Ginsberg died and even Norman Mailer stopped pushing himself to the top of the heap or anyway people stopped listening to him.

Now, as in many other respects, America provides a glimpse of the future — the globalization of literature, if you will. The bad news is that very few people will be able to make a living by writing or achieve the kind of public recognition of a Ginsberg or Robert Lowell, let alone a Vaclav Havel.

There is some good news. With new technologies widely available, multinational publishers will not be able to exercise de facto economic censorship. Software makes it much easier to produce camera-ready copy, and self and small press publishing is faster, easier, and cheaper than it has ever been. Little magazines are using the internet more and more, and though their sites may not get many hits, readers are more likely to find them on-line than in the few bookstores willing to carry very little magazines. Many writers belong to groups, live or virtual, in which the members read each others' work and offer critiques. Perhaps this is a new version of the practice in Renaissance England, circulating a few sugared sonnets among the writer's private friends.

None of these venues will bring the writer much money, if any, and the work will not be widely read. But this has always been the case in America. As one American poet said, poetry is a tough game because you send out a poem; then, if you're unsuccessful, you get your copy back. If you're successful, you get two copies of the magazine.

In short, if the rest of the world follows the American model, writers in Central Europe and everywhere else are going to have to give up the dream of making a living solely by writing. Former dissidents are familiar with the need to hold what American musicians call "a day job," something they do to earn money to support their artistic habits. Andrew Wachtel deals with some of the things that writers do besides, or increasingly, instead of strictly literary work in *Remaining Relevant after Communism: The Role of the Writer in Eastern Europe* (Chicago, 2006). Wachtel, who also edits the Northwestern University Press series, "Writings from an Unbound Europe," has provided the best general analysis to date of the economics, sociology, and psychology of writers in post–Communist Central and Eastern Europe.

Like many of the writers and editors I spoke to, Wachtel observes in more succinct terms that, in literature as in all other areas, "the most salient feature of actually existing socialism was its limitation of choice." Suddenly, after 1989, readers had a much wider variety of choices on which to spend incomes with markedly reduced purchasing power. More, it turned out, was less for most writers. Wachtel's charts put the situation in stark numerical terms. In the Czech Republic, for example, 759 periodicals and 4,115 nonperiodical titles were published in 1984. By 1999, when real prices were much higher, figures were 3,894 and 12,551. In Romania, literary works accounted for just over 25 percent of total production in 1990. By 1998, that had fallen to .91 percent. Print run figures were even bleaker: 3.65 copies per inhabitant in 1965 to .63 in 1998. In Poland, just over a thousand titles were published in 1985, a number that had tripled by 1999. But the total number of copies printed had fallen by a third. Hungarian figures reveal a different kind of shift: the incursion of books by Americans. In 1985, over two million copies of thirty-four titles by American authors were published compared with 8.5 million copies of 643 titles in 1998. Many of these — and an uncounted number of titles by English writers — were probably popular fiction that the communists had barred as decadent and escapist. In individual terms, the income of Moldovan Nicolae Rusu from literature in the late 1980s would have allowed him to buy a car, while in 2000 he couldn't have afforded a refrigerator.

At the same time, the cultural capital amassed by writers over the previous two centuries has been devalued because there are more immediate and potentially more powerful ways of affecting social and political change and because professions like journalism, law, and medicine no longer operate under nearly crushing political constraints.

The result, as the Serbian Mihailo Pantić puts it a bit melodramatically, is that "Artistic literature in the postsocialist cultural model has become socially unnecessary, an almost completely private affair which lacks any social importance and which is interesting only to narrow academic circles, to writers, and to rare dedicated readers who nurture their passion as other marginal groups nurture theirs. Some people belong to satanic cults, some to the Society for the Lovers of Bulldogs, and others, amazingly, read Serbian poetry."

As these new economic and social realities became clearer to writers, they must have asked, in different terms than Lenin's "What Is to Be Done?" Various attempts to find solutions occupy the last three-fourths of Wachtel's book. The most obvious strategy for a group who had been encouraged to regard themselves, in Shelley's terms, as the unacknowledged legislators of mankind, was to become acknowledged by going into politics. Noting that no writers who emerged after 1989 have gone into politics, Wachtel argues that "switching from literature to politics was a strategy adopted by already established writers [who still had some cultural capital amassed in previous conditions] as a way of remaining relevant to a (somewhat) postliterary society...." He concentrates on three figures, Václav Havel, Dobrica Ćosić, and Eduard Limonov, maintaining without insisting that the generalization applies to their colleagues, that "we can perhaps see their political activity as a kind of translation of their literary work from one medium into another rather than as a new chapter in their lives" and that they "tend to behave as if they were characters in their own literary works" without realizing "that in the world of politics a distanced irony from one's own words is impossible."

Another strategy for remaining socially relevant is for writers to attempt "to define the nation" in light of post-communist developments. Wachtel distinguishes between writers who deal with this subject in literary terms and those who, like Franjo Tuđman in Croatia and Corneliu Vadim Tudor in Romania, espouse in political practice and in journalism virulent proclamations of national and ethnic solidarity and superiority. But many writers look beyond national borders to create an "unstable but productive synthesis" of local and international cultures that is personal rather than "a (modernist) universal model of cultural synthesis." Neither culture is shown as entirely or necessarily superior or inferior; rather, the author holds out the possibility that they can be complementary. Of course, as Wachtel points out, both categories run the risk of offering clichés rather than serious analysis.

Wachtel's categories are not firmly fixed. For example, he has a separate chapter devoted to journalism, more highly regarded in the region since the fall of communism. Some journalists have become politicians and vice versa; much of the work written about national character and about East confronting West is nonfiction. Some mediocre poets and novelists have become very good journalists.

Wachtel's last two chapters, "Dealing with Transition Head-On" and "Learning to Love Popular Fiction," focus almost entirely on fiction. The discussions of two of the not many who do the former, Vladimir Makanin and Jáchym Topol, are among the longest in the book, less because they are representative than because Wachtel regards them as "serious novels that write themselves directly into the mainstream high-cultural tradition."

Many more writers have attempted to use Western genres like mystery and romance. The most successful keep in mind not only their own classical literary education but the unwillingness of readers from the same system to admit that "I want to read something fast-paced and mindless." But in *Bringing Up Girls in Bohemia*, Michal Viewegh obviously seeks a reader "with a reasonably high level of literary education," judging from the quotations he interpolates. Although critics "excoriate him for his bad taste and for pandering to the lowest common denominator," Wachtel wonders why Viewegh's novel is not accorded the same status as Kundera's *The Unbearable Lightness of Being*, no less a love story, and perhaps not much more. The difference, Wachtel thinks, may be "in the position that Kundera was able to make for himself in the cold war, as well as the literary reputation he achieved with the books he published during the liberal period of the mid–1960s."

Wachtel sees hope for Eastern European literature in works like Viewegh's "that at one and the same time incorporate genres of popular fiction and provide an ironic metacommentary on them." Nevertheless, he concludes, "it is safe to say that in this new environment the appearance of another Miłosz, Solzhenitsyn, or Kundera is all but impossible." However highly he regards literature, he cannot regard this as lamentable, for the conditions that led to the canonization of writers were socially, politically, and economically intolerable. As he says in the final sentence, "Lucky is the people whose literature need no longer be universally relevant."

Writers in smaller countries and languages often worry about being relevant at all. The editors of the Slovenian magazine *Apokalipsa* who initiated the Review within Review and other members of the consortium may not have stopped worrying, but they are acting. They attempt to get beyond the individual artist and nation in order to foster "inter–European collaboration among national cultures without the mediation of large languages." Journals from Slovenia, Montenegro, Macedonia, Croatia, the Czech Republic, Hungary, Austria, Macedonia, Slovakia, Poland, and (soon) Russia prepare material for special issues to be translated, entire, into other languages. This project moves beyond individual authors to give a sense of the broader editorial philosophy of the journal and therefore, by including political and broadly cultural material, of aspects of the country's culture. By 2006, there had been twenty-seven exchanges in nine languages, some book translations, and some multi-lingual editions. The Macedonian web journal *Blesok* (www.blesok.com.mk), published in Macedonian and English, is preparing a website for *Review within Review*.

Moreover, "publishers, editors, critics, translators, designers" and others meet annually to discuss further collaboration. *Apokalipsa* hosts a festival in Ljubljana, featuring international authors and magazines, and various other events, including a philosophy symposium with ten philosophers from five countries, and presentations of journals in translation are scheduled throughout the region. (*Review within Review* information pamphlet, 2006)

Perhaps less ambitious but increasingly international in scope is the Literature Live Festival held annually in Zagreb, sponsored by the Croatian PEN Center and the Croatian Writers Society, the which invites writers from as far away as South Africa, Iran, and the United States for readings, interviews, and discussions.

Many of these writers and editors and their colleagues will, for obvious reasons, be reluctant to abandon the notion of the writer as prophet or preacher and literature as a special repository of values. I mentioned in Chapter I a symposium on the topic, "Can Literature Save the World?" As a panelist, I had to say "No" for a variety of reasons that struck the audience as rather odd. The question itself assumes that Matthew Arnold was right when he said, more than a hundred years ago, that literature would replace religion as a source of values and of inspiration. (He had by that time given up poetry for criticism.) About fifty years ago, C. S. Lewis maintained that Arnold's "horrible prophecy" had been fulfilled. Now, at least in American departments of literature under the influence of French theorists of some forty years ago, we find that literature has been replaced by texts, authors by the iron whims of uncertain language, while students and even some former theorists long for pleasure in reading.

Some members of the audience were quick to make the connection between literature and salvation because they had become accustomed to writers who were effective proponents of ideas and even to writers who have been effective in practical politics. For example, in a symposium which I helped Gustáv Murín, the Slovak scientist-writer, to organize at the University of Oklahoma, one issue discussed was politicians as writers, writers as politicians. It was easy to think of a number of Central and Eastern European, Latin American, African, and Asian writers who have been deeply involved in politics, though few English or American writers could be found who shared that interest. And it is clear that what Americans call "creative writing" and "real writers" have had enormous influence in these regions.

But the question about literature saving the world contains three very slippery terms: "literature," "save" and "world." If the work is polemic or even primarily devoted to practical programs, is it literature? If it is primarily inspirational, like Dr. Martin Luther King's "I Have a Dream" speech, Patrick Henry's "Give me liberty or give me death," or the Declaration of Independence, are we talking about rhetoric or about literature? These are rarely included in any but the most politically correct anthologies of literature. I don't deny that poetry, fiction, and drama of the highest type can have polemical and even programmatic content, though my study of literary history tells me that these elements soon fade even for readers who are not specialists. Earlier I quoted Martin Šimečka's remark that new freedom should dispel "the perception that any intellectual effort, including writing, is only useful for rousing the nation from thick-headedness. This enlightening role of literature ruined the taste of writers until the second half of the century."

Then there's "save." Šimečka wants to save writers from being saviors. The word can, of course, have political or psychological or financial or physical implications, but the primary and inescapable meaning is religious. Anyone raised in traditional Christianity, even if she or he no longer subscribes to its doctrines, has a hard time believing that "the world" can be saved. Or, to put it in the terms of the Chinese heroic tradition of *Romance of the Three Kingdoms*, "Nations rise and fall. Kingdoms come and go."

Writers, like everyone else, would love to assume the position of benevolent dictator or guru, and some, most obviously the writers of utopian fantasies, have done so in their works. Ask yourself how eager you would be to live in any one of those societies, and not just Plato's *Republic*, from which all writers would be banished. And for that matter, how many of the works you would really like to read again.

We are all too familiar, some from direct experience, with the effects of self-contained systems of salvation. I won't name any countries or eras or religions because there is plenty of guilt to go around.

One advantage of literature is that it is disorganized. When it is organized, in literary cliques or in official centers of study, it has often, as Lewis pointed out, "taken on all the features of bitter persecution, great intolerance and traffic in relics." An example of relics: I recently visited the John Steinbeck Center in his home town of Salinas, California. At least for a time, Steinbeck was the kind of writer that PEN likes to think about, but the sub-text of the gleaming building is urban renewal. Empty spaces or empty stores line the street leading up to it. The building is full of memorabilia dealing with books that tried to solve problems that no longer exist and that earned Steinbeck the scorn and opprobrium of his fellow townsmen.

In fact, Steinbeck didn't save anyone. By the time *The Grapes of Wrath* appeared, some government programs for displaced people turned migrant workers had been put in place, though the book may have given impetus to still further action. But what really saved the Okies was America's entry into World War II, when the necessities of conscription and armament created full employment and solved the problem of production in excess of demand by creating new demands.

In any case, Steinbeck was like a lot of writers and for that matter humanity. His intentions were good, but his thinking was often muddled or contradictory or both, and it changed all the time. Would he have been able to save the world even if he'd wanted to? Not in his best moments as a writer.

William Butler Yeats was more directly involved in politics, and he wanted to save Ireland, if not the world. But at one point he questioned whether a poem of his "sent out / Those sixteen men the English shot," and he admitted that he had misjudged some of the men as well as the effects of his work.

Or take a fictional example: Joseph Conrad's Kurtz in *Heart of Darkness*. He practiced several arts, including writing, besides black ones, but his talents did not make him a, shall we say, guide to salvation. Marlow is faithful to his memory largely out of default — everyone else seems even worse — and partly because Kurtz had something to say about the world he created or inhabited, even if it was "The horror, the horror."

And that brings up the final term, "the world." In the first place, the world is always changing — mutability is the only constant. Besides, many if not most of the writers I value don't save a world; they create or recreate one. And many, like Scott Fitzgerald, Joseph Conrad, Henry James, and a host of others, deal with the failure of the characters to save the world or even themselves.

All this being said, I can now answer the question with a qualified yes. Literature can and does celebrate the world in its beauty, complexity, and imperfection. Perhaps people can be saved, though I am not convinced that it is the writer's job to do so. But they can be inspired, made better — or worse — by what they read.

So, from the tradition in which I work, I'd prefer the question to read, "Can literature change the world?" My answer is "Sometimes. A little." But it's much better at changing, or at least affecting, individuals.

If we stick to the original question, I'd still have to answer "No." But then I'd add that we have to act as though the answer were "Yes." Or perhaps, as Jake Barnes puts it at the end of *The Sun Also Rises*, "Isn't it pretty to think so?" Or even, as one of Henry James's dying writers, heroic in the measure of the knowledge that he has failed, says, "Our doubt is our passion, and our passion is our task. The rest is the madness of art." Sharing that madness can be intoxicating, but if we have learned anything from the century just ended, madness is no way to save anything, though in a very limited sense of *furor poeticus*, it is indispensable in making something enduring.

In any case, James precedes the passage just quoted with "We work in the dark." Very few of us know for certain that the work on the desk or screen before us will be completed; will, if completed, be published; will, if published, be read, let alone appreciated; will, if appreciated, endure. The solution, perhaps, is to take the work seriously — but not to take ourselves too seriously.

Appendix:
Memorial Poem
by Éva Tóth

On October the 23rd the mild and mellow autumn
we had that year the golden leaves the sparkling sunny day were as Pëtofi had
    wished them to be and because our last class was cancelled
we scoffed down our lunch with Erzi Gubics in the canteen
and went to the second-hand book shop in Market Street (in fact I don't
    think there was another one in Debrecen)
and for 2 forints I bought The Living Poet a posthumous selection of
    Kostolányi poems published in 1937
and marked it (as a kind of ex libris) showing that it was Éva Tóth's book
and the date too this was my practice at the time
Then we went to the Déri Museum it had a sunken garden where we used
    to play after the siege
when we were put up in the Bishop's Court in the flat of Tihamér Szendi
the pianist who fled to Nyírmihálydi from the bombs
while we moved into the cellar of Mr Csóka's pub on the corner of Jósika
    and Kassa (later Liberty) Streets
where the Russians marched in
and when our house was hit by a bomb (actually it wasn't our house we
    were just tenants in it)
that's when we went down to Mr Csóka's cellar to join some fifty others
We were afraid that the Germans would carry off my dad
he wasn't serving in the army because he drank caustic soda as a child
by accident at Aunt Juliska's on the farm on a wash day
because the caustic soda was in his mug and he was very thirsty because
    it was a very hot day
and he could reach the mug on the edge of the wash tub and gulped it down at once
but the Germans haven't harmed us mind you the first Russians haven't either
I slept next to the cellar door when they came in young soldiers every one of them
they laughed wept showed us photographs dandled the children on their knees
    as later in the films about the heroic liberating Soviet Army

they sang Volga Volga
one gave me a small brooch shaped like a fish but not like those made by
    Colonel Aureliano Buendía in Macondo because those are gold and he
    melts them all down and starts again
mine was made of red glass mounted in a bright golden yellow setting but I
    lost it soon somewhere
and didn't have another jewel until I reached twenty
because my ear clips Dad buried in the woodshed together with my mum's wedding
    ring and his own and two yards of tartan cloth
were dug out by our neighbor and when my dad discovered that he went across to him
and told him be very careful Mr Kovács because by noon I will be back with the police
and Mr Kovács was very careful and the police found nothing
and Mr Kovács had soon a bigger house built instead of the bombed one
Back to the Bishop's Court which was not the Bishop's court but a tenement block
anyhow when we lived there and used to play in the garden of the Déri Museum
we liked to climb on the Medgyessy statues it was easy to perch on them
on their arms legs knees even on their shoulders
a man holds a smaller man in his hand this is Ethnography
I liked Archaeology best a naked woman with a gentle face wearing a helmet
but since they were made of bronze it didn't matter that they were naked
The next Russians were not so kind and there were Romanians with them
they set up their field-guns against the wall of the pub and shelled the artillery barracks
a young soldier told Dad Germansky Germansky and shoved a tommy-gun into his
    mouth
Mum turned pale sent us there we screeched Dad Dad
an old soldier said something to the young one grabbed his arm and took him away
my dad by the way had a Charlie Chaplin moustache in those days wavy black hair
Dinaric type I think
my mum fainted when they shoved the young women up the cellar stairs with their
    rifle butts
she was twenty-five then mother of three
at the time I had no idea why she fainted and how lucky that was because they left
    her alone
although I was almost six years old and used to listen to the radio
while Mum did the washing or changed little Ilike's nappies maybe Bandi's too
and I sat in the little chair and listened and told Mum when they said enemy aircraft
    approaching Debrecen
then we ran to the bunker or to the woods or if it was too late
Mum stood in the kitchen corner leaning over the three of us
because she had heard on the radio that a house had collapsed but the child
survived because her mother was leaning over it
My mum was not afraid when the planes were coming
Bözsi and Kató were running up and down in the yard crying shouting throwing
    themselves on the ground
but I was afraid of the bombs and of the Stalin candles when the Gasworks blew up
and of the Stalin organs too and once I wetted my knickers
and it was in Oxford at the high table of St Catherine's College in 1989
that I realised why I was so upset whenever the radio or the TV was blaring at full blast
From Mr Csóka's cellar we moved to the Town Hall cellar
and when the Russians drove us out
we went along Market Street toward the Great Church with little Ilike and all our

Memorial Poem *by Éva Tóth*

possessions in the pram and it was getting dark and there was a curfew
and that's how we got to Bishop's Court and the flat was not Tihamér Szendi's but Emil Szabó's he was the one who went to Nyírmihálydi with his family
and Tihamér Szendi was a violinist and they had the key
and I had never seen such a beautiful large flat but Mum forbade us to touch anything
    in the other rooms although I wanted to see the piano
then the Russians came and took it away just as the Szabó family were coming up the stairs
but the Russians were kind-hearted and fond of children
and Mum sent us there to ask them for the snuff-brown eiderdown
and many other things and they let us have them and they had an interpreter with them and many things were saved this way
then we had to leave Bishop's but before that
my grandparents arrived on a cart from Bácska with Bazsa Maca and Zoli
we lived in Hatvan Street at Aunt Bözsi's
in the house of Fat Cat Balogh who was later branded as a kulak and deported
true enough Uncle Bandi was deported too never mind that he was a Wagon Works man but he made a threshing-machine and took on threshing jobs
Aunt Rózsi travelled up to Budapest on the roof of the train
she could speak with everybody with the Russians and Romanians too
then Sanyi and Jancsi returned from the front and Peti turned white at fifteen
Then we lived in the Peasants' Party opposite the Csokonai Theatre
but there was nothing to eat and we went to Püspöknádasd with my grandparents
    in a railway truck when land was given to them Dad came later at harvest time
Nádasd was a German village the Germans were deported but many of them escaped back
then my granny's little group became homesick and returned to Debrecen
they lived there in the Red Star Co-op out in a remote little house with the Sidó family they fled from Transylvania
when the Peasants' Party closed down we moved to the Böszörményi Street flatlets where the walls were damp
then to Dobozi Street by the abandoned cemetery where my Fehérati grandmother was buried
then to Rakovszki Street which became Sándor Fürst and you could see the spire of the Great Church from there but the kitchen was freezing cold
so when winter came we moved the cooker into the bigger room and the five of us all slept there and we heated water in a mess tin
handled it with a pair of pliers because it was hot and poured it into a hand basin and added cold water
and first I washed myself up to the waist then I took the basin down from the stool and sat in it
then I stood up in it and washed my feet too
every day after all I was a big girl I fell in love many times wrote poetry
I went to the theatre the movies concerts
I saw Hamlet and Il Trovatore heard the Les Préludes
and the Spinning Room at the Open Air Theatre with Rozó clinging on to the railing Kodály was there too with Madame Emma
I learnt French Italian Latin a little English
Finnish Romanian German and Russian of course
I fancied the Cyrillic characters and learnt them one afternoon from Aunt Luló's husband when he returned from the prison camp

I wrote on my exercise book Ева Андреевна Тотх
later I called myself Tóth fille in my Meteorological Study Circle notes where I wrote poetry too squeezed upside down starting at the bottom of each page
and a diary in ancient Icelandic runic script because the hieroglyphics I invented were not nuanced enough
I went often to Budapest once to Eger by the cheap train and to Tokaj
my first trip ever was to Kolosvár
having crossed the Királyhágó we were looking out of the train window at a field flush with autumn crocuses glowing in the early October sun
they were blue and mauve and at black buffaloes
and now we were leaning out of the window of the Déri Museum because we heard some noise outside
students from the University and the Fazekas Grammar School were shouting in front of the Party Committee Building and we ran out of the Museum
I had a lump in my throat it was like the fifteenth of March in 1848
and we ran breathless along Market Street into Kossuth Street to our school
and shouted into every classroom that there was a demonstration on come at once and we ran back
and marched to the Wagon Works and then to the Printing House
and János Görbe recited there the Call to the Nation which later got him into prison
they knocked down the red star it was made of glass it came down with a big crash
then we marched to the University and back to the Great Church
and suddenly the lights went out and the Security Police fired on the crowd
I wasn't hit and ran all the way home
then we listened non-stop to the radio picked up every leaflet and since Sándor Fürst Street is the continuation of Liberty Street
the Russians marched on the city right in front of our house
the tanks were coming day and night we could hardly cross the street between them
then we woke up to the sound of artillery fire it was the 4th of November
and my mum got me into an old black coat tied a black shawl round my head
and tried to disguise me as an ugly old woman before we went down to the cellar
but she had moderate success because I was quite pretty and not quite eighteen years old
luckily this time we had no Russians coming into our cellar
but they guarded the City Hall with tanks and fixed telegraph lines everywhere in our street too
my Russian was quite good in those days I told them to go home
but they said that they had to protect us against the imperialists
then there was a ban on public assembly martial law exodus to the West
I too thought of going away I was lugging for weeks an Attila József a Radnóti an Illyés and a Lőrinc Szabó volume in my small briefcase prepared for every eventuality
but I stayed in the end and last year Erzsi Gubics died of cancer
I said a few words at the graveside but I was choking with tears
the snow was drifting hard and I could barely be heard.

Written in 1996, translated by Peter Zollman in 1999
Reprinted with the permission of the author and the translator

Index

Acković, Dragoljub 174
Adcock, Fleur 149, 162, 164
Ady, Endre 100
Alexie, Sherman 18
Anderson, Sherwood 98
Andonovski, Venko 174
Andričik, Marián 140
Andriescu, Radu 158, 159
Arnold, Matthew 185
Austro-Hungarian Empire 3, 4, 5, 23, 67, 111, 113, 132, 145, 158

Babačič, Esad 37, 55
Balanescu, Grigore 160
Balassi, Bálint 100
Balla (no first name used) 117
Balla, Zsófia 88, 99, 117
Bánk, Zsuzsa 102, 103–105, 109
Barabás, Márton 110
Barbu, Ion 159
Bari, Károly 88, 100
Barth, John 50
Barthelme, Donald 39, 50, 51, 174
Bates, Bridgette 49, 64
Bátorová, María 136
Bayer, Gerd 109
Benedicty, Tamás (formerly Horváth) 98
Berceanu, Patrel 161
Bereményi, Géza 98
Berger, Aleš 27, 65
Bergmann, Ingmar 129
Berlind, Bruce 19, 96, 110
Berta, Cosmina 172, 173
Bettes, István 99
Biggins, Michael 1, 2, 13, 31, 62
Blaga, Lucian 159

Blatnik, Andrej 2, 5, 6, 29, 44–45, 56, 57, 60, 61
Blažkova, Jaroslava 135
Bleoca, Liviu 164
Bodor, Ádam 98
Bogataj, Matej 29, 39, 63
Bojetu-Boeta, Berta 55
Borbely, Stefan 159
Borges, Jorge Luis 82, 134, 175
Bowles, Paul 45
Braga, Corin 156, 159, 163
Brândus, Tom 164
Brecht, Bertolt 82
Buñuel, Luis 157
Burroughs, William S. 28, 36
Bútora, Martin 127–128, 129

Camus, Albert 82
Čander, Mitja 56
Cankar, Ivan 26
Čar, Aleš 55, 56, 57, 64
Cârneci, Magda 148, 154, 155–156, 163
Cărtărescu, Mircea 154
Cartland, Barbara 29
Cassian, Nina 149, 164
Castro, Michael 110
Čater, Dušan 56
Ceaușescu, Elena 149
Ceaușescu, Nicolae 38, 87, 144, 145, 147–152, 158, 160–161, 164
Celac, Sergiu 148
censorship 42, 88, 115, 117, 130, 131, 147–149, 154–155, 159, 164, 181
Central Europe 1, 3–4, 6–7, 9–14, 18, 20, 23–24, 38, 39, 45, 61–62, 66, 68–69, 88, 90, 92, 96, 111, 115, 127–129, 131, 146, 156, 165–181

Čeretková, Marína 136
Cesereanu, Ruxandra 156, 157–158, 159, 160, 163, 164
Chaplin, Charlie 190
Clement, Wolfgang 166
Cochina, Claudia 160
Codruţ, Mariana 158
Comănescu, Denisa 154
Conrad, Joseph 92, 186, 187
Coover, Robert 45, 50
Cornis-Pope, Marcel 155, 164
Ćosić, Dobrica 182
Coşovei, Traian 154
Crăciun, Gheorge 154, 155, 162, 163, 164
Crăsnaru, Daniela 149, 154
Cselényi, László 99
Csordás, Gábor 78
Čučnik, Primoz 55
Cyril and Methodius, Saints 137

Dalí, Salvador 157
Dalos, György 94
Danilov, Nichita 154
Dante 115
Deák, Nóra 81
Debeljak, Aleš 2, 11, 12, 19, 27, 29, 33, 44, 45, 50–51, 57, 60, 61, 62, 63, 64, 166–167, 175–178, 179
Debeljak, Erica Johnson 65
Dej, Gheorghe-Gheorgiu 147
Deletant, Andrea 164
Demeter, Gusztav 171
Dichev, Ivailo 115
Dinescu, Mircea 148, 153, 154, 164
dissidents 5, 115, 122, 124, 126, 153, 154, 155, 168, 178, 181
Djarova, Julia 109
Dobai, Péter 99
Dobozy, Tamás 102, 105–109
Dostoevsky, Fyodor 129
Dusa, Zdravko 65

Economou, George 12
Egyed, Emese 164
Eliot, T.S. 34, 42, 153
Elizabeth of Hungary, Saint 91
Engels, Frederick 150
Erdélyi, József 85
Eszterhazy, Péter 66, 89, 98

Fairleigh, John 160
Faraškova, Etela 135, 136
Farnoaga, Georgiana 164
Faulkner, William 61
Fázsy, Anikó 82–83, 99

Feldek, L'ubomír 139
Ferko, Andrej 129
Firan, Carmen 161
Fischer, Tibor 102–105, 109
Fitzgerald, F. Scott 9, 19, 187
Flamand, Dinu 154
Flisar, Evald 29, 38, 39, 41–45, 64, 65
Flora, Ioan 154
Fodor, George 112
Forgács, Éva 109
Frank, Anne 148
Frost, Robert 157
Fukuyama, Francis 18

Gális, Vladislav 117
Gašparovič, Ivan 112
Gautier, Théophile 93
Gergely, Ágnes 88, 94, 101
Ghelmez, Petre 154
Ginsberg, Alan 96, 181
Grafenauer, Niko 34, 35
Graham, Heather 81
Greenberg, Alvin 14–16, 17, 18, 20
Grendel, Lajoa 4, 87, 98–99, 133–134
Grigorescu, Oana Cristea 148
Guardijančič, Jože 60
Győry, Attila 99
Gyukics, Gábor 110

Haderlap, Maja 44
Haklik, Norbert 99
Halvoník, Alexander 129, 142
Hamsun, Knut 82
Hapsburgs 4, 5, 24, 25, 28, 109, 111, 115, 133, 177
Hasanović, Nisad 175
Haugová, Mila 139
Havel, Vaclav 91, 181, 182
Heller, Joseph 178
Hemingway, Ernest 9, 32, 45, 132, 175, 187
Henry, O. 39
Hiemstra, P. 76
Hirghidus, Ion 161
Hladnik, Miran 65
Hochel, Braňo 143
Holan, Vladimir 148
Holka, Peter 129
Horthy, Miklós 67
Hrastelj, Stanka 60
Huba, Mikuláš 4
Hudej, Mohor 56
Hudík, Pavol 143
Hughes, Ted 34
Hulik, Viktor 114
Hynie, Josef 132

Index

Ieronim, Ioana 147–148, 150–152, 154, 156, 162, 163, 164
Ihan, Alojz 44, 46–47
Ilić, Mikica 175
Illyés, Gyula 100, 192
Iova, Gheorghe 154

Jackson, Richard 42, 44, 46, 62, 64, 65
James, Henry 10, 187
Jančar, Drago 27, 38, 39, 65
Jansen, Wim 109
Jelnikar, Ana 64, 65
Jesih, Milan 39
Johanides, Ján 123, 130–131
Johnson, A. 179
Johnson, Samuel 101, 132
Jovanovič, Dušan 39, 60–61
József, Attila 100, 192
Jura, Anton 112
Juráňová, Jana 135
Jurešić, Valerij 168–170

Kádár, János 68, 71, 73, 88
Kadlečik, Ivan 116–117
Kafka, Franz 92, 116, 127, 174, 175
Kamber, Amir 175
Kányádi, Sándor 101
Kardos, György 93
Keats, John 31, 95, 157
Kerlik, Peter 119
Kertész, Imre 91–92, 93, 98, 110, 171
Kessler, Jascha 110
Keulemans, Chris 173
King, Dr. Martin Luther 185
King, Sharon 164
Kipling, Rudyard 39, 178
Kiss, Anna 9
Kiss, Irén 91, 99
Klimáček, Viliam 117, 139–140
Klinar, Meta 65
Klinec, Aleš 61
Klotz, Bea 172, 173
Klotz, Wolfgang 166, 172, 173
Kocbek, Edvard 1, 2, 11, 26, 27, 30–31, 34, 35, 36, 37, 47, 62
Kočevar, Marjanca 60
Kokelj, Nina 55, 57, 64
Kolšek, Peter 54
Komelj, Miklavž 37
Konrád, György 3, 93, 170
Kornis, Mihály 94
Korun, Barbara 49, 65
Kosmač, Tomaž 56
Kosztolányi, Dezső 97, 100, 189
Kovačič, Lojze 32

Kováčová, Eva 137
Kovalyk, Uršul'a 136
Kovič, Kajetan 14, 18
Kramberger, Taja 49
Kraus, Milan 137
Kravanja, Sonja 1, 2, 30, 31, 50, 62, 64, 65
Kukan, Eduard 112
Kundera, Milan 4, 183–184
Kúnos, László 76, 78, 81, 90
Kupcec, Ivan 138
Kušar, Meta 49

Lainšček, Feri 57–58, 64
Latham, Ernest 158
Lawrence, D.H. 16, 57
Lázár, Júlia 77, 101
Lefter, Ion Bogdan 154, 155
Lehenová, Tat'jana 139
Lenardič, Mart 56
Lenčo, Ján 129
Lengyel, Péter 94–95
Lenin 150, 182
Levchev, Vladimir 174
Lewis, C.S. 185
Limonov, Eduard 182
Lloyd, Harold 132
Lowell, Robert 69, 181

Macovszky, Peter 140–141
Madách, Imre 100
Mailer, Norman 81, 91, 181
Makanin, Vladimir 183
Makarovič, Svetlana 37, 49
Makkai, Adam 99–101
Mándy, Stefánia 93
Manea, Norman 148, 164
Manolescu, Ion 156, 158
Márai, Sándor 171
March, Michael 143
Marin, Mariana 148, 154
Marinescu, Angela 154
Marno, János 88
Martin, Mircea 153
Márton, László 94, 98
Marx, Groucho 132
Marx, Karl 82, 125, 104, 125, 132, 150
Matthais Corvinus, King 145
Maugham, W. Somerset 39
Maver, Igor 14
McConnell-Duff, Alan 64
McDonald, Walt 16, 18–19, 20
McLaughlin, Donal 64
Mečiar, Vladimir 112, 114, 115, 121, 122, 126, 147

Medgyesi, Emese 98
Merrill, Christopher 2, 25, 62
Mesterházi, Márton 78, 83–86, 98, 99, 101
Mikolaj, Dušan 141
Miller, Marlowe 131
Miłosz, Czesław 11, 44
Milošević, Slobodan 147
Milošová, Sharon 143
Mindszenty, József Cardinal 91
Mircea, Ion 154
Miu, Florea 161
Moon, Rev. Sun Myung 85
Morgan, Rachel 64
Moroiu *see* Ieronim
Mozetič, Brane 9, 44, 51–53, 65
Munteanu, Ion 161
Murín, Gustáv 74, 90, 115, 119, 120, 125–126, 142, 185
Mușat, Carmen 154, 161–162

Nabokov, Vladimir 132
Nádas, Péter 89, 94, 98, 99, 171
Nagy, László 85
Nash, Susan Smith 9
national identity, literature and 4–5, 11, 26, 63, 64, 91, 100, 112–113, 115, 118, 147, 166, 177–178
Nedelciu, Mircea 154
Negrici, Eugen 164
Németh, Ákos 98
Németh, László 85
Nero, Emperor 144
Nežič, Žakalon 179
Nimigean, Ovidiu 158–159
Nixon, Richard 112
Njatin, Lela Bajda 44, 48, 64, 65
Novak, Boris A. 32, 37, 43–44, 60, 64
Novak, Irene Zorko 37, 64
Novak, Maja 56
Novy, Lily 37

Oravecz, Imre 98
Orbán, György 79, 101
Orbán, János Dénes 99
Orbán, Ottó 13, 17, 19, 21, 74, 88, 93, 94, 95–97, 100, 110
Örkény, István 93, 98
Orwell, George 149
Osojnik, Iztok 13, 14, 18, 20, 26, 29, 38, 41–43, 61, 6a3, 65
Ottschovki, Hilde 164

Pannonius, Janus 99
Panța, Iustin 156–157
Pantić, Mihailo 182

Parker, Dorothy 45
Parti-Nagy, Lajos 98
Paštéková, Jelena 129
Pasternak, Boris 82
Pavček, Marko 37
Penescu, Razvan 171
Petőfi, Sándor 5, 11, 74, 91, 100
Petreu, Marta 154
Petrík, Vladimir 120, 143
Petro, Peter 143
Phillips, Arthur 69–70, 110
Pickens, Slim 112
Pikalo, Matjaž 37
Pišťanek, Peter 122–123
Plath, Sylvia 77, 157, 174
Plato 186
Plut, Katja 60
Pognačnik, Barbara 65
Pomogáts, Béla 87, 91, 98, 110
Popescu, Adrian 154, 160
Popov, Alek 174
postmodernism 12, 45, 83, 146, 154–156, 159–160, 173, 178
Potokar, Jure 44
Potpara, Lili 64, 65
Pound, Ezra 34, 36, 96, 140
Preda, Constantin 161
Prelipceanu, Nicolae 154
Prešern, France 5, 11, 22, 23, 26, 30, 35, 36, 49
Prokešová, Viera 141
publishing conditions 6, 9, 28, 29–30, 32, 42, 49, 53, 54, 61, 63, 69, 74, 76–83, 87, 116, 117, 118–120, 125–126, 142, 147–150, 153, 154, 159–160, 168–172, 173, 181
Pynchon, Thomas 45, 50, 70

Rad, Ilie 148, 164
Radnóti, Miklós 100
Rahv, Philip 9
Rakús, Stanislav 127
Ratzinger, Cardinal 25
Repar, Stanislava Chrobáková 49
Richter, Milan 115, 123
Robbins, Harold 29, 81
Rode, France 25
Rošanc, Marjan 24
Rushdie, Salman 81
Rzhevsky, Nicholas 143

Sabatos, Charles 126, 143
Šalamun, Tomaž 19, 34, 35–37, 54, 60, 62, 65, 170
samizdat 27, 34, 116, 124–125, 149
Šarotar, Dušan 55, 65

Index

Sartre, Jean-Paul 82
Semolič, Peter 20, 55
Shelley, Percy Bysshe 182
Šikula, Vincent 127
Silone, Ignazio 82
Šimečka, Martin 116, 117, 118, 123–125, 126, 143, 185–186
Šimečka, Milan 116
Simoniti, Vasko 27
Sloboda, Rudolf 116, 129–130
Smith, Wilbur 81
Somlyó, György 88, 93
Sophocles 115
Sorescu, Marin 150, 152–153, 164
Sorkin, Adam 147, 148–149, 153, 154, 155, 157, 158, 160, 162, 163, 164
Spiridon, Monica 155
Spiró, György 98
Stalin, Joseph 23, 44, 84, 103, 104, 145, 150, 190
Stănescu, Saviana 148, 156, 158
Štefanko, Ondrej 123
Štefoi, Elena 154
Šteger, Aleš 21, 26, 37, 53–54, 58–60, 65
Stein, Gertrude 132
Steinbeck, John 186
Stevens, Wallace 31, 34, 42
Stoiciu, Liviu Ioan 154
Strážay, Štefan 138
Strniša, Gregor 37
Šubert, Barbara 65
Suleiman, Susan Rubin 68–69, 109, 110
Šulej, Peter 141
Sun Tzu 78
Šuplata, Václav 127
Šušel, David 60
Šuštar, Alojzij 25
Sutherland-Smith, James 113, 116, 127, 135, 140, 143
Sutherland-Smith, Viera 118, 127, 135
Swift, Jonathan 47, 174
Szabó, Dezső 85
Szabó, László Cs. 100
Szabó, Lőrinc 192
Szántó, Gábor 95
Száraz, Miklós György 99
Szász, Endre 109
Székely, Magda 99
Szép, Ernö 93
Szilárd, Gabriella 81
Szirtes, George 86–87, 110
Szkárosi, Endre 99

Tăbăcaru, Adrian 164
Takács, Ferenc 71, 91
Takács, Zsuzsa 99
Tar, Sándor 98, 99
Taragel, Dušan 122–123
Tartler, Grete 153, 164
Tatarka, Dominik 113, 116
Taufer, Veno 13, 14, 18, 34–35, 37, 61, 65
Ťažký, Ladislav 128
Temesi, Ferenc 88–89, 91, 98, 99
Thomas, Dylan 54
Tito 6, 23, 24, 27, 28, 30, 38, 46, 57, 61, 64, 176
Topol, Jáchym 183
Török, András 83, 84, 110
Tőzsér, Árpád 98
Tratnik, Suzana 47–48
Tuđman, Franjo 147, 169, 183
Tudor, Cornelius Vadim 183
Turčany, Viliam 137
Turner, Frederick 91, 110
Tužinsky, Ján 129
Twain, Mark 10, 18

Udovič, Jože 31, 35, 55
Uličansky, Ján 127
Unamuno, Miguel de 82
Urban, Jozef 140
Uricariu, Doina 154
Ursu, Liaiana 154

Vadkerti-Gavorníková, Lýdia 139
Vajda, Miklós 83, 85, 90, 98
Válek, Miroslav 117–118
Várady, Szabolcz 89
Vášová, Alta 135
Velickovic, Nenand 171, 179
Verona, Dan 149
Vianu, Lidia 149, 153, 154, 164
Vidmar, Maja 48–49
Viegl, Svetloslav 137
Viewegh, Michal 183
Vilikovský, Pavel 3, 6, 113, 131–133, 143
Virk, Jani 45–46, 65
Vizenor, Gerald 11
Vondra, Alexandr 167
Vonnegut, Kurt 81
Vouk, Erika 37, 49

Wachtel, Andrew 2, 181–184
Walker, Brenda 162
Waugh, Evelyn 180
Weöres, Sándor 97, 100
Whitman, Walt 19, 31, 36, 54, 156
Williams, John Hartley 164
Wilson, Christopher C. 110
Wilson, Katharina M. 110

Wolfe, Thomas 85
Woolf, Virginia 136

Yeats, William Butler 31, 34, 78, 99, 186

Zagoričnik, Ifegenija 38
Zajc, Dane 32–34, 53, 65

Zalán, Tibor 88
Zawacki, Andrew 62, 64
Zelinová, Hana 118
Zeno 142
Žerjal, Aldo 37
Zsolt, Béla 93
Zupan, Uroš 20, 54–55, 60, 65

www.ingramcontent.com/pod-product-compliance
Lightning Source LLC
Chambersburg PA
CBHW032100300426
44116CB00007B/821